HOW TO BUY REAL ESTATE AT FORECLOSURE AUCTIONS

A STEP-BY-STEP GUIDE TO MAKING MONEY BUYING, REHABBING AND SELLING PROPERTY FROM SHERIFF SALES AND TRUSTEE AUCTIONS

Marc Sherby

Trafford
PUBLISHING™

Order this book online at www.trafford.com/08-0540
or email orders@trafford.com

Most Trafford titles are also available at major online book retailers.

Note for Librarians: A cataloguing record for this book is available from Library
and Archives Canada at www.collectionscanada.ca/amicus/index-e.html

ISBN: 978-1-4251-7652-5

*We at Trafford believe that it is the responsibility of us all, as both individuals
and corporations, to make choices that are environmentally and socially sound.
You, in turn, are supporting this responsible conduct each time you purchase a
Trafford book, or make use of our publishing services. To find out how you are
helping, please visit www.trafford.com/responsiblepublishing.html*

*Our mission is to efficiently provide the world's finest, most comprehensive
book publishing service, enabling every author to experience success.
To find out how to publish your book, your way, and have it available
worldwide, visit us online at www.trafford.com/10510*

Trafford PUBLISHING™ www.trafford.com

North America & international
toll-free: 1 888 232 4444 (USA & Canada)
phone: 250 383 6864 ♦ fax: 250 383 6804 ♦ email: info@trafford.com

The United Kingdom & Europe
phone: +44 (0)1865 487 395 ♦ local rate: 0845 230 9601
facsimile: +44 (0)1865 481 507 ♦ email: info.uk@trafford.com

10 9 8 7 6 5 4

This book is designed to offer accurate and useful information on the topics and subject matter covered. Real estate, by its very nature and the rules and laws that govern it are constantly being revised and changed. It is sold with the understanding that the author is not an attorney, accountant, or similar professional and this book should not be construed as offering any legal, accounting, or similar professional advice. It is recommended if you require these services you consult competent professional counsel in your area prior to engaging in any real estate transactions.

Dedication

This book is dedicated to my mother Arlene Sherby who I know is watching me from up there.

Acknowledgements

No written work of any caliber springs solely from the mind of the author without the efforts and assistance of others. Many folks have helped in the production of this book.

I would first like to thank my team: Editor Victoria White, of The Virtual Writer, whose mastery of the English language and punctuation far exceeds mine, and Kathleen McBride of Cranberryink for her creatively artistic talents designing the covers of the book. Writing a book involves a lot of commitment and hard work, and both their patience and creative insights were invaluable to me.

I wish to thank the following sheriffs who were kind enough to allow me use of their copyrighted terms and conditions of sale:
Sheriff Joseph F. McGinn, Delaware County, Media, Pennsylvania
Sheriff Richard C. Ketchem, Greene County, Waynesburg, Pennsylvania
Sheriff Daniel W. Beck, Allen County, Lima, Ohio
Sheriff David J. Mahoney, Dane County, Madison, Wisconsin
Sheriff William Elfo, Whatcom County, Bellingham, Washington
Sheriff John Whetsel, Oklahoma County, Oklahoma City, Oklahoma
Sheriff James Higdon, Kent County, Dover, Delaware
Sheriff Tracy Brown, Tippecanoe County, Lafayette, Indiana
Sheriff Ralph Froehlich, Union County, Elizabeth, New Jersey
Sheriff Paul R. Valteau, New Orleans, Louisiana
Sheriff Stanley Sniff, Riverside County, California

I also would additionally like to thank the following people for use of their copyrighted items: Alan Lecoff of Barry S. Slosberg, Inc. Auctioneers, for their real estate auctions newspaper ad; the Delaware County Bar Association for their listings in the Delaware County Legal Journal; Barron's Educational Services for definitions from their sixth edition of "Dictionary of Real Estate Terms"; and Trend MLS Listing Service for their MLS listings.

Many thanks to Len Halpern, CPA, real estate broker, and above all a great friend whose support, viewpoints, and insight I can always count on.

Also thanks to Bob Diamond, real estate attorney and guru for getting me involved in real estate to begin with and showing me the way of foreclosures.

To all of my friends and family who have not only lent their ears, which I bent heavily whenever we got together about my book, but also their support for this project. I thank you more than these words can express.

And finally, special thanks to:

My father, Lee Sherby, for always being there convincing me, as only a father can, that I can do anything if I set my mind to it.
My wife Connie, who is by far my biggest supporter and rooting section.
My daughter Abigael, and stepchildren, Amanda and Jay. Three of the best kids any father could hope for.

CONTENTS

INTRODUCTION
WELCOME TO THE WORLD OF FORECLOSED
REAL ESTATE PROPERTY AUCTIONS

There are lots of books explaining how you can profit from buying real estate at the pre-foreclosure (before it ends up at the foreclosure auctions) stage. Then there are books that tell you how to buy real estate at the post-foreclosure (*after* the sheriff sale from the bank or REO) stage. These books preach a multitude of methods designed to get either the homeowner or the bank to sell you the property *before* it ends up at the foreclosure auction with little or no money down. Or they tell you how to buy it *after* the auction from the bank. But none of them tell you where to find many of the *best* real estate foreclosure deals. They don't tell you how to actually *buy AT the foreclosure auctions.* And that is the purpose of this book. To tell you what you need to know so you can be successful buying property at the auctions.

When I began bidding on foreclosed properties at sheriff sale auctions, I was a greenhorn too. I found out that there was very little in the way of useful instructional "real world" information out there on what happens before, during and after the property goes through the auction process. How do I find out what properties are for sale? Where do they hold the sales? What do I need to know to correctly bid on a property? Who can tell me about rules and laws on this? What can I expect to happen *after* purchasing a property at the sale? In other words, *"How is it done?"* These were all questions I was trying to find answers to. And unless you are lucky enough to find someone who has previous experience with the process and is willing to spend the time mentoring you through it, it's sort of "learn as you go." The problem with that is "some learn from their experiences and others don't recover from them." You don't want to be one of the latter ones so you need to be able to avoid the foreclosure land mines out there. One mistake can literally spell financial disaster for you.

By walking you through the various types of auctions and all of the procedures involved with them, I will answer all of those questions and more. So that when you go to the auctions to bid, you will know how to do it like a pro and be well on your way to making money at the foreclosure sales.

CHAPTER 1
WHY BUY AT THE SALE?

Even though real estate foreclosures and auctions seem to be covered lately by the media on almost a daily basis, they are not something new. There have been sheriff sales, trustee sales and real estate auction sales going on for a long, long time. What's different now is the unprecedented increase in the amount of foreclosures currently being filed and those expected to be filed in the next several years. That figure will continue to grow at an alarming rate as problems with mortgages, housing and the economy persist. Many homeowners will see their adjustable rate mortgages adjust higher as the mortgage debacle continues to unfold. No region of the country has been immune to the rise in foreclosures. Especially hard hit are those areas that experienced a tremendous rise in real estate values over the past several years, with foreclosure rates increasing thirty percent and more over the previous year in some locales. And the worst is almost certainly yet to come.

This scenario presents a real buying opportunity, possibly never again to be duplicated on this scale, for making money by purchasing real estate at foreclosure auctions. It is not uncommon to be able to buy real estate for twenty to fifty percent below market value at auctions. That can put a very nice profit in your pocket. Think what you could do with that extra money: a family vacation, a new car, college tuition, and so on. But as in any new undertaking, you need to educate yourself on how to do it correctly. If this is your desire, then read on.

REAL ESTATE MYTHS

What is it that's so alluring about those real estate infomercials that people up at 3 a.m. are watching? Why do people want to go to buy houses at sheriff sales and foreclosure auctions anyway? While some go planning to buy properties to fix up, flip, and resell for a quick profit, others buy with the intention to hold long term as rental units. Still others go there looking to buy a house for their personal use, to live in. But the real reason why all of these people go is that sheriff and foreclosure auction sales represent *the* place where some of the best deals on real estate can be had. And like any other type of investing, along with the potential for profits can come the potential for losses. Be it the stock market, gold, bonds, or whatever else you decide to put your money into, if you don't know what the heck you are doing you can get burned big time. Investing in real estate is no exception. The landscape is littered with deals gone bad and just plain bad deals.

There are a lot of myths out there about sheriff and foreclosure sale auctions. Everything from "I heard you can buy a house there for a hundred dollars" (not likely) to "I saw this guy on television and he said I could easily make all this cash *with no money* buying houses" (even less likely). Contrary to what many books and infomercials would have you believe, it does take *some* money to make money, whether it's in foreclosures or almost any other business I can think of. Just exactly "where" that money comes from is a topic to be discussed later in the book. Let's just say for now there are ways to get the money you will need, some more creative than others. As you become more experienced and successful at buying and selling properties, you will find that the money you need will actually *find you*. Not a bad situation to be in, huh?

REAL ESTATE FACT vs. REAL ESTATE FICTION

Before going any further you need to understand how the real estate *fact* differs from the real estate *fiction* of many "get-rich-quick-no-money-down-no-risk" schemes pontificated by various books and TV infomercials. Many of the techniques preached in those books and infomercials are very difficult to pull off in the real world and some even border on illegal, depending on the state you are in. They would have you believe that real estate fortunes can be made virtually overnight for very little, if any, risk and almost no money or effort required on your part. Why, it's so easy you can even do it while walking the dog. *Bull poop!* If that were true, don't you think everyone would be doing it and we all would be tremendously wealthy? Don't we all want something for nothing?

First of all, the reality is real estate is a *get-rich-slow business.* Very few people become millionaires overnight investing in real estate, as many of those books and infomercials would have you believe. But people can and do become millionaires investing in real estate over the long haul. Second, this business takes *effort* and *persistence*. Let me state that again. *This business takes effort and persistence*. In fact, if you want to succeed in real estate, or *anything* else in life, effort and persistence are *absolutely required*. Being a success with any new endeavor requires four commitments:

1. Be willing to devote the time and patience to learn it.
2. Be willing to take the calculated risks associated with it.
3. Be willing to set the goals for it.
4. Be willing to take the action required to make it happen.

Learning how to buy and sell foreclosed properties successfully *does not* require any special skills, prior real estate experience, or even a Harvard MBA. It *does*, however, require *specific knowledge*, and a bit of your time, effort and creativity. Reading this book will give you the knowledge. But you also need to go out there and put that knowledge to practical use by calling in the other three (time, effort, and creativity) and actually buying your first property. Don't let "analysis paralysis" or the fear of failure hold you back from taking action.

Sure, there will be mistakes. No real estate investor or any other person I know for that matter has ever done anything new and not made a mistake. Even huge corporations with millions of dollars to spend make mistakes and don't always "get it right the first time." The idea is to learn from your mistakes and keep them "little." This type of investing will require you to get out of your financial comfort zone from time to time. However, by performing your proper "due diligence" (defined as "What a person does in making a reasonable effort to gather and examine accurate and complete information prior to making a business decision") before purchasing any property, you will minimize the chances of having something major go wrong. There is an old saying that goes, "If you always do what you have always done, you will always get what you have always got." It's true.

REAL ESTATE MAGIC

What is it about real estate that makes it seem magical to people? Many people think of owning real estate as only the domain of the wealthy or land speculators and wheeler dealers, but that is not completely true. Almost anyone with a little time, a little money, and a little desire can become a real estate investor. Real estate investors come in all sizes, from the person who does one flip a year to make some extra cash to the individual who has a couple of rentals, all the way up to the owners of large apartment buildings with hundreds of units—and everything in between.

Notice I used the word *investor* and not *speculator*. There is a *big* difference. A real estate investor is someone who buys properties below current market price based on the established values of those properties, *knowing* there is a profit to be made in the future. Speculators, on the other hand, buy properties without any established market price or values, gambling on the *hope* there is a profit to be made in the future. Buying raw land is an example of speculating and is very dangerous. Speculating does not make good business sense, and while the allure of a *potential* real estate windfall may seem tempting, stay away from it. If you want to understand speculating firsthand, go to Las Vegas or Atlantic City and watch all the speculators losing their money in the casinos.

WHY INVEST IN REAL ESTATE?

Why then should you consider investing in real estate? Well, real estate is generally considered a safe investment. Traditionally, most real estate increases in value over time. And real estate, unlike other investments, through the magic of something called "tax depreciation" actually allows you to *depreciate* for tax purposes the value of your real estate, even though it may have in reality actually *appreciated* in value. Depending on how much time you have to devote to real estate, you can do it part-or full-time. Many part-time real estate investors find it enjoyable and lucrative enough that they eventually become full-time investors.

Real estate investing can also be classified as *active* or *passive*. Buying foreclosures and flipping them is an example of active real estate investing. As long as you keep "active"—buying, rehabbing and flipping the properties—you make money. Stop buying properties to flip and the money stops. This type of real estate investing requires a certain amount of time and effort devoted to it. Many people are drawn to the large payouts, or what I call the "chunk cash," when they sell the property, and they don't like to give it up. Passive investors, on the other hand, are those who after buying and rehabbing the property choose to hold on to it and rent it out. This produces a "passive" stream of rental income every month as well as added tax benefits and long-term wealth accumulation. Besides, it's a nice feeling to know that the property you bought is actually being paid for by your tenants. But landlording and dealing with tenants is not for everybody, and you should talk to other landlords or read books on it before deciding to become one.

Realize also that while real estate is a good vehicle for long-term appreciation and wealth building, is it not an asset that can be liquidated quickly for cash, like stocks and similar items. However, depending on the extent of your equity (the amount your property is worth over and above what you still owe on it in mortgages and loans), you can tap into that money in the form of an equity line of credit. Equity lines of credit, as you will learn in a later chapter, are one of the ways you can use to finance buying your foreclosure properties.

BEFORE WE BEGIN

In this book, I will explain the process of how to buy foreclosed properties *profitably* and *legally* at auction sales. As I said before, some of the best deals can be had at the foreclosure auctions, and also some of the worst **IF** you don't know what you are doing. To be successful at buying foreclosed real estate you need to be completely familiar with how the entire foreclosure process works, and yes, there is a definite order to that process. Buying at the actual sale is not that difficult once you know "how the game is played." That is why I recommend that for the first sale or two you attend, just go and "sit on your hands" so to speak, observe what is happening and take notes.

In this book, I will walk you through the research process and show you how to conduct your due diligence on the properties, bid and buy at the sales, and learn the language of the sales. And I will tell you the tricks that I have learned along the way so that when you bid, you can bid with confidence. I will go through the do's and don'ts of rehabbing the property so you can see which repairs and remodeling efforts will bring the best return and which ones to avoid. I will also tell you little inexpensive repair and remodeling tips that can bring a big return when you resell the property.

But before I get started explaining foreclosures and how the sheriff and foreclosure auctions work, the following concept needs to be kept in mind, as it applies not only to the foreclosure process itself but to the auctions as well. The sheriff, trustee and real estate auctions, including the entire foreclosure process, are *not* a standardized cookie-cutter procedure. It is *not* administered by the federal government. Laws concerning each type of foreclosure are administered by the individual state and local counties, and vary accordingly. Actual rules governing the sheriff sale for your specific area can be found at your county courthouse. I do my purchasing in the counties surrounding Philadelphia, Pennsylvania, which happens to be a judicial foreclosure state. The individual rules regarding the sheriff sale are different for each of the five counties surrounding the city of Philadelphia as well as for Philadelphia itself. So in a radius of about seventy-five miles, there are six different sets of rules in place. At times, I will refer to paperwork and procedures that are standard for Pennsylvania and the surrounding counties. Similar procedures may be found in your area also.

At the back of the book, I have listed brief synopses of the foreclosure procedures and guidelines for all fifty states as well as sample sheriff sale rules from various counties throughout the country, illustrating differences in the rules and regulations governing sheriff sales at the county level. And while there are differences in both state and county laws and procedures, there are also threads of commonality that run through the foreclosure and sheriff sale process in most of the states and counties that practice it. Rules regarding trustee auctions in states that practice the power of sale method of foreclosure are customarily spelled out by whoever is conducting the auction for the lender or trustee prior to the sale. Like the rules for sheriff sales, rules for trustee auctions also vary, so once again you need to verify these before you bid.

The aim of this book is to show you **how** to find and **apply** the information you need to gather to properly bid at your local sheriff sale and foreclosure auctions. I will tell you what to expect before, during, and after the sale. So while the specific information I offer will vary from location to location, the concepts are universal. Since many of these rules are area-specific and do change, I urge you to seek out a competent local *real estate* attorney (explained further on in the chapter about building your team) who can explain to you these rules and laws as they apply to the local area that you plan to do your purchasing in.

I will go into more details on this later in the book, so let's get started!

CHAPTER 2
FORECLOSURES

THE DIFFERENCES BETWEEN SHERIFF, TRUSTEE, AND REAL ESTATE FORECLOSURE AUCTIONS

Sheriff, trustee, or real estate foreclosure auctions are conducted throughout the United States. Depending on where you are located will determine what type of foreclosure auction you will primarily be dealing with, and even that can vary. To begin with, not all states have sheriff sales. That is why you may not be able to find a sheriff sale auction in your state. Sheriff sales are basically only conducted in states that subscribe to the judicial form of foreclosure. In states that practice the "non-judicial power of sale process" trustee auctions are their primary way to dispose of foreclosures, even though the auctioneer might be the sheriff. I say "basically or primarily" because even though a state may subscribe to only one type of foreclosure, that doesn't completely rule out it's using the other type in special circumstances. Complete details on judicial and non-judicial foreclosure methods will be discussed later on. Sheriff sale auctions are usually held at the county seat of government in their courthouse building and are carried out by that county's sheriff. Trustee and real estate foreclosure auctions, on the other hand, are typically held at the foreclosed property itself or at a predetermined location and are, in most cases, run by an auctioneer hired to conduct the sale.

WHAT IS FORECLOSURE?

What is foreclosure and how does someone get into foreclosure? Since you will be bidding on and purchasing properties that are in foreclosure, you need to understand the process and how it works. First, foreclosure as it applies to real estate, can be defined as follows: *"A legal process undertaken that allows a creditor (bank, mortgage company, tradesperson, taxing authority, etc.) to acquire title and ownership of real property from a defaulting borrower by forcing the sale of the defaulting parties' real estate to satisfy the debt."*

While a foreclosure action can be initiated by any number of various sources, such as local real estate taxing authorities, IRS, or a defaulted judgment for non-payment of a bill, in most cases you will find the foreclosure action is initiated by a financial institution (usually a mortgage company or bank) for non-payment of the mortgage, deed of trust, or similar note. Normally if payment is not received after 30 days beyond the due date, the lender will send out a letter politely reminding the borrower that perhaps the payment was "accidentally overlooked" and to kindly remit as soon as possible. If there is no payment after 60 days, a less kindly letter stating that payment is past due and to avoid late fees remit immediately. If after 90 days payment has not been made, at that point the next letter sent will serve notice that a foreclosure action will be started against them. Typically by 120th to the 150th day (4 to 5 months) past due the creditor will have already begun setting the foreclosure process in motion.

Lenders (meaning banks, mortgage companies, or similar financial institutions) do not like having to go through foreclosure. It is both expensive and time-consuming. Lenders will use foreclosure as a last resort if all else fails. Depending on the primary foreclosure method used in that state, from the time a lender starts foreclosure until the actual auction takes place can be anywhere from three to 12 months, or more. And with any legal intervention on the part of the debtor it can drag out much longer.

TYPES OF FORECLOSURES

There are essentially four types of foreclosure used in the fifty states today:

- **Judicial Foreclosure**
- **Non-Judicial Foreclosure**
- **Strict Foreclosure**
- **Entry & Possession**

The first two, Judicial & Non-Judicial, are the most common. Strict Foreclosure and Entry & Possession are rare and only practiced in a few states. All four types differ, and the state you are located in determines which foreclosure method applies. Let's examine how each of them works and their differences. (For a full list of all fifty states and their foreclosure methods, please see the reference list and resources section in the back of the book.)

Judicial Foreclosure: Judicial Foreclosure is the legal process whereby the debtor's property is sold through the courts via the sheriff sale. While judicial foreclosure is "technically" available in all states, it is practiced only in states that use a mortgage to secure the purchase of property. After the debt notification period to the borrower has expired (this varies but usually after 90 days past due the borrower is considered in default), the unpaid creditor contacts their lawyer, who files a foreclosure lawsuit. Notice is also served to all persons or entities having an interest in the property subsequent to the foreclosing entity's interest. A *Lis Pendens* (Latin for "suit pending") is filed in the Prothonotary's office at the county courthouse to make public notice that a lawsuit has begun against the borrower. If the borrower does not respond to defend against the suit, then the creditor receives a judgment by default against the borrower. If the borrower does choose to defend against the suit in court and the decision of the court is against the borrower, the court then issues a judgment in favor of the creditor.

A writ ("writ" is legalese for a formal command issued by a court to carry out a particular act) of execution follows, enabling the foreclosed property to be scheduled for sheriff sale. The court then tallies up the total amount due (typically interest, fees, penalties, any past due taxes, etc.) and directs the sheriff's office to conduct the sale of the property. The property must, depending on local law, be advertised in at least one or possibly several local newspapers and/or legal publications a certain minimum number of days before the foreclosure sale. If the debtor does not pay the total amount due by the day of the sale, the property is then sold at the sheriff sale. If the property does not sell for enough to satisfy the amount the lender was owed, then some states allow for a deficiency judgment, depending on where the property is located. In a deficiency judgment, the creditor can pursue additional legal actions against the original borrower, such as wage attachment or the seizure of cars or personal property, to recover the additional monies due. So depending on the particular state's foreclosure rules and any motions filed by the debtor, such as bankruptcy, using right of redemption (if available), and so on, all in all this whole process from notification of debt to actual sale can take from as little as three or four months to several years.

NON-JUDICIAL FORECLOSURE: Non-judicial foreclosure allows the creditor to foreclose without filing a lawsuit and without court authority. This is accomplished through what is called "Power of Sale." Non-Judicial foreclosure is practiced in states where a "Deed of Trust" rather than a mortgage is used as the security instrument to purchase a property. In a deed of trust, the borrower *(trustor)* gives a deed of trust to an intermediary party *(trustee)* to hold for the lender *(beneficiary)*. In the case of a default by the borrower, the intermediary on instructions from the lender serves what is called a **Notice of Default (NOD)** to the borrower and is empowered to sell the property at a foreclosure sale. The NOD is also recorded in the public records at the courthouse. The power of sale clause is a part of the deed of trust and waives the borrower's right to a judicial or sheriff sale in the event of default. The lender, by invoking the power of sale clause, not only saves money compared to the cost of a judicial sheriff sale but also saves time by shortening the foreclosure timeline significantly, in some cases to as little as 90 days.

Conversely, if there is an extraordinary set of circumstances connected with the foreclosure the lender can still order a judicial sheriff sale even though non-judicial means are available to them. Non-Judicial foreclosures using power of sale auctions are usually conducted by either a public auctioneer, trustee, or the trustee's agent. Sales can be held at the property location, local courthouse, or other specified location. You will typically see listings in the local general interest newspapers advertising the sale and possibly online at the auctioneer's website. More often than not the property is sold to the highest bidder; however, depending on the type of sale, it could be returned to the lender if an acceptable high bid is not received.

Less than half of the states use the non-judicial method as their primary means of foreclosure. And even though some states have both methods available, depending on the circumstances of the default, they predominately will use either one method or the other. If you are unsure which is used in your area, check with your county office.

STRICT FORECLOSURE: Currently only three states—Connecticut, New Hampshire and Vermont—use strict foreclosure method, which does not call for a sale of the property at all. The lender formally requisitions the court to terminate the debtor's right to redeem the property. If granted and once the process is started, the debtor has a pre-determined amount of time to pay the amount owed. If it is not paid in that specified time frame, the title reverts back to the lender.

FORECLOSURE BY ENTRY & POSSESSION: Only four states—Maine, Rhode Island, New Hampshire and Massachusetts—currently allow foreclosure by entry and possession. In this form of foreclosure the lender petitions the court to take peaceable possession of the property in the company of a witness and by filing a certificate with the courts.

Sample- Notice of Lis Pendens

IN THE COURT OF COMMON PLEAS OF DELAWARE COUNTY, PENNSYLVANIA

CIVIL ACTION – LAW

: NO. 06-3456

Big City Mortgage Co.
100 Main Street
Anytown, PA 19000

Plaintiff : IN MORTGAGE

VS. : FORECLOSURE

John Q. Homeowner
25 Big Elm Dirve
Springfield, PA 18000

NOTICE TO DEFEND

TO: John Q. Homeowner

You have been sued in Court. If you wish to defend against the claims set forth in the following pages, you must take written action within twenty (20) days after this Complaint and Notice are served, by entering a written appearance, personally or by attorney and filing in writing with the Court your defenses or objections to the claims set forth against you. You are warned that if you fail to do so, the case may proceed without you and a judgment may be entered against you by the Court without further notice for any money claimed in the Complaint or for any other claims requested by the Plaintiff. You may lose money or property or other rights important to you.

YOU SHOULD TAKE THIS PAPER TO YOUR LAWYER AT ONCE. IF YOU DO NOT HAVE A LAWYER OR CANNOT AFFORD ONE, CONTACT THE OFFICE BELOW TO FIND OUT WHERE YOU CAN GET LEGAL HELP.

LAWYERS REFERENCE SERVICE
MEDIA, PENNSYLVANIA
(610)-555-1212

FOLIO NUMBER 1010-04-789-3

STAGES OF FORECLOSURE

There are three different stages in the foreclosure process where a property can be purchased.

These are, in sequential order:

1) Pre-foreclosure
2) Foreclosure sale auction
3) REO

Let's look at numbers 1 and 3 first.

Pre-Foreclosure: To purchase the property you would deal directly with the homeowner or the bank before it ends up at the auction. The advantages of pre-foreclosure are that you can usually inspect, to some degree, the property both inside and out before making an offer and you have time to arrange financing and title insurance before you buy. One of the disadvantages is that the homeowner may owe so much money on the property in mortgages, home equity loans, back taxes, etc. that there may be little or no equity at all in it. Or worse, it is "upside down," meaning more is owed than it is worth. At that point you will have to negotiate with each of the creditors to accept less money than they are owed (known in the industry as a "short sale") if you plan to make a profit on the property. While this can be done however, it can be very time consuming. You need the complete cooperation of the homeowner, who is willing to go along with the entire short sale process and not declare bankruptcy or commit some other action along the way, sabotaging your efforts. If you cannot be guaranteed this cooperation, you will just be wasting your time. There are books and seminars available on how to do short sales, and I would advise you to study them thoroughly before ever attempting one.

REO: REO is banking and real estate lingo for **R**eal **E**state **O**wned. This is what happens when the property goes back to the creditor, usually a bank or mortgage company, if it does not sell at the sheriff sale or foreclosure auction. In other words, the property did not receive a high enough bid at the sale to cover the creditor's costs and basically they purchased it back. After the creditor gets the property back, it's turned over to a realtor who specializes in REO properties. The realtor will evict the previous owners if needed, clean out any of their junk, make the property saleable by making minor repairs or fixing any code violations, and sell it for the creditor. Many times real estate investors end up being the purchasers of REO properties. REO realtors generally work with a handful of banks and mortgage companies and are constantly getting a supply of properties from them to move.

The advantages of buying REO properties are you can inspect them inside and out and that they are sold with clear title. The disadvantage is that banks typically want top dollar for them, so deals can be hard to come by. However, depending on the number of unsold properties the bank has taken back and has in its inventory, as well as the time of the year (banks are generally more flexible on price at the end of a quarter or year), and before winter sets in up north (they won't have the expense to winterize it), you stand a better chance of finding the bank willing to deal. And while you can finance an REO with a mortgage, you will find most buyers of REOs do their purchasing with cash and no contingency offers. This is because banks as a rule want quick settlements with the least amount of conditions or stipulations.

Foreclosure Sale Auctions: The second stage of foreclosure, the Sheriff Sale and Trustee Auctions, is what this book is all about, so let's go!

CHAPTER 3

YOUR PLANS and GETTING THE LISTS

Before jumping into getting the lists of foreclosed property sales, let's take a quick moment to go over your plans. You do have a plan, don't you? At this point you should have some idea in the back of your mind what *kind* of property you are looking for and *what* you plan to do with it after you get it.

WHAT ARE YOUR PLANS?

Listed below are the three basic options. These three will also be examined in greater detail later on in the book, but for now let's briefly look at each of them:

- Either reselling it immediately, or rehabbing and then reselling it, known as "flipping"
- Holding on to it as a rental
- Living in it as your personal residence

RESELLING/FLIPPING: You can do flipping one of two ways. You can buy the property, make no repairs or improvements and resell it immediately to a real estate wholesaler. The plus side of this type of flip is that you make your profit right away. The downside is you make less profit. Or you can buy and rehab it, reselling it for a potentially larger profit than you would make selling to the wholesaler. The biggest advantage either type of flipping provides is that you receive a relatively large sum of money (the profit) that I call "chunk cash" when you sell the property. The biggest disadvantage of flipping is that the chunk cash does not come at regular intervals. In light of that, and accounting for the time spent finding the properties and the cash required for holding and/or rehabbing, flipping properties should be regarded as a good supplemental second income source to your regular job, at least in the beginning. So don't quit your day job just yet.

This is not to say you cannot make a very nice living eventually doing just flips. You can. You just need to have a system in place that keeps the flips coming in and going out regularly so your chunk cash does also. However, a word of caution here. Depending on how many properties a year you flip, you could be considered a dealer in the eyes of the IRS and that can cause you substantial tax headaches. There are no clear-cut IRS guidelines as to how many flips constitute a "dealer," but you should definitely consult with your accountant if you find yourself doing more than four or five a year.

RENTALS: Buying property at foreclosure for rental purposes can make very good sense. Depending on how much you spend purchasing and rehabbing the property, you may actually be able to make money when refinancing it long term with a mortgage. Your accountant can explain how to do this to you. Renting is wonderful, in the fact that *your* tenant is ultimately paying off *your* property's mortgage for you. Plus, you should have extra money each month from the positive cash flow that the property throws off after all the expenses have been paid. In addition, you save, since rehabbing for a rental generally requires less work and expense than rehabbing for a flip.

While owning rental properties is a great way to build extra income and long-term wealth, there is a lot more to it than just owning the properties. Your accountant can go over the tax advantages and record keeping that go along with owning rental properties. And just be sure you are ready for the role of landlord. Besides dealing with tenants, there are many state and local regulations you need to be aware of. There are a slew of books out there on all the aspects of landlording. Be sure to read them before you go down this road.

PERSONAL RESIDENCE: Buying a house for personal use at a foreclosure sale is a great way to buy more house than you could have probably bought otherwise. Some of the pluses:

- You are buying much lower than retail price.
- You can outbid the rehabbers, since you don't have their concerns with turning it for a profit.
- You are saving by not having to pay a realtor's commission.

The minuses are that you may have to wait longer and be more flexible about finding the exact house you are looking for. But if you can deal with that, you can definitely save some bucks!

DIFFERENT TYPES OF REAL ESTATE

There are many different kinds of real estate out there to purchase:

- Single family homes
- Duplexes
- Triplexes
- Apartment buildings
- Garages
- Commercial and industrial buildings
- Raw land

If you are just starting out, the best type of property to begin with is the single family home, or SFH. These can be a stand-alone house, a side by side twin, or a row home. Why do I say these are the best? First of all, is the sheer number of SFHs out there to choose from. Second, they are the easiest to rent or flip. Third is stability. Most people's aspirations are to live in a single family home, and once they get there they tend to stay a long time, whether through ownership or rental. If your desire is rental properties, then a duplex, triplex, or small apartment building (four units or less) is the way to go. Above four units the rules change, and landlording becomes more complicated. If you are looking at larger apartment buildings, be sure to read up on what is involved with them.

Renting garages is a great way to make "easy" money. They need very little in the way of mechanical systems (heat, plumbing, etc.), don't require much maintenance and have few tenant problems. Commercial and industrial buildings can be a tricky animal. Flipping and/or renting those properties can be very difficult. Whereas a SFH appeals to almost everyone's basic needs (bedroom, kitchen, bathroom), a commercial, industrial, or office building must fit the *individual* requirements of the person or company looking at it. And that is why it can potentially take a LONG time to rent or sell it, driving up your holding costs. These are not the kinds of properties to begin cutting your teeth on. Leave these to the seasoned investors. The same is true with raw land. It takes a long time and a lot of work and money to make it developable, if it is developable at all. Save your time and money for another kind of better deal.

GETTING THE LISTS

"Where do I get the list of properties for foreclosure auctions?" is a common question. Well, there are several ways to get them. Depending on whether you are in a judicial foreclosure state looking for sheriff sales or a non-judicial foreclosure state looking for trustee auctions will determine where you want to look. To begin, let's look at the difference in frequency between real estate foreclosure/ trustee auctions and sheriff sale auctions.

Real estate foreclosure auctions that are carried out in non-judicial power of sale states occur as the need arises, while sheriff sales are generally conducted at regular intervals, usually on a monthly, weekly, or bi-weekly basis. Notices advertising sheriff sales, real estate or trustee auctions are generally published in the local newspapers at least thirty days prior to the sale, depending on local custom and law. Many times sheriff sales are also published in the local legal journal. You should get the lists as soon as they are made available, as this way you will have the maximum amount of time to do your due diligence work.

JUDICIAL FORECLOSURES – SHERIFF SALES

There are several possibilities for getting the sheriff sale lists:

1. Get the list from the sheriff's department at your local courthouse

The cheapest (usually free or for a small fee) and easiest place to obtain this list is the sheriff's office at the county courthouse, where the sheriff sales are typically held. Ask the clerk for the list of properties that will be offered at the next upcoming sale. They are usually available three to four weeks before the actual sale. Also ask if they have a copy of the rules pertaining to the sheriff sales. I will refer to them later in the book. If the courthouse is not convenient, many county websites now post the sheriff sale listings and rules online—the counties where I buy do. That is where I get my lists from. Simply go to the website and print them out. Available for the taking at courthouses in my area are the large individual paper handbills that list the details for each of the properties up for sale that month. These are the same handbills that many times you will see placed at the property location, making public notice that the property is up for sale.

2. Local newspapers and legal journals

Two additional places to get sheriff sale lists are the local newspaper and the local legal journal. Most states require that before a foreclosed property goes to sheriff sale it be advertised at least once, and in many cases twice or three times, in a countywide newspaper at a minimum thirty days prior to the sale. Some locales also require advertising in the local legal newspaper or journal. In Pennsylvania the rule is three times prior to the sale in the local legal journal if available and newspaper. The reason for all this advertising is twofold. First, it serves notice to all parties with a financial interest in the property that it is going to be auctioned at sheriff sale. Second, advertising of the sale will attract bidders and hopefully bring a good price for the property. By the way, the local legal journal is a good publication to subscribe to when you are starting out, since all properties going into foreclosure will be listed in it. You do not need to be a lawyer to subscribe to it. Contact your local bar association for more information.

3. Subscribe to a foreclosure listing service

Another source of lists is the foreclosure information reporting companies that have proliferated online. If you go online and type in "real estate foreclosure lists" you will see a myriad of choices to select from. Personally I'm not a big fan of the idea of buying something you can get for free. Both sheriff sales and non-judicial auctions are advertised in several publications and sheriff sales also at the county office or website. Buying the lists almost always involves having to sign up as a member. Some services for a small fee will allow you to "try them out" on a limited basis, but to get the complete detailed information often requires purchasing a more extensive and (hint) more expensive package. But of most concern is how often these services *update* their lists: daily, weekly, bi-weekly or monthly. This will determine whether the information they give you has value or is hopelessly outdated by the time you get it. These companies do foreclosure lists on a nationwide basis, so be certain to find out how often the list *for the area you plan to buy in is updated.*

It probably sounds like I don't endorse signing on with one of these foreclosure listing services. They can however put a lot of information at your fingertips, and if you plan to purchase foreclosures and sheriff sales *outside* your immediate area, they are probably the quickest and easiest way to get those lists, since *time is money*. All I am saying is check with several different ones to see what you are getting *before* giving them your credit card number to sign up.

NON-JUDICIAL FORECLOSURES – TRUSTEE & REAL ESTATE AUCTIONS

If you decided to subscribe to a foreclosure reporting service, you should see listings for trustee foreclosure auctions also in your reports. If not, look in your local newspaper where the sales would be advertised. Sales and auctions are usually listed in the classified, legal, business, real estate, or auction sections of your local newspaper. You can also do an online search. Type in "real estate auctioneers" with your state and that should bring up a plethora of listings for auctioneers in your area. Just go through the websites. When looking at the advertisements describing the auctions you need to be able to differentiate between trustee auctions, real estate auctions, and private real estate auctions. While they are all technically real estate "auctions" the rules and the auctions themselves are different. The next chapter will explain these differences.

Sample newspaper listing for property auctions in Philadelphia

Auctions	Auctions	Auctions

☆☆REAL ESTATE AUCTIONS☆☆

**32 Properties Will Be Sold Individually
on Thursday, October 25, 2007 at 1 PM
at our location 2501 E. Ontario St., Phila., PA 19134**

The Philadelphia District Attorney's Office Auction of Seized Properties

OPEN HOUSE INSPECTION SCHEDULE

Monday, October 22, 2007, 9:00-10:00 AM
1. 6141 N Woodstock St — 19138
2. 467 W Queen Ln — 19144
3. 5112 N Broad St — 19141
4. 4727 C St — 19120
5. 3741 Frankford Ave — 19124

Monday, October 22, 2007, 10:30-11:30 AM
6. 4620 N Marvine St — 19140
7. 4516 N Smedley St — 19140
8. 1609 W Erie Ave — 19140
9. 3423 F St — 19134
10. 628 E Cornwall St — 19134

Monday, October 22, 2007, 12:00 PM-1:00 PM
11. 2629 N 12th St — 19133
12. 2238 N 12th St — 19133
13. 2811 N Darien St — 19133
14. 2536 N Palethorp St — 19133

Tuesday, October 23, 2007, 9:00 AM-10:00 AM
15. 2043 N Van Pelt St — 19121
16. 2210 Seybert St — 19121
17. 2025 W Master St — 19121
18. 2451 W Berks St — 19121

Tuesday, October 23, 2007, 10:30 AM-11:30 AM
19. 2438-48 W Lehigh Ave — 19132
20. 2214 N Chadwick St — 19132
21. 2353 N Beechwood St — 19132
22. 2460 N 18th St — 19132

Tuesday, October 23, 2007, 12:00 PM-1:00 PM
23. 2440 N Stanley St — 19132
24. 2856 N 25th St — 19132
25. 2843 N Garnet St — 19132
26. 3102 N Stillman St — 19132

Wednesday, October 24, 2007, 9:00 AM-10:00 AM
27. 5329 Chestnut St — 19139
28. 51 N 52nd St — 19139
29. 5635 Market St — 19139
30. 5707 Thomas Ave — 19143
31. 1259 S 54th St — 19143
32. 6173 Upland St — 19142

REGISTRATION: Begins at 10AM. Must Show I.D. & secured funds. Title reports may be review at that time. TERMS: $3,000 non-refund. dep. in cash reqd. at knockdown for ea. prop.

Barry S. Slosberg, Inc.
Auctioneers/Appraisers
215-425-7030

AU-1487-L
www.bssauction.com

Sample listing in a local legal journal for sheriff sale properties in PA

DELAWARE COUNTY LEGAL JOURNAL VOL. 84 No. 41 10/12/05

No. 12345   16.   2005

MORTGAGE FORECLOSURE

1034 Main St.

Anytown, PA 19000

In the Township of Madison

Beginning at a point on the Southeasterly Side of Main St. at a distance of 300.20 feet Having an irregular lot.

IMPROVEMENTS CONSIST OF:

Residential dwelling.

SOLD AS THE PROPERTY OF: Anna Smith.

Hand Money: $3,987.25

Louis Lawyer, Attorney

No. 56789   17.   2005

MORTGAGE FORECLOSURE

Prop. In the City of Madiaon, beginning at a point on the Southeasterly side of Ace St. Front: 25' x 106.34'

BEING prem: 89 Ace St.

IMPROVEMENTS CONSIST OF:

Residential property

SOLD AS THE PROPERTY OF:

Matthew How a/k/a Mathew W. How

Hand Money $4,900.78

Louis Lawyer, Attorney

No. 34567   18.   2005

MORTGAGE FORECLOSURE

Prop. In the Borough of Downville, beginning at a point of intersection of the Southeasterly corner of First St. Elm Ave. Front: 25.60 feet Depth: 136.87 feet.

BEING Prem: 345 Darby Rd.

IMPROVEMENTS CONSIST OF:

residential property

SOLD AS THE PROPERTY OF:

John Brenner and Ellen Brenner.

Hand Money: $19,345.03

Brian Barrister, Attorney

No. 11934   19.   2005

MORTGAGE FORECLOSURE

ALL THAT CERTAIN property situated in the Twp. of Lemon in the County of Delaware, and the Commonwealth of PA, being described as follows: Parcel 12-34-56789-01 in the deed recorded 06/30/1998 in book 230 and page 1015

SOLD AS THE PROPERTY OF:

Jahn Aye

Hand Money: $2,000.00

Brian Barrister, Attorney

Sample Handbill of property for Sheriff Sale

SHERIFF'S SALE OF REAL ESTATE

AT THE

COUNTY COUNCIL MEETING ROOM

COURT HOUSE, MEDIA, PA

FRIDAY, JANUARY 18, 2008

11:00 O'Clock A.M. Prevailing Time

NO. 10858   **MORTGAGE FORECLOSURE**   2007

Property in the Township of Tinicum, County of Delaware, Commonwealth of PA on the Easterly

Front: IRR   Depth: IRR

Being Premises:

IMPROVEMENTS CONSIST OF: a single family residential dwelling.

SOLD AS THE PROPERTY OF:

TAKE NOTICE that a Schedule of Distribution will be filed within thirty (30) days from the date of sale and said distribution will be made in accordance with the Schedule of Distribution unless exceptions are filed thereto within ten (10) days thereafter. No further notice of the filing of the Schedule of Distribution will be given.

, Sheriff

Hand Money $15,588.20

CHAPTER 4
READING THE LISTS

SHERIFF SALE VOCABULARY

Listed here are definitions for many words and phrases that you will likely encounter at the sheriff sale no matter where it is being held. You should become familiar with them if you want to be successful and bid like a pro.

As Is/Where Is: Property is sold "As it Is and Where it Is" with no guarantees or warranties whatsoever.

Attorney on the Writ: The foreclosing attorney whose name appears on the writ of execution.

Bankruptcy: The financial inability of the property owner to pay their debt, thereby seeking relief through the courts. Any of the three types of bankruptcy (chapters 7, 11, 13) will stop the sale process for a minimum of three months and possibly longer.

Continued or Postponed: This is when the plaintiff and/or their attorney, or the lender and/or their attorney, or the court causes the sale to be continued or postponed to a later specified date. A continuation or postponement can occur for any number of reasons. One such example of this would be a technicality, such as improper advertising of the sale of the property.

Deficiency Judgment: A deficiency judgment occurs when the price a property sells for at auction is less than the balance of the unpaid loan. The lender (creditor) then seeks a deficiency judgment against the mortgagor (previous property owner) to recover the shortage plus expenses. Not all states allow deficiency judgments.

Ejection: The removal of persons and/or their possessions from a particular address who *no longer have legal claim to ownership of the real property*. Example: Persons whose house was lost to foreclosure but refuse to vacate. Differs from eviction in that persons ejected previously *had* legal claim to ownership of the property. Ejectment is usually carried out by the sheriff or constable.

Eviction: The removal of persons and/or their possessions from a particular address that have *legal claim only to occupy the property* but are in violation of those terms of occupation. Differs from ejection in that persons evicted never had legal claim to ownership of the property. Evictions are ordered by the court and are enforced by the sheriff or constable. Example: Renters who have defaulted in their rent and are ordered by courts to vacate the premises.

Hand Money: The deposit money that you are required to pay at the time you purchase the property at the sale.

Knock Down: The fall of the auctioneer's gavel. Going once, twice, three times...SOLD.

Marshaled: How liens are assembled in order and paid in that order.

Poundage: Term used for the commission that the sheriff's department receives for conducting the sale. Poundage varies, but it is usually in the one to three percent range of the sold price.

Right of Redemption: Specific period of time in which the former owner may buy back or "redeem" the property from the successful bidder. A complete detailed explanation is given in a later chapter.

Sheriff's Deed: The type of deed you receive from the sheriff showing transfer of the property from the sheriff to you as the new owner of the property.

Stay or Stayed: Denotes that the sale of the property has been stopped and the property will not be sold at that sale. A stay can occur minutes before the property is to be auctioned off. Stays happen for a number of reasons. The owner may have filed bankruptcy protection (called an automatic stay). It could be the homeowner or their attorney reached a payment agreement with the lender, or possibly the homeowner sold the property. For whatever the reason, as this information is generally not disclosed, the sale has been stopped. While a stayed property usually will not reappear for sale again, a property stayed due to bankruptcy however may reappear for sale if the bankruptcy filing is dismissed at a later date.

Subject to Mortgage: In this situation the property is *not* being foreclosed upon by the first mortgage holder but by a subsequent mortgage or lienholder. This means that if you are the winning bidder, you will not only be responsible for your bid but also for the *first and any other* mortgages or liens preceding whoever was foreclosing on the property.

Upset or Reserve Price: Maximum dollar figure that the foreclosing attorney will bid for the property. Basically, it is the starting point for the bidding. Your bid will have to be higher than that upset price to buy the property. Typically, the foreclosing attorney announces the upset price before bidding on the property commences. The upset price can include any of the following: the outstanding mortgage amount, past due and any other real estate taxes, attorney's fees, sheriff's costs, and any other costs directly related to the sale of the property. If the foreclosing creditor (in most cases a bank or mortgage company) did not bid to their upset price to cover their costs, then they would lose money if someone else bid less and won. If no one bids higher than the upset price, then the property goes back to the creditor. If the creditor was a bank, in most cases the property will become an REO and then be resold by an REO realtor.

Writ of Execution: Written court document issued by the Prothonotary commanding a person (in this case the sheriff) to carry out a particular action such as execute on a judgment.

SHERIFF SALE LIST

There is no standard format for how the information on a sheriff sale list of properties is presented. While the layouts will vary, the information presented will have many things in common. Below is a page from a sheriff sale list in one of the local areas that I attend. Chances are the format does not resemble the arrangement for the list used in your area. However, information such as names, property addresses and monies owed will be there. This particular county's listing only gives a bare skeleton of information. Many lists go so far as to include the property's legal description, name of the foreclosing entity (bank), etc. If there is any part of your list you do not understand, ask the clerk at your sheriff's office to explain it.

Now, let's look at this list in detail to see what all the information means and how to use it.

Sample Sheriff Sale List of Properties

No. **A**	Location **B**	Term&No. **C**	Name **D**	Debt **E**	Attorney **F**
1.	Darby Boro 766 Raven Rd.	06-1234	Ralph Jones	$56,234.89 **E1** $ 5,623.49 **E2**	Louis Lawyer
2.	Haverford Twp. 865 Seahorse Rd.	05-678	Al Johnson	$77,234.00 $ 7,723.00	Brian Barrister
3.	Thornberry Twp. 16 Holly Rd.	07-4788	Veronica Stevens Archie Stevens a/k/a Archibald Stevens	$135,978.50 2,000.00	Elliott Esquire
4.	Chadds Ford Twp. 2578 Poplar Drive	07-9342	Karen Singer	$28,435.00 $2,843.00	Brian Barrister
5.	Ridley Park 23 Hillside La.	06-9034	Allen King Administrator of the Estate of J. Kingman, Deceased	$93,406.80 $9,340.68	Brian Barrister
6.	Chester 1057 Scotts Way	07-0134	Bruce Martinson Ethel Martinson	$18,923.40 $1,892.30	Louis Lawyer
7.	Marple Twp. 56 Big Bux La.	03-4012	Stewart Flounder Sally Ann Smith	$467,903.50 $46,790.25	Brian Barrister

Beginning with column **A** on the far left, that is the reference number of the property on the list. Its only significance is to indicate the order that the sheriff follows when auctioning off the properties. Properties that are continued for sale at a later date will refer to that number and date of sale again. I also use it as my reference number when I categorize the properties.

Column **B** shows the property address and the "township or boro" where it is located. In some instances, for mailing and registration purposes, the actual town will differ from the township or boro listed.

C is "Term and No." (This is more commonly referred to as the "Docket Number.") It is important because it indicates the date and numerical order of the civil filing. Civil actions, which foreclosures are, also include divorces, lawsuits, judgments, and so on. The first two numbers indicate the year that the action was initiated. For instance, "07" means that the foreclosure action was filed in 2007, "06" indicates 2006, and so on. The second set of numbers "1234" indicates that it was the 1,234th civil action filed that year in the county court. That gives us an important timeline on how long the foreclosure action has been going on. This is important because the longer the foreclosure action drags out in court, the more interest, attorney fees, back taxes, and so on accumulate. This adds to the upset price and ultimately the property's price. You want to be wary when bidding on properties that have docket dates that are three or more years old and are coming up for sale again. More on this later.

Column **D** shows the person or persons named in the foreclosure. It may be one individual, a husband and wife, a business entity, or a property that is part of an estate. This name may or may not be occupying the property at the time of the sale.

E: The debt gives us two important dollar figures. First, the top figure (**E1**) is the amount of the foreclosure that the judgment is for. It is not the price at which the bidding for the property will start. That is known as the "Upset Price" and will be discussed later on. It is, however, a starting point for how much debt the creditor is looking to recover. You will use this figure as your starting point when you begin evaluating the properties to determine which ones are worth pursuing and which are not. The second figure (**E2**) is what is referred to as the "Hand Money." This is the money you will need **ON HAND** if you are the successful bidder on the property. In this particular county the amount of the hand money is a pre-determined fixed amount. Payment of hand money is typically cash or bank check at the time the sale is knocked down. You **must** have this money with you at that time to give to the clerk. You cannot run out to a bank to get it and come back. Credit cards are **NOT** accepted, nor are personal checks. If you do not have the correct hand money to pay the clerk, you forfeit the property and it returns to the auction block for re-bidding.

The last item **(F)** is the attorney handling the foreclosure. As you attend more foreclosures, you will notice that the same groups of attorneys handle most of the cases. Look up their phone numbers then write them down, as you will be referring to them again in the future.

TRUSTEE, REAL ESTATE & PRIVATE REAL ESTATE AUCTIONS

Unlike the lists for the judicial sheriff sales, which in some cases are exactly that, just lists with little or no information about the property other than the owner's name and address, in the listings for non-judicial trustee or real estate auctions you will typically see more information presented, and in the case of real estate and private real estate auctions most likely a picture of the property also. The layout in these three types of auction listings is a bit more standardized, as you will see. The descriptions and rules listed below regarding trustee auctions, real estate auctions, and private real estate auctions should be considered general in nature. Before attending any type of auction you need to *read and completely familiarize yourself with that particular auction's rules first.*

TRUSTEE & REAL ESTATE AUCTION VOCABULARY

Listed here are the definitions of many words and phrases that you will encounter at a trustee or real estate auction sale. Again, you need to be completely familiar with them if you plan to bid successfully.

Absentee Bid: This procedure allows someone to bid without actually being present at the auction. Consult the auctioneer for rules governing this type of bidding.

Absolute Auction: Also known as a no-reserve auction. An auction where the property sells to the highest bidder with no minimum bid amount.

As Is/Where Is: Same definition as sheriff sale.

Ballroom Auction: An auction involving multiple properties typically held in a large meeting room.

Bank Letter of Credit: Letter from a bank stating that the person named on the letter has been given a certain level of credit from that bank.

Broker Participation: Means third party brokers register bidders for properties sold at the auction in return for a commission paid by the auction firm or property owner.

Buyer's Premium: A stated percentage of the winning bid or a flat fee that is added to the winning bid as total cost to be paid by the buyer.

Caveat Emptor: Latin for "Let the buyer beware." Legal term denoting the buyer assumes all risk regarding the condition of the property purchased. (Goes with the term "As is/Where is.")

Collusion: An illegal practice where two or more people agree not to bid against each other in an attempt to lower the bidding price. Also known as bid rigging.

Estate Sale: Sale of property left after death of owner.

Hammer Price: Price of the last bidder acknowledged by the auctioneer before dropping the gavel or hammer.

Minimum Bid Auction: Auction in which there is a stated minimum price that the property must sell at or above, or be withdrawn from sale.

Minimum Bid–No-Reserve Auction: Auction in which there is a stated minimum bid price that the property must sell at or above, but in which the seller has no right to accept or decline a bid at or above the stated minimum.

Opening Bid: The first bid of an auction.

On Site Auction: Auction conducted on the site of the property being sold.

Reserve Auction: An auction in which the seller has the right to accept or decline any and all bids. Auction may also contain a reserve price, which is a minimum bid price the seller will accept.

Special Warranty Deed: A deed to property in which the Grantor (such as a trustee) warrants that the title issued to the Grantee (winning bidder) to be free from defects or claims only during the period that it was held by the trustee. It does not warrant against any defects or claims that existed before that period.

TRUSTEE AUCTIONS

Here are two hypothetical examples of trustee auction listings: the first from an auctioneer's website and the second one a typical example from a local newspaper's classified legal section.

Auctioneers Website

HYGHBID AUCTION COMPANY
www.HYGHBIDAUCTIONS.com

Type of Auction: Trustee
Date of Auction: September 15, 2006 at 1:00pm sharp
Auction Location: On site
Previews: One hour before sale

PICTURE

OF

PROPERTY

Property Location
Address: 525 Locust Ave.
City: Mytown
State: PA
Zip: 12345

Property Description: Three bedroom, two bath, brick exterior, Cape Cod. Eat in Kitchen, finished basement. New deck. Hot air heat with central air. Refrigerator Washer/dryer included. 1,590 sq. feet. Property .46 acres. Zoned R-2. Annual Property taxes $3,450.

TERMS & CONDITIONS of SALE:
1. Bid registration begins one hour before sale. Please have I.D (drivers lic.) for identification.
2. A 15% deposit due at sale knockdown. **CASH or CERTIFIED CHECK ONLY** unless other payment terms agreed to by trustee. Balance of payment due within 45 days of sale.
3. Property is sold **AS IS/WHERE IS.** Buyer is responsible to conduct any independent investigation they deem necessary to verify information provided by Trustee or Auction Company.
4. **ALL SALES ARE FINAL**
5. Property is sold by Trustee, pursuant to terms contained in the Deed of Trust. Property is conveyed by Trustee Deed
6. Trustee retains the right to cancel sale or reject any and all bids prior to knockdown.
7. Announcements made on the day of sale take precedence over all prior announcements.
8. A Buyers Premium of **TEN PERCENT (10%)** will be added to the high bid amount to determine sale price.
9. Auction Company represents the seller.
10. For additional information call (123) 456-7890

Local Newspaper Classified Legal Section

Mortgage Foreclosure Sale Default having been made in the payment of the indebtedness described in and secured by that certain mortgage executed by John Q. Public to Big City Mortgage Co. dated July 1, 2005 and recorded in book 1234 and page 567 of the records in the Judge of Probate in Rickville County, Oregon. Notice is hereby given that the undersigned as holder of said mortgage will under power of sale contained in said mortgage, sell at public outcry for cash to the highest bidder during legal hours of sale on March 19, 2008 at the front door of the Rickville County Courthouse, 133 Main Street, Prospect, Oregon 56789. The following described real property in the County of Rickville, in the State of Oregon, being the same property described in the above referenced mortgage. LOT 5, HAPPY ACRES SUBDIVISION IN THE OFFICE OF THE JUDGE OF PROBATE IN RICKVILLE COUNTY, OREGON. Said sale is made for the purpose of paying said indebtedness and the expenses incident to this sale, including reasonable attorney fees. Big City Mortgage Co. holder of said mortgage. Phillip Williams Attorney 711 W. Oak St. Conroy, PA 45678

Trustee auctions are similar to sheriff sales in many respects. First, you need to do much of the same research work regarding liens, judgments, title work, minimum bid, etc. that you would do prior to bidding at a sheriff sale. However, unlike sheriff sales which are officiated by the sheriff, trustee sales can be officiated by an auctioneer, sheriff, constable or the attorney representing the trustee. Trustee sales generally are conducted at the property but can be held at the courthouse or other large public meeting room. In the listing, besides the property's street address, you will most likely see its legal description and possibly some information about the debt and debtor, in addition to the date and time of the sale. It is advisable to call the day before the sale to verify if it has for some reason been cancelled or rescheduled. The terms of sale will be spelled out on the listing as well. Read them carefully but take notice—there usually is a sentence stating any announcements made on the day of sale take precedence over any prior releases, including the one you are reading.

You should go out and look at the property's exterior at least once prior to any formal inspection time. If it is unoccupied, you can do a more detailed walk around the exterior. Try to peek in the windows if possible to get a look at the interior, and take lots of notes. Asking neighbors about the property is also a good source of information, as I will explain in greater detail further on. You'll need to look at the auction listing to see if and when the property will be open for inspection. Generally it is one hour before the sale, but this can vary. Most trustee sales require a good faith deposit be paid when you register to bid. This amount can range from several hundred to thousands of dollars. This is customarily paid by bank check or cash, but verify this ahead of time so you have the proper form. If you are not the successful bidder or the property does not sell, your deposit monies are returned to you. The purpose of the deposit is to be certain the persons registering are serious qualified bidders.

Pay particular attention in the listing to whether the property is being sold as **free and clear** of all mortgages, liens and judgments or is being sold **subject to** any existing mortgages, liens, and judgments. A property being sold "free and clear" means just that. When you go to settlement and pay the balance due, you will receive a property that is free and clear of any liens or judgments against it. If this is so, then you do not need to spend money doing a separate title search before bidding; however, you may want to purchase title insurance before going to settlement on the property, just in case some prior lien was missed that you could be held liable for. If the property is being sold "subject" to all previous liens and judgments, then you will have to do your title work due diligence before bidding. You need to find out if there are any senior, junior, IRS, or tax liens not disclosed that will be "subject to" the sale of the property. If there are any and they are not discharged or wiped out at or before the sale, and you are the successful bidder, they now become **your** liens and **your** responsibility.

Be sure you fully understand the part in the terms of sale that deals with how payment for the property is handled. Is there a buyer's premium that you need to account for when determining your final bid price? Buyer's premiums vary with the auction and can be **five percent or more** of the bid price. Who is responsible for paying transfer taxes and other fees? As a rule, the buyer is responsible for those costs and fees, so you will need to add that figure to your bid calculations. How much money will you need with you at knock down if you are the winning bidder? Settlement can be in as little as several days after the sale to 45 days or more, so be sure you have your financing in place ahead of time. If for some reason you decide to renege and don't return to pay the balance due, you could be subject to the loss of your deposit money plus fines, so be sure of yourself when bidding. If you have *any* questions at all regarding the auction, contact the person listed for verification.

REAL ESTATE AUCTIONS

In contrast, real estate auctions are almost always conducted by an auction company hired by the creditor (bank, city, county, etc.) that took the property back after default. Again, the auctions are usually held at the property, the exception being if a large number of properties are to be auctioned off, in which case a ballroom auction will likely be used. There is also a relatively new third type of what I refer to as a "private real estate auction" that you might see. I call it that because the property is being auctioned "privately" at the request of the homeowner and not due to the fact it is being foreclosed on. Some homeowners are trying out this route, hoping to realize a higher selling price rather than selling it through the traditional realtor channel. I would stay away from these. By and large, there are few if any bargains to be found there.

RESERVE VS. ABSOLUTE

Real estate auctions come in primarily two varieties, **reserve** and **absolute**. You need to read the auction ad to determine which one it is and the details of the sale.

Example of an add for an Absolute Auction

REAL ESTATE
AUCTION

SATURDAY MAY 3rd @ 11AM SHARP
Ordered ABSOLUTE Auction
No Minimum Bid/No Seller Reserve

This is a great buying opportunity for those wishing to buy in Happy Valley County. All three homes to be sold by auction without reserve regardless of price. All homes are 4 bedrooms/2 baths with eat in kitchens.

Previews Thurs. & Fri. May 1st & 2nd 12-3 pm

TERMS OF SALE: $10,000 cashiers check to bid.
10% Buyers premium
30 day closing
Clear title guaranteed
Property sold As is/Where is

**For full details call Wayne Lowry Auctions
(123) 456-7890**

Example of an add for a Reserve Auction

REAL ESTATE AUCTION
WITH RESERVE
SATURDAY MAY 3rd @ 11AM SHARP

This is a great buying opportunity for those wishing to buy in Happy Valley County. All three homes to be sold by auction without reserve regardless of price. All homes are 4 bedrooms/2 baths with eat in kitchens.

Previews Thurs. & Fri. May 1st & 2nd 12-3 pm

TERMS OF SALE: 10 % down day of sale in cash or certified funds.
30 day closing
Property sold As is/Where is

For full details call Wayne Lowry Auctions (123) 456-7890

Reserve auctions, more often than not, offer fewer opportunities to make a good buy since the seller establishes a minimum "reserve" price that the property will not sell below. This price may or may not be disclosed at the beginning of the auction. And even if the bidding rises enough to go above the reserve price, the seller still can accept or reject the final bid. If the auctioneer cannot get the bidding to go above the reserve price, the property is withdrawn and is returned to the owner. Be careful not to confuse the term "minimum reserve" price with "minimum bid" price. While a property might be advertised without a published minimum reserve price, a minimum bid price is almost always published so you know going in where the bidding will be required to start at.

Conversely, in an "absolute auction" there is no reserve and the property is guaranteed to sell to the highest bidder, regardless of price. Absolute auctions, by virtue of this fact, represent the better opportunity versus reserve auctions to make a good purchase. In almost all cases the properties sold at reserve and absolute auctions are free and clear of any liens or judgments. In other words, other than purchasing title insurance you do not need to conduct your due diligence title research before bidding on the properties. You will notice many conditions in the terms of sale for the trustee auctions (buyer's premium, payment terms, cash needed on hand, deposits, etc.) also appear in the terms of sale for real estate and private real state auctions. As always though, read and familiarize yourself with the terms of sale of that particular auction.

TAX, JUDICIAL & REPOSITORY SALES

Besides the previous discussed sales, there are three other types of foreclosure sales in Pennsylvania: the **Tax** sale, the **Judicial** sale, and the **Repository** list. You may have similar sales where you are. Check with your sheriff or tax claims office for more information on them. Out of the two sales, the judicial sale probably represents better opportunity to profitably purchase properties.

TAX SALE: There are really two different types of tax sales depending on what state you are in: tax deed sales and tax certificate sales. Refer to the state tax sale list in the reference lists and resources section of the back of the book for the complete list. "Deed States" are so named because the property is foreclosed on by the municipality and at the tax sale the "deed" is auctioned off to recover the delinquent tax money. In "Non-Deed States" a public sale or auction is held for the right of an individual to collect on a delinquent taxpayer's debt. The winning bidder pays the past due taxes on behalf of the delinquent taxpayer and receives in return first lien position. Then if the tax debt, including interest, is not repaid within the specified time period, the purchaser of the lien forecloses. Rules for these sales vary tremendously, so a clear understanding of them is an *absolute must.*

Pennsylvania, being a deed state, has a tax sale known in my area as the "Upset Sale." The date varies but is usually in September. A good faith deposit is required to bid at the tax sale and is returned to you if you do not end up purchasing any properties. The list of properties and date of the sale is found at the county's tax claims office as well as online, and is advertised in local newspapers. As with sheriff sales, you cannot gain entry into tax sale properties to inspect them prior to the sale. Rules for the tax sale differ somewhat from those of the standard sheriff sale. I would advise that prior to bidding on any property at a tax sale you consult with your attorney and title company to see if they are aware any inherent problems you could encounter. The minimum bid for the property must be enough to cover the unpaid taxes, municipal liens and any associated costs.

One of the glitches you should be aware of when buying property at the tax sale is that the property is being auctioned to satisfy the past due taxes and/or municipal liens *only.* Any mortgages, non-municipal liens, or judgments in place on the property at the time of sale stay with the property when sold. So if you are the successful bidder, then any of these mortgages, liens, or judgments now belong to you. You need to do your title work due diligence in regards to the mortgage, lien, and judgment situation before bidding at the sale. Whereas in a traditional sheriff sale there is always the chance of junior lienholders being wiped out, this is not the case in a tax sale property. Once again, the rules in your location may be different, so check first to be sure.

Another reason making it difficult to find a good deal at the tax sale is that, as in my area, you have to be a minimum of two years past due on your taxes before the property is even considered for the tax sale. You would think that would leave the owner a lot of time to catch up. But most often you will find that the day before or even the morning of the sale the delinquent taxpayers are lined up at the tax claim office to pay their taxes, or at least set up a payment plan. Doing either will result in their property being removed from the tax sale list. You will find that most properties on the list prior to the sale end up being removed.

JUDICIAL SALE: The Judicial sale, usually held in the spring, auctions any properties remaining from the previous tax sale to the highest bidder, free and clear of all tax or municipal claims, mortgages, judgments, or liens due at the time of the sale. As with the tax sale, a good faith deposit is required to bid. The list of properties, again, is available at the tax claims office, the county website, and published in local newspapers. Rules for the judicial sale are similar to the tax sale. Because of the fact that properties are sold free and clear of all debt (you do not need to do title work due diligence), there is a better chance of finding a good deal at the judicial sale. Unfortunately, as is the case with the tax sale, owners can come in, clear up delinquent taxes or claim they were not properly notified of the sale and contest it, which would remove the property from the sale list. As before, just because a property is on the list does not mean that it will ultimately make it to the sale.

REPOSITORY LIST: The repository list is not actually a foreclosure auction per se but more of an ongoing sale. If a property ultimately fails to sell at either the tax or judicial sale, it ends up on the repository list. Many areas have a repository list. You can obtain the repository sale list at your county's website or courthouse. These properties can be purchased at any time, but use caution. Many times they are either vacant pieces of land that cannot be built on, properties in war zones, or those with such environmental issues that nobody wants them at any price. Every once in a great while though you find a worthwhile property there that somehow got missed, so it is not a bad idea to check the repository list from time to time. Who knows, it might be you that finds that "diamond in the rough!"

CHAPTER 5
PICKING & FINANCING THE PROPERTIES

PICKING THE AREAS

The first step to picking the properties is to look over your lists and decide which areas you plan to buy in. Don't look at the amount of the debt just yet. Concentrate on the areas for now. We will deal with dollar amounts next. A good rule of thumb is to pick your properties within a forty-five minute driving radius of where you live. Why? Because while you are doing any rehab work for a flip or rental, the cost spent in time and fuel driving up and back to the property will certainly begin to add up. Plus if the property is ultimately ending up a rental, think about this statement: "I'm really glad my rental is only a short drive when I get that eight p.m. phone call to go clear a stopped-up drain."

If you plan to just quickly flip it to a wholesaler and move on, then this point is not really as critical. Look for properties in areas where property values are at least stable or hopefully increasing. Looking at properties in areas that are experiencing decreasing values and *hoping* for future increase is speculating, and not recommended. On the other hand, if you are planning on purchasing property to hold as a long-term rental and you're looking in areas where the surrounding neighborhoods' values are increasing, and your knowledge leads you to believe this trend will continue into your prospective area, then looking there is probably a good idea. This is when it's **REALLY** important to *know your local areas*. I can't overemphasize this point enough. A great deal in a lousy area is not a great deal.

Read the local newspapers to keep abreast of trends and developments, especially anything concerning the local school district. School districts weigh heavily upon a buyer's decision when choosing an area to live in. When looking at prospective properties I try to keep in mind the following question: "If I were buying this house, would I feel safe and comfortable living here?" If your answer is no, then cross it off the list. Unless you have a really, really good reason, one type of area that I recommend staying away from is what is commonly referred to as the "war zones." These are areas where drugs and crime are rampant. It doesn't make any sense, no matter how good the deal is, to put your life or anyone else's for that matter in danger renovating a property. Cross those properties off the list. Finish looking at the remaining property locations, checking the ones that you feel good about.

Now it's time to look at the dollar amounts of the foreclosure debt. Until you actually go out, see the properties and ascertain as best you can the amount of rehab work they will need, this step is merely to establish a starting point from which you will develop the list of property(ies) to ultimately go see. Right now you should have a fairly good idea of the price range of properties you should be looking at. Be realistic. If you only have access to $ 100,000 in capital you probably should not be looking at $ 300,000 properties unless you have a plan to bring in partners or get access to more funding.

At this time, review each of the properties you previously picked based on their location and determine if they fit your funds. After doing your due diligence and crunching the numbers, many of the properties will be eliminated for various reasons, so you want to try to get as many properties on the list in the beginning as possible. If your list starts out with only two or three properties on it rather than say ten or twenty, odds are they will be eliminated and you won't end up having anything to bid on at the sale. So don't just focus your efforts on a few properties. You need to have a large list in the beginning.

I HAVE TO PAY FOR IT WHEN and HOW???

That is the response I hear most often when talking about buying property at foreclosure auctions to the uninitiated. This is the part most people don't realize about all sheriff, most trustee, and some real estate auction sales. In almost every instance all properties are to be paid for in cash, bank check, or certified funds **ONLY.** This is one time you can leave home without your Visa card, since you can't pay with credit cards. Depending on what type of sale you will be attending—sheriffs, trustee, or real estate auction—you'll need to find out *in advance* from either the sheriff or the auctioneer conducting the sale what the terms of payment and rules for the sale are. For sheriff sales, these terms can be as short as full payment due within two hours after the sale (as in Douglas County, Kansas) to 30 days from the date of sale (as in Philadelphia, Pennsylvania), and everything in between. Expect trustee and real estate auctions to have similar time frames. In my local five-county area, full payment is due anywhere from ten to thirty days from the day of sale, so that sale date is very important.

Sheriff sale properties are typically **not** sold with clear ownership at the time of the sale. Depending on what is typical for your location, you should receive what is known as a Sheriff's Deed, usually in 60 to 180 days after the sale. Your attorney can tell you what is typical for your location. What's more, because of the very nature and risk of sheriff sale properties, *traditional mortgage companies will not give you a loan to buy them.* That is not to say there isn't some banking institution out there somewhere that will lend on a sheriff sale. If, however, you rehab and hold onto the property for either personal use or as a rental, once you have the sheriff's deed, *then* you can refinance it with a traditional mortgage. Trustee sales and real estate auctions do offer you the chance to obtain pre-approval for a loan or mortgage. You need to be certain you are approved (with a pre-approval letter stating so) because if not, you could be in default if you are not able to fulfill your obligation to purchase the property. If found in default, you'll lose your deposit and you can be held liable for financial damages suffered by the seller. But don't get discouraged if you do not have the money. The next chapter will tell you how to get it.

CHAPTER 6

GETTING THE MONEY

So how do you buy properties at sheriff sales or trustee auctions when you can't get conventional financing to pay for them? Believe it or not, there are options available to you. Some are easier to obtain than others. Listed below are these options, categorized two ways:

YOUR OWN MONEY	OTHER PEOPLE'S MONEY (OPM)
Savings accounts	Lines of credit from banks
Self-directed IRA	Credit cards
	Borrow or loans from family or friends
	Hard money lenders

YOUR OWN MONEY

In terms of getting your hands on money, the quickest and easiest way is to simply use **your own money.** This can be cash you have in a savings account or stuffed in an old mattress. It can be CDs, stocks, bonds, or any other instrument that you can redeem or borrow against. Or it can be money you pull out of a *self-directed IRA.* If tapping into an IRA, it must be a *self-directed* **IRA,** and not any other type of IRA, such as a Roth, or you will incur penalties. Check with your accountant to be sure about directing the use of the money. Simply stated, depending on how much cash you have will determine how much property you can buy. Now I'm not saying that I *recommend* using your own money for purchasing and rehabbing the properties; sometimes you have no other choice. I'm just saying sometimes using your own money is the *easiest and quickest* way to do it. But you *never* want to use your own money for these projects if you can use other people's money (OPM) instead. The problem with using all your own money is it's finite. When it runs out there isn't any more. And you don't want to run out of money mid-stream on the project. Once you have invested it in the property, you can't get it back until you either sell or refinance it and plow the profits back into the next project. When you're using OPM usually that is not the case. That doesn't mean OPM is not finite, it can be. But as the old saying says, "There's more out there, you just have to know where to find it."

OPM (OTHER PEOPLE'S MONEY)

LINES OF CREDIT: If you own a home, probably the easiest OPM to obtain is a Home Equity Line Of Credit, or "HELOC" (pronounced he-lock) in banking lingo. A HELOC is actually a revolving line of credit/second mortgage you can obtain from your bank. This is a **secured** line of credit, which means if you default on it the lender can foreclose on your house. Banks don't actually care what you do with the money. You can use it for whatever you wish and pay it back over time with interest. But you do have to pay the money back...*eventually.* Interest rates and repayment times vary by bank, so be sure to shop around. Another nice thing about a HELOC is interest; in most cases it is tax deductible. Another option is a personal **unsecured** line of credit, whereby your good name and bank relationship are what is pledged for security. Unsecured lines are typically made for smaller amounts of money, since there is no collateral for the bank to hold. The two most popular payment options for lines of credit are interest-only payments and principle and interest payments. The difference is that on interest-only you make payments only on the interest (no principle) of the money you borrow, resulting in a lower payment amount. On principle and interest the payments are higher, since you are paying back not only interest but principle too.

CREDIT CARDS: Credit cards are another way to access fast cash. I know of many people who have bought properties with money borrowed from credit cards. While most situations will not allow you to actually pay for the property with a credit card, you get a **credit advance** and borrow money from the card(s). Check the last page of your credit card statement. Many times credit card companies issue "checks" as part of your monthly statement. These can be used just like regular checks to withdraw money against your credit card up to the amount of your credit advance limit. Bear in mind that you will have less credit available to you with that card if you need it for something else, as credit advance money counts toward your total credit limit. Check with the credit card company(ies) for full details on their requirements and interest rates. And one more thing, that interest rate in most cases is negotiable, so this will give you an opportunity to test those skills.

FAMILY and FRIENDS: A third way to acquire OPM is to borrow from family and friends. Explain to them fully *what* you are doing and *how* you intend to do it. Expect them to be skeptical. Tell them of your expected profits as well as the risks involved. Offer to pay them simple interest on their money. Another source for raising even larger amounts of capital from people you don't know is by making a public offering that also goes by the term "private lending." Borrowing money by making offers to strangers is more complicated than borrowing from family and friends, since public offerings are regulated by the Securities and Exchange Commission, or SEC as it is commonly referred to. You will need to comply with their rules, and failure to do so can result in some stiff penalties and huge amounts of aggravation. If you decide to go this route, I strongly urge you to read up and research fully the correct procedures for your state. A fellow named Alan Cowgill has an excellent book and conducts seminars that explain how to raise capital from private sources where he walks you through the compliancy laws of your particular state's SEC rules. I would urge you to look into it if you plan to use this type of fund raising in the future. For more information, his website is www.PrivateLendingMadeEasy.com, or call 1-866-831-3540.

PARTNERING: Another option is to get a partner. While having a partner is not always the best thing (you have to split the profits at the end), it can lighten both the financial and workload of the project. It always helps if one or both of the partners happen to be a tradesman and can perform some of the rehab tasks. In any case, if you decide to partner with a friend or family get everything, and I mean *everything* in writing. Keep in mind you need to treat this as two or more people entering into a *business* relationship and not as you and your friend, uncle, or whoever rehabbing a property. Partnerships between friends or family can be devastating if things don't go as planned. I strongly recommend you have a lawyer draw up the partnership agreement. It should spell out **everything** in complete detail. Consider it cheap peace of mind. Many friendships have been ruined or family relations destroyed by people who think they can do this on a casual handshake.

HARD MONEY LENDERS: The fourth way to acquire OPM is by using what are known as "Hard Money Lenders." When I speak about hard money lenders I am not speaking about the burley shylock-style loan sharks from the movies; however, these people do exist and are out there loaning money, and I urge you to steer clear of them. You will find the hard money lenders I am speaking about are *real* companies, staffed by hardworking and knowledgeable business people. Hard money lenders loan out money for short-term use. Like banks and mortgage companies, they loan money for the purchase of real estate. Unlike banks and mortgage companies, hard money lenders base their loans more on the value of the property and project and less on you and your credit history. Hard money lenders typically loan money for projects that banks will not. Not every hard money lender loans for sheriff sale properties, but many will. You need to contact each of them and find out which ones do. A sample of a hard money lender's ad might look like this.

Sample Hard Money Lender Advertisement

INVESTOR'S FRIEND

INVESTOR FRIENDLY HARD MONEY LENDING

- No down payment
- Quick 48 hour approvals
- We finance <u>all</u> types of deals
- Low rates
- Easy interest only payments up to 6 months
- Loans up to 100% of sale price
- No minimum credit score requirements
- For all your financing needs

CALL US AT 321-234-5678 TODAY!

Investor's Friend Lending
567 Main St.
Anytown, PA 67890

One of the easy ways to locate hard money lenders is to check with your local real estate investing group. Members in the group who have used hard money lenders can recommend to you the best ones to work with. You can also go online and do a search under "hard money lenders" and pull up listings for them. Hard money lenders can be good friends. Especially when you are first starting out. But there are pros and cons dealing with hard money lenders. Most if not all hard money lenders will have you fill out an application before they loan you Dollar One. Before signing anything, make sure you read over and understand exactly their terms and conditions, and ask questions if you are unsure of anything.

Now, the **PROS...**

One of the biggest advantages of using hard money lenders is they get you the money fast. Where it can take a bank *weeks* to get you funds, hard money lenders can have the money to you in *days.* Hard money lenders are more concerned with how much the property will cost to rehab and its value fixed up rather than what your credit score is. If this is your first project, you might find it a good idea to use a hard money lender. From their experience, they can give you ideas on what to and not to do in rehabbing the property. Depending on the project, you may find they can lend you most if not all the money you need to buy and improve the property. Most hard money lenders use the sixty to seventy percent range of the properties **After Repaired Value (ARV)** as their basis for lending. ARV represents the value of the property after all repairs and renovations are completed. So depending on the ARV, you may or may not have to put up any money of your own. Most hard money lenders will go out to look at the property before approving the loan. If they think what you want to do looks shaky at best, they will tell you so and most likely not loan the money. I would take their advice to heart and move on. They understand the business. What they *don't* want back as payment is your half-baked project that didn't work out. They are in the selling money, not finishing rehabs business. Hard money lenders sound like a good way to go, so you may be asking, where is the fly in the ointment?

And, the **CONS...**

First and foremost is cost. Hard money lenders don't come cheap. Because they fund projects with higher risk factors that don't conform to traditional banking standards, they have to charge more. This comes as a real shock to many people just starting out. Hard money lenders charge both points and interest rates that are typically higher than what a bank would charge. Points, as they are called in the lending biz, are one percent of the amount you borrow and are typically paid up front. Hard money lenders typically charge four to eight points, sometimes more. So if you are looking for $ 100,000 you would have to pay $ 6,000 if it is a six point loan. Interest rates are also typically higher than what a bank charges. Expect them to be in the ten to fifteen percent range.

You may be wondering, why so high? It's because hard money lenders take on riskier short-term loans that traditional banks wouldn't touch. For example, typically a traditional bank or mortgage company won't loan money for a property that needs extensive work done to it, or is missing the kitchen or bathrooms. Most hard money lenders loan their money for usually no more than six months at a time. After that point, they expect you will have completed the rehab and refinanced with a conventional mortgage if you are going to rent it out, or sold it if it was going to be a flip. Hard money lenders as a rule collect only interest on the loan while you are doing the rehab. This helps keep your out-of-pocket financing costs to a minimum while the rehab is under way. Their payday comes at the end when you sell or refinance the property, so they want to be as sure as possible it has a happy ending.

HOW MUCH SHOULD I SPEND TO BUY A PROPERTY?

At this point you should have a pretty good idea of your strategy for financing the property (ies) you plan to bid on. Be creative. Mix and match different sources and techniques if your own personal finances will not cover the complete cost of purchasing. Just don't be tempted to think, since I have $ 100,000 I can spend $ 100,000 to buy a property, right? Well, not exactly. There are lots of additional costs that will come out of the $ 100,000 before finally selling or renting the property. Like any new endeavor, sometimes it is better to start small then work your way up to bigger, more expensive and complex projects. Rehabbing foreclosures by its very nature requires you to be conservative when calculating costs. Not overextending yourself makes more sense than realizing halfway through the rehab you do not have enough money to complete it. If you have $ 100,000 total for your first rehab, you may find that after using the formulas you calculate that you can only afford to spend $ 60,000 acquiring the property, the rest is committed to rehab and holding costs.

HOW MUCH PROFIT CAN I EXPECT TO MAKE?

That is a common question asked and a hard one to answer. To say you should make "X" dollars profit every time you flip a property is difficult. There really is no "standard" profit. The amount of profit is really up to you. There are certain *percentages* you *need* to make for the project to be worth your time, money and effort. Also, keep in mind that bigger projects do not always translate into bigger percentages of profit.

Let's look at the following example. The figures shown for holding costs, realtor commission, and capital gains are for example purposes only and not representative of any actual amounts.

EXAMPLE

You buy small house "A" at an auction sale for $ 65,000. You put $ 10,000 in to rehabbing it and sell it in four months for $ 125,000, yielding you a gross profit of $ 50,000. After deducting your holding costs for four months, the realtor's commission to sell it, and the capital gains tax all of which total $ 15,000, you realize a net profit of $ 35,000, or a forty percent return on your $ 75,000 investment. Not too shabby for four months work. Do that three times a year and that's an extra $ 105,000 in your pocket.

Now, for comparison, let's look at a bigger project. You buy a larger house "B" for $ 180,000 and put $ 50,000 into rehabbing it, but because it's bigger it takes six months to rehab and sells for $ 320,000, yielding a gross profit of $ 90,000. After deducting your holding costs for six months, the realtor's commission to sell it, and the capital gains tax, all of which total $ 40,000, you realize a net profit of $ 50,000 or a twenty-two percent return on your $ 230,000 investment. Do that twice a year and that's an extra $ 100,000. Not too bad either. But even though you made a greater net profit on the larger house, you made a *greater percentage* of profit with less capital outlay with the smaller house.

	"A"	"B"
Purchase price	$ 65,000	$ 180,000
Rehab costs	+ $ 10,000	+ $ 50,000
TOTAL	$ 75,000	$ 230,000
Selling Price	- $ 125,000	- $ 320,000
Gross Profit	$ 50,000	$ 90,000
Holding costs	- $ 15,000	- $ 40,000
NET PROFIT	**$ 35,000 or 47 percent**	**$ 50,000 or 22 percent**

This illustrates that while bigger projects might make you more actual cash than smaller ones, the difference you had to lay out in money to buy and rehab do not always translate into a greater *percent* of net profit after all is said and done. Now I am not saying only do little projects. Pick the right larger project and you may make $ 100,000 with net profits of forty percent or more. Mix up the size and scope of your rehabs as you gain experience doing it. It all really comes down to carefully choosing the property you plan to bid on. If it looks like the numbers just aren't working out and your profit percentage is below the minimum, then pass it and move on. There are lots of other properties and opportunities out there. Leave that property for some one else to buy and not make any money on. Here are, in my opinion, the standards you should observe:

- You want to end up with a minimum **NET PROFIT** of at least *fifteen percent.* Any less than that and it's just not worth your while. Wait for a better property.
- You want to shoot for between a *twenty to forty percent* **NET PROFIT** as your **IDEAL** target range goal.
- Above *forty percent* **NET PROFIT** you hit a home run, congratulate yourself. Go out to dinner and celebrate!

CHAPTER 7
GOING OUT TO SEE THE PROPERTIES

FIRST, KNOW YOUR BUYER

As you're getting ready to begin the process of looking at properties, you should give thought to what kind of buyer you are looking to attract when you go to sell or rent it out. Who do you want to target? Do you understand the market for the area where you plan to buy? Is it an area where people live for only a couple of years and then move on up, or a stable, older neighborhood where houses only come up for sale once in a while? What types of people live in the neighborhood? Is it predominantly couples just starting families, with younger children and mini-vans, or older retired folks looking for peace and quiet? Or maybe single professional people who like to party a lot?

You need to give this some thought when looking at the properties. Does the house only have two bedrooms in the land of three and four bedrooms? Without building an addition for that third bedroom (a rehab no-no) will make it difficult to resell or rent to almost any one other than a single person or a couple with no kids. But yet there is a market for two bedroom houses. You just have to know your buyer and how to present it to them. Make it appealing to that professional single or that childless couple who doesn't want extra rooms to clean and can see that second room as the multipurpose spare bedroom/office/computer room equipped with all the high-tech computer hook-ups ready to go when they move in. Is the property you are looking at a nice four-bedroom colonial that unfortunately happens to be located on a busy road? That's also a tough sell, as most people don't like the noise and traffic associated with living on a busy road, especially if it's a family with young children. Older folks downsizing after the kids have moved out like houses with the convenience of all of the living space on one floor, such as a ranch house. These are all points to consider when looking at the properties.

GROUND RULES

Well, don't go hopping in your car and driving off to look at the properties just yet. You need to understand the ground rules of looking at properties first. And the ground rules begin with the fact that there are two types of properties out there: **Unoccupied** and **Occupied.** With unoccupied property, the former owners have abandoned them. More or less, they loaded up the car or truck with as much stuff as they could carry and disappeared into the night, leaving no forwarding address. With the occupied property, the owners are still living there. If you are looking at sheriff sale properties, whether occupied or unoccupied, you *cannot* get inside to inspect them before the sale. It is the same circumstance with trustee and real estate auctions. *However* with trustee and real estate auctions, in most instances you will be able to inspect unoccupied properties inside, usually an hour or less before the auction commences, depending on the auction rules. And even if the property is occupied and you cannot gain entry inside, you can still inspect it from the outside.

When driving or walking by you want to be as inconspicuous as possible, in case the property is still occupied by the owners. A flashy car with music blaring is sure to call attention to you. You want to appear like the unassuming pizza delivery man looking for an address. When making your outside inspection, you are looking for several things. First, the style of the house: Cape Cod, colonial, rancher, twin, duplex, triplex, row, etc. You need to know this when getting your comparables, or "comps," which are selling prices for similar properties in the area. Not all properties in any given neighborhood will always be the same, so you need to be sure when comparing them you are doing apples to apples.

You also need to determine the condition of the property to get some idea of what fix-ups will be needed. Take notice of the neighborhood. Are the streets clean or are they full of litter and trash? Lawns maintained? What types of cars are parked there? Are they prosaic-looking sedans representative of a working, middle-class neighborhood or are they abandoned and up on milk crates? You get the idea. Does the area fit the rule: "If I was buying this house to live in, would I feel safe and comfortable living here?"

WHAT TO BRING WHEN LOOKING

Let's see what items you should bring when you're out looking at properties. First, carry a note- book to jot down information about each place you look at. Also, a pair of binoculars is handy to get a close look at the condition of a pitched, shingled roof. I carry a small folding two-step stool if needed for peeking in windows if I'm sure the place is unoccupied. You'll need a camera to take pictures of each property you look at. If you don't have a digital camera, you'll need to get one. Mine has a neat feature that lets me record the property's name and address. This is important because after looking at dozens of properties they all begin to look the same and it helps you to remember the details from each of them. Just download them into your computer. Now that you know what you need, let's get ready to get out and go looking.

PLANNING YOUR ROUTE

By now you should have your list narrowed down to properties that fit your criteria. Depending on how many properties you plan to see (sometimes I look at ten or more in a day), you need to plan a route so you're not wasting time and gas driving all over the place. Before GPS units I used one of those book maps to laboriously plan my routes, and that took a lot of time. Now with the affordability of GPS navigation units, they are without a doubt the way to go. All I do is plug in the property locations and the GPS plans the route for me. I still use the map but only to get an overall idea of where the properties are located in relation to each other. However, the map is a great tool for getting "the big picture" of the area I plan to look at, since it shows all kinds of other things, like parks, lakes, public transportation, and lots more. This can be very handy knowing that a school and a shopping center are located nearby a property I plan to bid on, possibly increasing the property's desirability to certain buyers and ultimately making it easier for me to resell. So I still recommend getting yourself a map, if only for reference sake.

LOOKING AT CONDOMINIUMS

If the properties you are going to see happen to be condominiums, here are some things to keep in mind. Most condominiums will probably be located in either a high or low rise building, and depending on exactly where in the building the unit is located might make it virtually impossible to actually see any of it. Condominiums are actually a form of ownership whereby you own a dwelling unit up to the interior walls of that individual unit. All exteriors of the building, including the common areas and mechanical systems, are owned by an undivided interest and the condominium association is responsible for their upkeep. The cost of that upkeep is reflected in the monthly dues that the condominium owners pay. Those "condo fees" are one of the reasons I don't like buying condos for flips or rental. While you are rehabbing, one of your holding costs are the monthly condo fees. If the fee rises dramatically or is high to begin with, that could hinder your ability to profitably rent or quickly flip the unit. And if unbeknownst to you the building is in need major repair work, such as a roof or other large scale repair projects requiring assessments, then you will have to bear those costs also. My advice, unless the condo represents an exceptional deal, steer clear of condos.

UNOCCUPIED PROPERTIES

Since unoccupied properties are the easiest to deal with I'll cover them first. Even though a property is unoccupied, you still cannot gain access into them. The sheriff's office, foreclosing lender, or trustee will have had the doors locked shut. Many times the handbill for the pending sheriff or trustee auction sale will be posted on the door. But that doesn't mean you cannot *find out more* about the property and what's inside.

Your first step is to ask the neighbors. Neighbors love to talk. Chances are good the house has been unoccupied for some time now and it's starting to look a bit ratty. The grass probably needs a good cutting or the weeds have taken over, and the neighbors don't like that look. When you knock on the neighbor's door, explain to them that the property is going to be sold at a foreclosure sale and *your* intention is to buy it and fix it up to make it really nice. You will be the answer to their prayers. "It's bringing down the value of the neighborhood" is a comment you will most likely hear many times over. They will tell you everything you want to know about it. For instance: "Whenever it rained the Smiths would start a bucket brigade from the second floor window on the right." That tells you there is a problem with a leaky roof—and probably the ceiling under it as well. Listen carefully and take notes. After chatting with the neighbors, it's time to look around at the house.

If the foreclosure is occurring in colder climates during the winter months when there is potential for below freezing temperatures, the property may have been winterized to prevent burst pipes. Winterizing is the process whereby the water supply to the property is shut off, all the water in the pipes inside the house is drained out, and non-toxic anti-freeze is pumped back in its place. A tip-off that it has been done is a tag noting this, usually placed on the door by the company that did the winterizing. This is a good thing, since many times you'll find the utilities shut off due to lack of payment by the previous owners, and with no electric to run the heating system freeze-ups can happen. Had the property not been winterized, and for some reason the water supply coming into the property was not shut off and a pipe bursts, you might end up purchasing a property with an indoor swimming pool you had not planned on. Another tactic to finding more information about a property's condition is to check with your local code enforcement, or License and Inspections (L & I) department as they are sometimes called, to see if there are any uncorrected building code violations on record.

EVALUATING THE PROPERTY

Start at the roof and work your way down. If it's a shingled roof, use your binoculars to get a better look the condition of the shingles. If they are the standard asphalt type and curling around the edges or a lot of the little gravel on them is missing, figure on most likely needing a new roof. If it is a flat roof, you will not be able to see it, so unless the structure is of very recent vintage (less than ten years old), a good rule of thumb is to figure in the cost of a new roof anyway. Even if it only ends up needing just a patch or two, it's better to be ahead in your estimate costs than behind. Next have a look at the windows. If they are old, possibly damaged single pane glass with wooden or aluminum frames without storm windows and you're planning on rehabbing and flipping the property, expect to be replacing the windows with new ones. One of the first items buyers look for are new, energy-efficient windows. Maintenance-free vinyl tilt-in style windows are the most popular for replacement and come in a variety of styles and price ranges.

What is the exterior like? Is it brick, vinyl or aluminum siding, asbestos shingles, or something else? Does it need to be painted or just power washed? Depending on the area, look at the other nearby properties and they will show you what needs to be done. Older buildings with painted exteriors can be cleaned and if necessary repainted. Power washing is inexpensive and can improve the look of dirty vinyl siding, brick, stone, or stucco dramatically.

Moving on, look at the foundation walls. You are looking for large cracks or gaps, which can indicate structural or foundation problems. This can be caused by several things, such as excessive settling or a defect in the walls. Cracks, especially large ones, can be extremely expensive to fix, and not being able to see what the inside walls look like, you might want to pass on that property.

If the property you are looking at is in a climate that requires heat in the winter months, it helps if you can determine what type of fuel is being used. Why is that important? Well, if it uses gas to heat it and the heater needs to be replaced, a gas heater typically costs less than a comparable unit that burns fuel oil or solid fuel. Gas heaters burn cleaner and require less maintenance than oil or solid fuel units, saving you on tune-up costs. Also, you don't have the creosote and soot deposits in the chimney associated with oil or solid fuel units, which may require a chimney cleaning. Is there a large white cylindrical tank visible outside, like in picture #3? If so, it's probably a propane gas tank, and that's good. If you see a grey metal box with a round disc attached to it with pipes coming out it and it looks like the picture #1, you have natural gas. That's also good. If you do not see either a propane tank or gas meter, then you may have electric heat. Or if the property you are looking at is located in a rural area, it might be that you have a heater that burns coal, wood or some other similar solid fuel. Or you might see something that looks like picture #2.

#1 Natural Gas Meter

#2 Fuel Oil Filler Neck

#3 Propane Tank

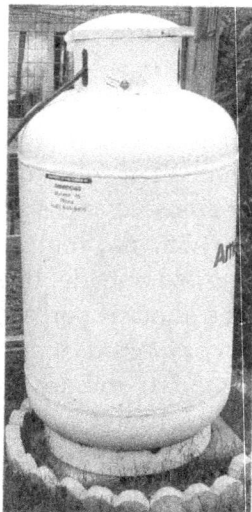

#4 Outside Oil Fill Box

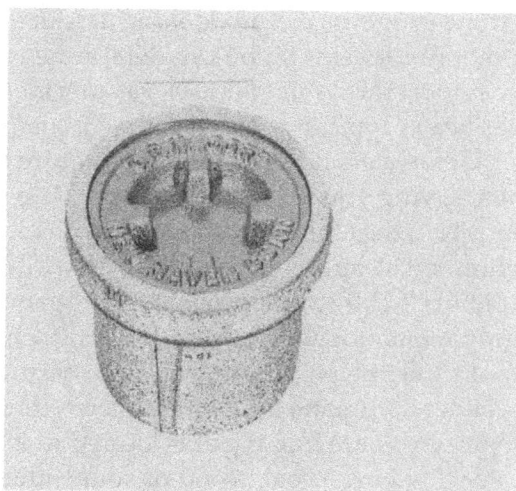

That means your property heater burns fuel oil. It is the filler neck for a basement fuel oil tank. If you do not see *any* of these but instead see a pipe with a cap on it, sticking out of or flush with the ground or pavement that maybe looks like picture #4 then, **BEWARE.**

I say beware because most likely it indicates that the property has a fuel oil tank that is buried underground, and that is something to stay away from. Here's why. Underground steel tanks, especially older ones from the 1950s through the 1980s, can rust out and leak into the ground, and that is what you need to beware of. These tanks were mostly made of single wall steel and had capacities of 500 gallons and more. It will not be disclosed to you if there is an underground oil tank at a sheriff sale, and may or may not be disclosed if it's a trustee or real estate sale. If you do unknowingly end up purchasing a property with an underground tank, having the tank pressure tested will determine if it has a leak. And if the test comes back indicating a leak, you need to find out if it leaked any of its contents into the ground.

Unfortunately if it has, you have problems. **BIG PROBLEMS.** As the new owner of the property you will be liable for the costs to have the tank removed and the soil cleaned and remediated. Depending how much and how far the contents leaked into the ground, the cost to have this done can easily run in the tens of thousands of dollars. So much for any profit made. And you cannot sell the property until you have completed the remediation. So why take the chance buying a property with a buried fuel oil tank. In fact, you want to avoid any properties that have any potential for possible environmental problems. This includes residential as well as commercial properties. By commercial I mean any property that may be, is, or was, a factory, gas station, dump, or anything that processed, stored, manufactured or dealt in hazardous toxic chemicals or compounds. It's just not worth the huge potential for problems that could exist.

Have a look at the landscaping. Is there any landscaping at all or are vines and weeds taking over? Do the trees need trimming? What will you have to do to give the place "curb appeal"? Curb appeal is real estate lingo for how attractive the property and the land improvements look when viewed from the street. Nicely mulched flower beds with colorful flowers are an example of curb appeal. The idea is that you want your property to look better than all the other ones in the neighborhood. It is said that most buyers decide within ten seconds of driving up to a property whether or not to purchase it. All of your improvements done inside won't mean a hill of beans to a potential buyer if they drive away because your property does not look inviting to them when they pull up. Curb appeal is so important! Even if you only plan to rent it out you need it to have an inviting first impression for prospective tenants.

If the property has sidewalks and curbs, you should look for any cracks or breaks in them. Most municipalities have something called a U & O certificate, which stands for **U**se & **O**ccupancy, and it states that the property is in compliance with the municipality's codes. Unless the property is being sold with the understanding that it is the buyer's responsibility to obtain it, the seller normally provides this certification from the local municipality before transferring ownership. If the seller does not obtain this U & O, or the property fails the inspection, in most cases the buyer cannot occupy the property until all violations are corrected. There is a saying that sometimes U & O stands for yoU fix Our sidewalks. In most cases if there are sidewalks and curbs the municipality will look at them; and if they are damaged or cracked, *YOU* will be responsible for the cost to repair or replace them. It can cost upwards of $ 200 to $ 400 to have each square of concrete sidewalk cut out and replaced. This can get expensive really fast, especially if you have several squares of sidewalk or curb that need replacing, so keep that in mind when doing your cost estimates. As long as you are looking at the curbs and sidewalks, look at the driveway too. Buyers are not as particular about the driveway, but unless it has completely fallen apart you should not have to replace it. If it is asphalt, many times a good coat of sealer will cover the cracks and imperfections and make it presentable.

It has been my experience when trying to get a peek inside of a building that if there are blinds or curtains in the windows, the former occupants probably left them closed. In their situation, they were not happy people and did not want to look out at the world, nor did they want the world looking in. But sometimes the blinds are not totally down or the curtains are not drawn closed and there is a gap you can peek through. If the windows are up too high, use the step stool to get a better look inside. Many times I've peeked through a half-inch gap, and that can be just enough to get a lot of information on the condition of the interior. Look for any holes in the walls or ceilings, old wallpaper that will need to be removed, *anything* that will give you some idea of the work that will need to be done. One of the rules of thumb I use if I can't get a look at the inside is this: If the outside of the house looks bad, the inside is not far behind, and if the outside looks good, then the inside should be decent also. Remember, these people were not making their mortgage and probably other payments as well, so you can be sure they were not keeping up with maintenance either.

OCCUPIED PROPERTIES

Occupied properties are just that, still occupied by the owners. You may ask how they can auction off a property with the owners still in it. In many cases the owners are still fighting the foreclosure in one way or another. There are laws and rules for dealing with the owners of properties. One of these is known as the "Right of Redemption" law and it varies from state to state. It's possible the owners are aware of that state's right of redemption law and that is why they are still in there. You will need to know and completely understand this law before you bid on any property. Your local sheriff's office may be able to provide you with a copy of it. I will explain right of redemption in detail later on in Chapter 14.

The sheriff or person conducting the auction is not responsible for removing the occupants at this stage of the process. You will find the bulk of sheriff sale properties are still occupied by the owners. Because of this, you must be both careful and creative in how you evaluate these properties. An occupied property will probably no longer have the notice of sheriff or trustee sale posted on the door. Chances are good if it was posted there the owner removed it. If you are unsure whether a property is occupied or not there are several ways to tell. One is to find out what day the trash is picked up and ride by. If all the other residents in the neighborhood have put their trash out that day and the property in question has not, chances are good it's unoccupied.

Another way is to ask a neighbor. You already know the occupant's name, so ask the neighbor if they still live here. If the neighbor asks why, tell them you saw that the house was up for foreclosure sale and you were thinking about bidding on it, but do not offer them any other details. As a bonus you may be able to glean additional information about the property from the neighbors—information you otherwise wouldn't have been able to get just from looking at it. Remember, let them do the talking and you do the listening.

At this point if you still can't tell, ride by the property in the evening at several different times and look for any lights on or any other signs of activity. If you see nothing after one or two passes, chances are good it is unoccupied. If you find that it is occupied, I don't recommend you make contact with the owner unless you are planning to try to buy the property pre-foreclosure as a short sale.

CHAPTER 8

BUILDING YOUR TEAM

Now is a good time before going any further to discuss building your team. Look at any owner of any sports team franchise and you will see carefully selected managers, coaches, and players standing along side them. These people were selected because of the individual talents each of them possesses and their ability to work together to produce for the owner the goal of a winning sports *TEAM.* The owner knows that by themselves they do not possess the time, knowledge or talent required for all that is necessary to produce that winning team. Neither do you. As much as I hate to tell you and as much as you might hate to admit it, you don't either. *You cannot do it alone.* No one can. You need to seek out the "players" and "coaches" that will be *your team* to help you achieve your goal. Members of your team will have the knowledge to save you time and money, helping you avoid mistakes by showing you the tricks and shortcuts they have learned over the years. Here is my list of team members that you will need to assemble as you continue in your real estate endeavors. Depending on the scope of your talents and abilities your list may be different.

Local Real Estate Attorney: You did seek out and develop a relationship with a local RE attorney, didn't you? If not, the time to start is *now!* This person can be worth their weight in gold. You can locate attorneys several ways. One is to call your local bar association and ask for the names and contact information of real estate attorneys that are members. Another is to look in your local yellow pages under "lawyers" and you should see pages of listings that are broken down by category. A third is check with a local real estate investing group. What you want is an attorney whose primary area of expertise is **REAL ESTATE LAW** and who practices it in the area you plan to do your buying. Real estate law is a specialized field unto itself, just as divorce, criminal, or negligence law are all fields unto themselves.

What you don't want is a jack-of-all-trades lawyer. While they may charge less for their time, the problem is they know a little about a lot. Describe to the attorney your plans, explaining that you want to buy properties at foreclosure auction sales. What you want to find out is how much they charge for their services, including explaining the laws and interpreting any documents or reports you obtain. Let them know this relationship will be an ongoing one over time and see if you can reach an agreement on their rate based on that premise. In other words, see what you can negotiate. Besides being able to explain how local real estate laws impact you, the attorney should be able to interpret any title searches as well as any legal issues that may crop up, handle settlement when you sell property, and advise you on any possible rental issues. Yes, good attorneys don't come cheap, but mistakes made by having the wrong one or not having one at all can be vastly more expensive. As with most members of the team you are assembling, you may have to interview several prospects before finding the one you feel comfortable with and fits your needs.

Realtor: Besides the attorney, a local real estate agent is probably the second most important person on your team. When you begin your search for a real estate agent, I recommend that you look for one that has an office in the area and deals in the price range of properties that you intend to buy. This way, they will already be familiar with what and where you'll be doing your buying and selling. If you plan to buy and sell houses in the $ 100,000 to $ 200,000 price range, interviewing a realtor who sells million-dollar McMansions will probably not do you much good. Begin your search with the smaller local realtors and work your way up to the larger franchised offices that cover greater market areas. Smaller, independent realtors are typically very familiar with the local housing and rental markets and tend to be more in tune to working with investors, especially when you are just starting out.

Several places to begin your search are, again, the yellow pages or the local real estate groups. Look under "real estate" in the phone book and you should find lots of listings. Pick out ones in your area and start calling them. Ask lots of questions. As you did with the attorney, explain that you plan to buy property at foreclosure sales and fix them up to either resell or rent out. Don't be surprised if you get a quizzical look or sound from the agent. Many real estate agents are not familiar with foreclosure sales. Ask the agent if they personally have had experience rehabbing or owning any rental properties. You may find that many agents don't. Try to find one that does. They will understand firsthand what you are doing and can offer you lots of added insight as you get started. They can also find you potential deals on properties not in foreclosure. Realtors especially worship loyalty. It's the foundation of their business and is one of the primary things they strive for. One of the easiest ways to build a relationship with a realtor is agree to use them exclusively when you list your properties for sale. So find a realtor you feel comfortable with and stick with them. You will have probably found your most important asset to help you buy and sell real estate profitably.

Title or Abstract Company: You will need the services of a title company for several reasons. Number One before you bid on *any* property, you must find out what liens and mortgages there are on it. This is where a "Title" or "Abstract" company comes in. An Abstract, or Abstract of Title as it relates to the title of real property, is nothing more than a historical summary listing of all of the documents (mortgages, liens, etc.) and all actions that would affect the title to a property. This is what the title company's research provides you with. A good title company is an important part of your team, as you will need their services for every property you plan to bid on. Not only will they provide the title information you need, they can also interpret it for you. This is information you must know and understand. After purchasing a property at foreclosure, you may need to buy title insurance to protect yourself from any unexpected problems that may crop up with the title and the costs to defend against them. This is something the title company also can provide for you.

General Contractors & Tradespeople: Unless you are very handy with tools, building construction, and you are up to date on all the building codes, then finding a good *licensed* general contractor (GC) or good licensed tradespeople such as plumbers, carpenters and electricians can be invaluable to you. Why? Because they do this sort of thing *every day*. Not only do they have experience and are familiar with these types of projects, they can probably save you money in the long run. They know how to do the job properly and make it proceed smoothly. If you can't do it yourself, then these people need to become your next new best friend.

Accountant: If you do not already use the services of a Certified Public Accountant (CPA), I recommend you hire one, preferably one with knowledge of real estate as it applies to accounting. If you plan to buy and sell real estate with any regularity, a good CPA is absolutely essential. Besides just preparing your taxes, a CPA keeps up to date on the ever-changing tax laws as they apply to real estate, and that is important. They can guide you with proper record keeping, allowable tax deductions you were probably not even aware of, and much more. And speaking of taxes, remember that old saying: "Nothing is certain but death and taxes." If you decide to flip that rehab project, you will have taxes to pay on the profit you make. A good accountant can help you legally minimize those taxes. That in itself makes a CPA an essential part of your team.

Insurance Agent: You probably already have an insurance agent you use for your home or auto needs. But does that agent have the knowledge needed for your upcoming real estate requirements? Getting the proper insurance at the right cost when you are rehabbing an unoccupied or occupied property is essential. There are agents and companies out there that specialize in insurance for rehab work and are accustomed to working with people who flip or rent properties. Be sure the one you choose is. Get the wrong kind of insurance and you could have big problems should a claim arise. Or you could find out after the fact that you paid too much for the insurance you got. Ask questions if you are unsure of anything before you sign or pay for the policy. If you are having a hard time finding someone, ask the other members on your team or your local real estate group to help you find the proper agent or company.

Bankers & Money Lenders: You will need a consistent source of money to buy and rehab the properties. And unless you are borrowing money from family and friends, or have a very large savings account from which to draw, you will need the services of a banker or some form of money lender. These people are vital to your team. Don't believe those infomercials that say you can buy property with virtually no money down. To buy foreclosed property at auction sales you need cash money. There is a humorous old saying that goes, "Banks only loan money to people who don't need it." While not completely true, banks or other lenders don't make money until they "sell" you money and you pay it back. So you need to establish yourself with a source for money. That "source" could be the traditional bank you regularly deal with or it could be a non-traditional "bank" such as a hard money or private lender. Or both. Either way, you need to form a relationship with these people who control the money *before* purchasing or bidding on anything. Get your accounts set up ahead of time. Know how much money you have access to. Reward your banker or money lender by paying your loans back on or *ahead* of time and they will reward you with even more money the next time. That's the kind of partnership you want.

Home Inspector: You might be wondering why I am including a home inspector as part of your team since you can't get into the properties to inspect them before you bid anyway. And aren't home inspectors typically associated with someone the *buyer* brings in to check out the property before you sell it to them? My reason for adding a home inspector to your team is this: after you take possession of the property, have the home inspector come in and evaluate it for you. They will find the obvious and less obvious things that need to be fixed, things that you might miss. They will crawl around in all the dirty spots so you don't have to, to find the hidden problems. If you are rehabbing and flipping the property, these are problems that the *buyer's* home inspector *will* find and you will have to fix *after* the rehabbing is done. And that is the wrong time to be doing it. Fixing the problems *before* the buyer would be made aware of them gives your rehab more credibility in their mind and doesn't make them second-guess buying it. Peace of mind is worth the price of the inspector.

Local Real Estate Investing Groups: If you have one of these in your area, joining it can be one of the best and least expensive investments to furthering your real estate career. These groups can be an invaluable source of information and education, for everything from recommendations and finding other team members to avoiding the land mines of real estate investing—and everything in between. Membership costs are typically very reasonable, and you can make lots of contacts networking with people who are doing the same thing you are. I belong to a great local real estate investment group called Diversified Real Estate Investment Group, or "DIG" for short. I have listed in the back of the book many of the large real estate groups in the country and the areas they cover. I urge you to check into joining one.

CHAPTER 9

VALUING THE PROPERTIES

Before we begin this chapter, a word of caution. As you begin researching the financial and public records of the properties, keep in mind that not all information you gather will always be error free. Mistakes occur on the MLS due to information incorrectly provided by the listing realtors. Incorrect information can happen in the public records too. Things get misfiled, filed late, or not at all. You need to do your due diligence with all of the information gathered. If it does not look correct, and sometimes even if it does look correct, recheck it if possible by going back to the source where it came from and verifying it. That is why it helps having the other people on your team (attorney, realtor, etc.) with the experience to be able to tell when something doesn't look right before you bid on it at the auction.

By now you should have inspected the properties as best you could. If feasible, you walked around the property taking pictures and scrutinizing the exterior of the structure as well as the property grounds. If possible you peeked in the windows, examining any hints of the interior you could see. If there was a shingled roof, you used your binoculars to determine the condition of it. If there were neighbors nearby, you made an effort to speak with them and gathered as much information as possible. If you have done all of this, you are ready for the next very important step: determining the value of the property.

WHAT ARE COMPS?

In real estate jargon, getting the "comps," or comparables, means finding out what nearby properties similar to yours *recently* sold for. The reason you need comps is to establish a dollar value starting point for what the property is worth as it sits now and will be worth after rehab *compared to* what the foreclosing dollar amount is. If after getting a comp and determining the property's value you discover that the foreclosing amount is *higher* than the property's comparable value as it sits plus any repairs or rehab, then the property is referred to as being "upside down." In other words, it is worth less than what is owed on it and should be crossed off your list as a bad deal.

For example: The house you are considering to bid on you determine to be a three-bedroom, one bath colonial (referred to as a 3/1) that has a foreclosing debt of $ 150,000. You want to flip it and figure it needs about $ 20,000 in total rehab costs. You get comps on two other similar 3/1 colonials in the same neighborhood as yours in A+ condition and find they recently sold for $ 130,000. You would not want to bid on that house as it is upside down. More is owed than it's worth or could be worth after rehab, so you wouldn't make any money on it. Now let's look at the same example again, only this time the foreclosing debt on the house is only $ 60,000 with the same $ 20,000 in rehab expenses, for a grand total of $ 80,000. This would be a very good house to bid on as your research shows 3/1 colonials in A+ condition go for $ 130,000, giving you a potential profit of $ 50,000. In some instances, a property will be offered for sale at less than the foreclosing price, but at this time just consider it a bad deal and cross it off the list.

GETTING THE COMPS

How and where do you get the comps? While there are several ways to get comps, by far the most accurate way is the one I will be referring to, and that is the **Multiple Listing Service,** or MLS as it is generally known. You will need the assistance of a realtor to access information on the MLS. You cannot do it without one. You did add a realtor to your team, didn't you? If you didn't, you need to get on board with one ASAP. If you *absolutely* cannot beg, borrow or compel by almost any means possible the services of any realtor to help you, there are other ways to get the comps, but they will almost certainly be less accurate and require a lot more effort than the MLS.

One way to start is to go to any of the multitude of websites that list houses for sale, such as Realtor.com, Zillow.com, Domania.com, and so on, and look up other properties in your area to see what they are listing or selling for. A word of caution first. Many of these websites that provide comps, depending on where they get and how they calculate their data, can be wildly off target with their numbers. If you get a comp this way and it seems out of line, either verify it or just disregard it. The details, for example, on Realtor.com are provided by the property's listing realtor. You will need to hunt through the listings for other *similar* properties on the street or in your nearby area. The problem with doing it this way is that these websites only list properties that are *currently* for sale. Most do not list properties that have sold or the prices they sold for. And that can be a problem if houses in that area are *ultimately* selling for five to ten percent above or below their listing price, since you will not be made aware of this from the listing. By doing it this way, you can't get as true an idea of what the property should *actually* be worth as you would from the MLS. Another technique is to drive around the neighborhood where the property is located and look for other similar properties that are for sale. Sometimes realtors attach information boxes to the For Sale sign that contain details about the property as well as the asking price. If there is no box and you want to get more information on the property, call the realtor whose name is on the sign and ask them for the particulars and the price on it. A way to see the prices for sold properties is to look in the local newspaper. In their real estate section typically they list the completed real estate transactions for the various local areas. The drawback with this is the postings usually lag behind the actual settlement date by several months or more, so your information is that much out of date.

You can also go down to the local courthouse and ask where the real estate records are kept. They are public domain and available to view. Tell the clerk that you want to look through the records for properties that have recently sold in your particular area. The records will contain information including legal descriptions of the properties as well as their selling price. While these methods all will give you information, they will not give you the *scope and detail* that can be obtained in one place from the MLS.

ABOUT THE MULTIPLE LISTING SERVICES (MLS)

The MLS contains not only the listings of properties for sale by members of the NAR (National Association of Realtors) and the CREA (Canadian Real Estate Association), but also information covering a wide scope of real estate data. The MLS is administered by various private companies and those companies set the rules as far as availability of the information. While some bits and pieces of those listings are made available to the public, the majority of it is only available to realtors who subscribe to their local MLS service. The MLS is considered the bible of the real estate industry. It contains the detailed listings for all properties in its coverage area that currently are for sale, have been sold, expired, withdrawn, re-listed, etc. for the past twenty or so years. While membership in the MLS is not required in order to be a realtor, it is generally considered vital, so almost all realtors and brokers subscribe to some form of MLS service. In my area, the Philadelphia region, the company that administers the MLS is called Trend. Depending on where you are located it goes by different names. The Washington DC region has the largest MLS service and goes by the name Metropolitan Regional Information Systems, with over 60,000 subscribers. So when I make references to MLS information, I am basing that on the format that Trend presents it in. Yours may be different. Check with your realtor.

WHAT THE MLS TELLS YOU

The first area of the MLS you want to look at is the section called Public Records. By entering the address of the property into the public records section of the MLS, the following information can be accessed:

• Property location

- Property tax ID or folio number
- Previous owners
- Property classification
- Estimated annual taxes
- Lot size
- MLS history information
- Transaction history of property's previous owners

Shown below is what a sample MLS public records listing may look like.

Sample MLS Public Records Listing

123 Main St.
Anytown, PA 56789
Apple Township, Unreal County

Summary Information

Owner	John Smith	Property Class	Residential
Owner Address	123 Main St.	Record Date	6/1/2005
Owner City, State	Anytown, PA	Settlement Date	5/12/02005
Owner Zip	56789	Sale Amount	$150,000
		Annual Est. Taxes	$ 3,500

Geographic Information

School District	Apple	Tax Map #	33
Neighborhood	Happy Valley	Lot #	567.123N

Tax & Assessment Information

Tax Year 2005

Estimated Annual Tax	$3,120	Taxable Land Assmt.	$40,300
School Tax	$2,100	Taxable Building Assmt.	$95,300
County Tax	600	Taxable Total Amount	$135,600
Municipal Tax	$ 420		

Lot Characteristics

Square Ft.	37,240	Roads	Paved
Acres	.86	Traffic	Moderate
Zoning	R2	Topography	Level

Structure Characteristics

Building sq./ft.	1650	Exterior	Brick
Residence type	Single/Detached	Basement type	Full
Residence design	2 story	Basement description	Finished
Residence style	Colonial	Heating system	Hot air
Total rooms	9	Heating fuel	Nat. gas
Bedrooms	3	Cooling	Central air
Full Baths	2	Water	Public
Year built	1965	Sewer	Public

Codes & Descriptions

Land Use	Res. Single family	County legal description	Lot 31

MLS History & Information

Listing Number	Status	Status Date	Price
123456	STL	6/01/2005	$150,000
234567	STL	6/03/1990	$ 54,000

Transaction History

Record Date	6/01/2005	Book	2445
Settlement Date	5/12/02005	Page	6789
Sale Amount	$150,000		
Owner Name:	John Smith		
Record Date:	6/25/90	Book	1456
Owner Name:	Sally Homeowner	Page	8123

Mortgage Record date	6/15/2005	Lender	Big Money Mortgage Co.
Mortgage amount	$100,000		
Mortgage Record Date	7/16/1990	Lender	Dime National Bank
Mortgage amount	$ 40,000		

Reading down the sample listing, this tells you who the current owner is and the address, which should match up to the information you have on the foreclosure. Next, the school district and what that particular area's neighborhood is called. A very important number listed next is called the **TAX ID** number. Sometimes it is referred to as the **folio** number or account number. This number is important because it is the property's "address" that identifies it on all the tax maps and property roles. If you need to gather more information about the property at the courthouse, this is the number they use to identify it. Also shown are the lot and building characteristics, which tell you the size and sometimes the shape of the lot plus the property's classification.

The MLS History Information is probably the most important information on the page, besides the Tax ID number. If there are listings under this heading, they are the gold you are seeking. Those MLS numbers represent a listing every time the property has been put up for sale on the MLS and will have information about the property that should tell you what you want to know. If there are MLS numbers listed, ask your realtor to pull them up and print those listing reports. The listings may be current if the property is occupied and the owner is trying to sell it before the foreclosure sale. Or they may be older, previous listings. It really does not matter.

What matters is the *information contained in the remarks section of the listing.* This is where the realtor writes the sales pitch for the property. Trend until recently allowed up to six pictures of a property to be shown with the listing, but it has now upped that to twelve. Hopefully, the listing realtor posted the maximum allowable pictures of the property and its interior. In this section you will find all of the property's pluses described in detail. It's like the peacock showing off its feathers. This information can give you a *really* big head start as to what rehabbing you can expect will need to be done when you determine your bid price. If you do not see anything listed under MLS history, one of two things is possible: The property was sold privately by the owner and not through a realtor, so it would not have appeared on the MLS. Or, it probably predates the records kept by the MLS if the house has not changed ownership in a long period of time, say over twenty years.

Your realtor can explain to you what the cryptic abbreviations and terms on the listing mean, but here is the information you really want to know:
1.   The property address
2.   Classification of the property (Residential or commercial, if there is a question about it.)
3.   Square footage of the structure, and/or rooms if noted
4.   School District (If people have children they buy or rent based on the school district.)
5.   Beds/baths (Very important for comparing properties of similar size.)
6.   House design and style. (Again, very important when comparing similar houses.)
7.   Real estate taxes

8. Type of utilities. (Gas, oil or other for heating and hot water, central air if so outfitted, public water and sewer if present.)
9. Parking (On or off street. Garage?)
10. All information noted on the interior and exterior of the house and any remarks
11. DOM (Days on Market) How long did it sit before it sold?
12. Opening price (What was the price when it was listed initially?)
13. Selling price (What did it ultimately sell for?)

MLS Listing for a property that I bought at sheriff sale, rehabbed and resold

Boothwyn, PA		RES	$254,900

MLS #:	4762	Beds, Baths:	3	1/1
MLS Area:	10409	Ownership:	FeeSimple	
	U Chichester Twp	Type:	Single/Detac	
County:	Delaware	Design:	2-Story	
Zip Code:	19061 -3652	Style:	Colonial	
Tax ID #:		Basement:	Y	
Subdiv / Nei:	None Available	Age:	39	
School Dist:	Chichester	Int Sq Ft:	1,500/ S	
- High:	Chichester	Unit Floor #:		
- Middle:	Chichester	Central Air:	Y	
- Elem:		Internet:	Y / Y	
Directions				

Cross Street: Map Grid: 8269D6

Room Dimensions

		Other Information
LR/GR: 18 x 12 M Main BR: 14 x 12 U Family R: 21 x 10 M		Total Rooms:
Dining: 10 x 10 M 2nd BR: 12 x 12 U Basement: 21 x 21 B		Bath Full: 0M 1U 0L
Kitchen: 12 x 10 M 3rd BR: 11 x 10 U		Bath Part: 1M 0U 0L
Family: 21 x 10 M 4th BR:		Model:
Inclusions: All Appliances & Window Treatments		Builder:
Exclusions:		

Tax Information	Association Info	Lot Information	
RE Taxes / Yr: $3875 / 2006 Blk	Condo / HOA: N / N	Acr / SqFt: 0.75 / 32,670	Land Use: Zoning: RESID
Assessment: 99910 Lot 422-000	Assc Fee / Freq:	Lot Dim: 92X240	Waterfront: N

Features

Utilities: GasHeat, HotAirHeat, GasHotWater, CentralAir, PublicWater, PublicSewer, 100-150AmpEl
Parking: NoGarage, 2-CarParking   Exterior: Sidewalks, StreetLights, ShingleExt, ConcreteFoun, IrregularLot, ShingleRoof, Deck, NoPool
Bsmt: FullBasement, UnfinishBsmt   Interior: AccessPanel, NoFireplace, W/WCarpeting, CableTVWired, NoModifs/Unk, BsmtLaundry   Kit: EatInKitchen, GasCooking, BuiltInDishW, Disposal
Finance: ConventnalFi, FHA   Cond: Average+

Remarks

Public: WELCOME HOME to this lovely colonial on large 3/4 acre partially tree lined lot in quiet neighborhood on CUL-DE-SAC street in Upper Chichester Twp. House totally renovated in 2006. Brand new energy efficent heating & central air system with new hot water heater. New wall to wall carpet and paint throughout. Three nice size bedrooms feature generous closet space. Elegant second floor bathroom features polished brass faucets and has ceramic tile tub area with a RADIANTLY HEATED ceramic tile floor. New vinyl tilt in windows with energy efficent Low-E glass. Check out the remodeled kitchen with new granite look countertops and lots of cabinet space. New roof. Spacious new family room/den with powder room has large front triple window and rear slider opening to a large new deck. Huge back yard offers privacy as well as space for a pool. Basement is ready to finish as you wish. Within minutes of major highways and shopping centers. Act quickly this one won't last long.

Brokerage Information

Leonard B Halpern	HALPERN		SBr:	OPr:	
ListAgent: Leonard Halpern	60009675		BBr:	LDt:	06/29/2006
CoListAg:	Appt Phone:		TBr:	XDt:	12/31/2006
Show: Call	for appointment to show.				
Show: CallToShow, ComboLockBox Poss: Immediate		Agmt:	EA		
		Sign:	Y	DVB: N	OMD: 09/04/2006
		BkInt:	N	LBon: N	LMD: 09/22/2006
Owner: MARC SHERBY		Disclosure:		PrExc: Y	DOM: 68

© Copyright 2008 TREND MLS - All information, regardless of source, including square footages and lot sizes, should be verified by personal inspection by and/or with the appropriate professional(s). The information is not guaranteed. This report contains some confidential information for use by TREND members only. Created: 05/12/08 11:03 AM.

All of this information will help you evaluate the property and get an accurate comp. Now what you need the realtor to do is this: Get a list of all the properties on that street or surrounding neighborhood that are similar to yours and have recently sold. This is where it can get tricky. If the property you are looking at is in a development and all are basically the same size and style, then finding a comparable sold property should be easy. If you are looking in an area where the building style and sizes vary widely, then it becomes more of a challenge. Your realtor's experience should be able to help you come up with some comparables. You want to obtain the most recent listings possible for properties that were *sold.* Properties that are "pending," while being an indicator, should not be used for comparison until after the property goes to settlement, since the final selling price will in all probability be different from the listing price. Here are some items to carefully consider when reading the MLS report on your property versus the comparables:

ADDRESS/CLASSIFICATION: Is the address on the foreclosure list the same as what's on the MLS list? Be certain the classification is **"RES"** if you are looking at a residential property or a **"COM"** designation if you are looking at a commercial property.

SQUARE FOOTAGE/BEDS & BATHS/DESIGN & STYLE: Is the square footage or style of the property you plan to bid on similar to the other comparable properties? Do not try to compare a two-story colonial to a single floor ranch. Are the number of bedrooms and bathrooms similar? After the property's location and/or its school district, the Number One thing people look for next is the number of bedrooms. Why? Because if they have children or plan to have more children, that then dictates how many bedrooms are or will be needed. Besides, adding a bedroom many times means adding an addition on to the house, an expensive construction project most people do not want to tackle just after moving in. It's far easier just to buy a house with another bedroom already there.

Bathrooms are not as big of a buying influence as bedrooms. All houses have at least one bathroom. However if a house has a bathroom *and* a powder room, you improve your chances of selling or renting it. A note of caution though: beware of older houses with four or more bedrooms and only one full bathroom. Houses like that are referred to as being "functionally obsolete." Four bedroom houses nowadays simply have more bathrooms. This is not to say that it is impossible to resell or rent a 4/1 house; it might just take you longer.

SCHOOL DISTRICTS: As previously noted, people buy or rent properties in a specific area for two reasons: location and school districts. How fast a property sells or rents and at what price depends on one or both of these determining factors. People will often pay more for a smaller, comparable property that has a better school district. Take note of the school district in which the property you plan to bid on is located and its state ranking.

TAXES: First, do the taxes seem especially high in relation to the value of the property for the area? This can occur in places where there is little industry or commercial business to carry the majority of the tax load, after which it then falls on the residents of the town to make it up. If the area is depressed and taxes are on the rise, it may hinder your ability to flip the property quickly or rent it profitably. Most municipal taxes are due in the spring, usually in the March to June range. Typically school taxes do not follow a calendar year and customarily run from July to July, with payment due some date shortly thereafter.

Depending on when you buy, you may be responsible for taxes yet to be paid. For example, if you won the bid on a property bought in June, in most cases the taxes that are currently due, which are pro-rated, and those, if any, which were past due are included in the bid price that you paid and will be paid up to the time when the deed is issued. It is the taxes that are due *after* you receive the deed (if you still own the property), that you will be responsible for, such as the school taxes, which will be due sometime after July. What you need to due is budget for those taxes in your holding costs. Holding costs, which will be discussed in greater detail later on, are *ALL* the costs (rehab, insurance, financing & interest, real estate taxes, settlement, etc.) that you will incur from the time you buy the property to the time that you sell or rent it. For instance, if you plan to rehab and flip, and it takes you ultimately six months from the time you won the bid until you actually go to settlement and get paid, and assuming the municipal taxes run from June to June and the school taxes run July to July, with the total annual taxes due of $ 4,000, you will be responsible to pay your percentage of taxes due, which is $ 2,000 for the six months you owned the property. Those taxes due will be deducted from your check at settlement.

What you don't want to happen is that you forget to account for the real estate taxes in your holding cost budget and now that money has come out of your *profit*. And while **capital gains tax** is technically not a holding cost (it comes out when you pay your income taxes), it is a very real expense you need to account for as a cost. Determining these costs will be discussed later on in the book as well as how to figure them in your maximum bid price. For now, just know that you have to be aware of the tax issues.

FEATURES: Look at the utilities section of the MLS report for each property. Do you know if the nearby properties use the same fuel to heat them? From a cost and maintenance standpoint gas fuel is preferable to oil or solid fuels, such as wood or coal. Has the heating and/or air conditioning system been replaced? While central air conditioning is not a necessity (unless you are buying down south or out west where it is considered standard equipment), it has become more common and is definitely a plus. This will be especially apparent if most of the other nearby properties have it and yours doesn't. Is there public water and/or sewer? Private wells and especially septic systems can be expensive to repair or replace if they failed. Are there any notations about the electric system being upgraded? Many older properties still have outdated 60 amp systems with fuses in place. Modern electrical circuit breaker systems now have an absolute minimum of 100 amp incoming service, with 200 amps or more quite common. If yours still has an outdated electric service, you may have to update it to meet current electrical code.

REMARKS: Information shown in the remarks will give you a lot of clues as to what you will or will not need to do to the property if you plan to rehab and flip or rent it. Most realtors will trump up any and all improvements made to the property in this section. "New or newer" windows means you probably won't need to replace outdated windows with new energy-efficient ones, almost a required improvement now if you plan to flip. Other clues to look for: New or "newer" roof. Brick, stucco, stone, and vinyl exteriors are pretty much maintenance free. All that might be needed to make them look new is have them power washed. If your exterior is wood, old style asbestos siding or a similar material, a fresh coat of paint may be in order. Remember curb appeal! Does the property have a pool? Above ground pools are easy to remove if needed. Stay away from properties with inground pools, unless they are a common item in your part of the country where almost every house has one, because the pool's filtration, piping systems and even the pool itself might need repairs, and that can be very expensive. Also, if you are flipping, you need to find someone who wants a pool, and not everyone does.

Has the kitchen or any of the bathrooms been recently updated? Is the kitchen eat-in? Is there new or newer wall-to-wall carpeting? Hardwood floors? Ceiling fans are a plus. Finished basement? Are there any notations of repairs that might be needed but not done by the previous owner? Any information you can garner from the listing will help determine what rehab work will be required. This will allow you to be more accurate with your bid price, thus giving you an advantage over other bidders who maybe didn't do their homework.

DOM/OPENING & SELLING PRICE: The **DOM,** or Days On Market, is a very important number, especially when looked at in conjunction with the opening and final selling price. This gives you an indication of how long similar properties took to sell and what price you can *realistically* expect your property to sell for in the current market. Be conservative with these numbers. If it took 100 days on market and a price drop from $ 150,000 to $ 140,000 before a comparable property sold, that tells you properties are selling for $ 140,000 *NOW* and that should give you an indication of the trend currently in that area.

CHAPTER 10

MORTGAGES, DEEDS OF TRUST, LIENS, JUDGMENTS & TAXES

Of all the topics covered in this book, this one is probably the most critical and the most misunderstood. Not understanding how liens, mortgages, deeds of trust, and judgments tie into the foreclosure process can spell the difference between a good profitable purchase and a disastrously costly one. Be sure to check with your real estate attorney to help you understand the specifics and applicability of mortgages, deeds of trust, liens, judgments and taxes for your area, as laws governing any of these can and do vary from state to state. I cannot overemphasize your knowing and understanding this information so when you go to the foreclosure sales you can bid with confidence.

DEFINITIONS

First, let's begin with the definitions of what a mortgage, deed of trust, lien and judgment actually are. Barron's Dictionary of Real Estate Terms defines a **mortgage** as "A written instrument that creates a lien upon real estate as security for the payment of a specified debt." It is a common misconception about mortgages that it is actually the *borrower* that *gives* a mortgage which pledges the property as collateral. It is the *lender* that provides the loan and *receives* the mortgage. A **Deed of Trust** is defined as "An instrument used in many states in lieu of a mortgage. Legal title to the property is vested in one or more trustees to secure repayment of the loan." Barron's defines a **lien** as "A charge against property making it security for the payment of a debt, judgment, mortgage, or taxes; it is a type of encumbrance." And it defines a **judgment** as "A decree of a court stating that one individual is indebted to another and fixing the amount of the indebtedness."

MORTGAGES: Let's start with mortgages, since falling behind on this one generally results in the other two, liens and judgments. Most people when they want to purchase a property go to a lender to obtain a loan. Depending on their finances, they decide on a repayment term usually fifteen, twenty, thirty or more years for this debt and are given a corresponding interest rate. A lot of papers are signed, one of which is called the ***promissory note*** or simply the "note." This note acknowledges the debt that they promise to pay back under the terms specified in it. It also spells out the procedure for action to be taken by the lender to cure this debt if they default on the payments. They will also sign a ***mortgage*** document which will pledge the home to the lender as the collateral for the note. This initial or first loan is usually referred to as a ***first mortgage***. Most first mortgages are also known as "closed end mortgages" since the initial amount borrowed cannot be changed for the pre-determined life of the loan.

Now, let's say the owner's been living in the house for five years. He's making the loan payments on time, and decides to make some improvements to the property. He stops by a local lending institution for money to fund the improvements. The lender finds the owner's track record on payments so far is good and the property has had some modest appreciation in value, so the lender gives the okay. The lender gives the homeowner a home equity line of credit **(HELOC).** A HELOC is technically known as an "open-ended mortgage," meaning that unlike a first mortgage you *can* change the initial amount borrowed for the pre-determined life of the loan. A HELOC sets up an account or "credit line" with a predetermined maximum amount that the homeowner can draw monies from as needed. The homeowner only pays interest on the money drawn out from the account, not on the total amount available if set up that way.

HELOCs can usually be repaid several ways. In many instances the borrower can elect to pay only the interest due on the principle, reducing the amount of the payment, or he/she can pay interest and a portion of the principle, resulting in a higher payment due. Usually the interest paid on a HELOC is tax deductible, same as the interest on the first mortgage. That's why homeowners like HELOCs. And you can stretch the repayment period out on a HELOCs for a long time, as much as ten years in some cases. Lenders like that, as they make lots of interest on that money. And it's secured by the property. That's why banks like HELOCs. Lots of homeowners have used them. What many homeowners don't realize is a HELOC is actually a **SECOND MORTGAGE** on their house. If you stop paying on it and default, the lender can foreclose and force the sale of the house even though you were still paying your first mortgage on time. Many people are not aware of this and have gotten into trouble with HELOCs and have had their houses foreclosed on.

DEEDS OF TRUST: In many states the instrument used to secure the loan to a property is not a mortgage but a document known as a deed of trust. And while some states use only a mortgage, others use only a deed of trust, and still others can use both. Below is a listing of states and their preference.

MORTGAGE STATES

Alabama	Kentucky	New Mexico	Vermont
Arkansas	Louisiana	New York	Wisconsin
Connecticut	Maine	North Dakota	
Delaware	Massachusetts	Ohio	
Florida	Michigan	Oregon	
Hawaii	Minnesota	Pennsylvania	
Indiana	New Hampshire	Rhode Island	
Kansas	New Jersey	South Carolina	

DEED OF TRUST STATES

Alaska	Mississippi	North Carolina
Arizona	Missouri	Virginia
California	Nevada	Washington DC

DUAL STATES

use both deeds of trust and mortgages depending on local custom.

Colorado	Montana	
Georgia	Nebraska	Utah
Idaho	Oklahoma	Wyoming
Illinois	Oregon	Washington
Iowa	Tennessee	West Virginia
Maryland	Texas	

Even though a mortgage and a deed of trust do basically the same thing, there are several important differences. A mortgage involves two parties, the borrower and the lender, while a deed of trust has three: the borrower (trustor), the lender (beneficiary), and the trustee. The trustee, a neutral third party typically an attorney or title company, holds the title until the equitable lien is paid in full. The deed of trust is then cancelled and the title transfers over to the homeowner. The biggest difference however between a mortgage and deed of trust only comes into play if the borrower defaults and the property goes into foreclosure. At that point the trustee has the "power of sale" clause in the deed of trust to sell the property at the direction of the lender. The lender must provide proof to the trustee of the default; the trustee cannot take action against the borrower for no reason. The state in which the default occurred will determine how the foreclosure proceeds. It is not required to go through the lengthy court process a sheriff sale does in a mortgage state, thereby making it a much less expensive and quicker procedure.

LIENS: There are basically two types of liens against real property, equitable or statutory. Equitable liens are imposed by an agreement (mortgage or deed of trust) between the lender (creditor) and the borrower. They are also known as consensual liens because they are levied against an individual with the person's knowledge or "consent" of this happening. Statutory liens, on the other hand, are imposed by statute of law. These laws give the creditor legal right to lien real property of the debtor. Statutory liens typically involve unpaid federal, state, or municipal taxes, mechanic's liens or monetary judgment liens. Statutory liens are also referred to as non-consensual liens, since they are done without the person's consent. Within those two categories are liens attached to properties for various reasons. Listed below are some of the more common liens you are likely to encounter from those two categories, with their classification.

MORTGAGE or DEED OF TRUST LIEN: This is the most common real property lien you will see. It is brought about by the borrower failing to make the monthly payment, causing the lender to lien the property and foreclose. **Equitable**

PROPERTY TAX LIENS: These liens are brought about by local taxing authorities when the homeowner fails to pay their local county, city or school taxes. **Statutory**

FEDERAL IRS TAX LIENS: If the owner was remiss in their payment of federal taxes, the IRS will file notice to attach a lien to the property. **Statutory**

CODE ENFORCEMENT LIENS: These are liens for penalties placed by local municipalities for code enforcement violations for everything from trash or debris in the yard to who knows what. These liens are usually smaller monetary amounts and are enforced when the property is sold or foreclosed on. **Statutory**

MUNICIPAL LIENS: Placed by the local municipality when the homeowner fails to pay for municipal services such as water, sewer, etc. **Statutory**

MECHANIC'S LIENS: If a licensed contractor, tradesman, architect or materialman supplied work or material to improve the property and was not paid, they can file a lien against the property. In most states unlicensed contractors do not have lien rights. **Statutory**

MARITAL & CHILD SUPPORT LIEN: Depending on the type of support due, this lien can be placed by state or federal governments for non-payment of support. **Statutory.**

JUDGMENT LIENS: This lien is associated with a monetary award given to the plaintiff (person filing the lawsuit) against the defendant (person whom the suit is against) resulting from a lawsuit filed for bad debt. This type of lien can be against both real and/or personal property. **Statutory**

LIEN PRIORITY

We defined what a lien is. Now let's look at what a lien does. A lien assigns creditors a position in line for payment when the property is sold. Depending on where in that hierarchy of liens the creditor falls determines their chances of being paid from the proceeds if the property goes to foreclosure sale. So it only goes to say the higher you are in the order, the better your chances of collecting monies from the sale. This is what is known as "Lien Priority" or "Lien Position." In many cases there is not enough money collected from the sale of the property to satisfy all lienholders so lien priority is critical. Lienholders who were too far down in priority to receive any monies from the sale are "divested," or more commonly said to be "wiped out at the sale" and lose their hold on any future financial claims to the property.

There are two dates associated with a mortgage or lien you need to be concerned with. The first is the original date that the instrument (mortgage or lien) was drafted or written. The second and most critical is the recording date. That is the date the instrument (mortgage or lien) was actually *recorded* in the public records at the courthouse. It is that recording date that determines a lien's position. The only exception would be superior liens, which have priority over everything and are explained in greater detail below. The earlier a creditor's lien is recorded in the public records, the higher the priority of that lien respective to the recording dates of other liens, and it will be the first to get paid with the proceeds from the sale of the property. For example, a lien drafted on July 23 and recorded on July 28 would have priority over a lien drafted earlier on July 10 but *recorded* later on July 30. When you are looking at title search reports or doing title searches yourself, be sure to use the recording date as your basis for lien position and *not the drafted date.*

LEVELS OF LIEN PRIORITY

There are four levels of lien priority, **Super Priority, Superior, Senior and Junior**, each explained below.

Super Priority Liens: Super priority liens are not very common and are usually associated with a purchase money mortgage. A purchase money mortgage is a method of financing a property whereby the buyer actually borrows money from the seller instead of or in addition to a lending institution, such as a bank. Also known as seller financing, this type of funding is used when the buyer cannot qualify for the full amount with a traditional mortgage. Super priority liens can jump ahead of all other mortgages in terms of priority but not ahead of superior liens. If you encounter a super priority lien in your title search, check with your real estate attorney as to how these liens are handled in your particular area.

Superior Liens: A superior lien is a trump card for the holder of it. Superior liens have priority over *all* other liens, even if their recording date is *after* the recording date of any mortgages or other senior or junior liens. Superior liens are generally the following: local municipal or county taxes, such as school and other real estate-based taxes, and water and sewer bills that are administered by local government. Water and/or sewer bills that are from private companies are not superior liens and fall into the standard lien priority based on their recording date. As you do your title due diligence work, you will likely find homeowners in foreclosure who also have outstanding debt with the IRS. It just seems to work out that way. Ironically, IRS liens are *not* considered superior or even senior liens but fall into the category of junior liens and are explained in that section.

Senior Liens: A senior lien is any lien whose position is ahead of the lien-holder that initiated the foreclosure. That would be by virtue of the fact that the recording date on the senior lienholder's original document, most likely a mortgage or deed of trust, was recorded *before* the foreclosing entity's document. You will find that the senior lien position, also known as "first position," is usually held by banks, mortgage companies, or the lender that made the original loan to purchase the property. Banks or mortgage companies, as they are more often than not the largest creditor against a property, are typically the first to become delinquent and therefore usually the first to initiate a foreclosure action against the homeowner. Banks or mortgage companies as a rule will not make a loan on a property where they have to go beyond being in a second lien position. This means they will never end up further down in lien priority than right below the initial mortgage lender. This greatly increases their chance of getting paid in the event of foreclosure. If you are third, fourth or greater in lien position, chances are good you will end up being wiped out and not get paid if the property goes to foreclosure sale. Banks won't take that chance. If a junior lienholder is fore-closing and the property sells at the auction, the senior lienholder simply goes along with the transfer of the property to the winning bidder, and now it is their responsibility. The senior lienholder can now demand payment from the new owner for its lien or can even foreclose on the new owner of the property! Some locales however will allow a senior lienholder to receive monies against their lien if there are excess proceeds from the sale available. Your real estate attorney can advise you if this is applies to your area.

Junior Liens: A junior lien is a lien whose position is below that of all other liens. This is because the junior lienholder's recording date occurred *after* that of the senior lienholder. This is why junior lien holders stand the greatest chance of not receiving any proceeds from the sale of foreclosed property and are usually wiped out, losing their claim against the property. Because of this, all states have as part of their foreclosure statutes a requirement stating that all junior lienholders must be notified when a senior lienholder initiates a foreclosure action on a property for default. In fact, all creditors (superior, senior and junior) with any financial interest in the property must be notified in advance of the sale. This gives the junior lienholders the opportunity to defend their liens before possibly having them wiped out if the property goes to the foreclosure auction. If a junior lienholder is not properly notified by the foreclosing lender and the property does sell at the auction, then that lien remains active and stays attached to the property and now becomes the responsibility of the new owner. Mistakes do happen and creditors, particularly those with liens lower in priority, sometimes do unintentionally get missed. Perhaps they moved their business location and the forwarding order expired. Courthouses handle tons of papers and things do get misfiled. I cannot overemphasize enough that as you go along check, recheck and verify all of your paperwork.

Junior liens can be for non-payment of things like HELOCs, medical bills, credit cards, work done by tradespeople such as plumbers and landscapers (known as "mechanic's liens"), or federal taxes to the IRS. IRS liens include a unique stipulation known as "right of redemption." In this, the IRS has up to 120 days of redemption time to exercise their right to reclaim monies owed it through the buyback and resale of your purchased property. If the IRS decides to exercise their option, they will buy back your property from you for what you paid at the auction plus interest for that period and any expenses you paid for the preservation of the property, such as fire insurance. The good news is that in most cases the IRS does not exercise this right, as it does not really want to be in the real estate biz. I said most, but not all cases. If there is a lot of equity in the property you bought and the IRS realizes this, they can buy it back from you and use that money to satisfy their tax lien. Here is the catch: if you do any repairs or rehab work to the property during that 120-day redemption time, and the IRS decides to exercise its right on the 118th day, they will *not* pay you for any of that work you did. They would buy it back with those free repairs from you and *they* would list it for sale with other IRS Tax Lien properties at their sale and apply the profits to satisfy their lien.

Many real estate investors are not aware that you can request the IRS to relinquish their lien against the property before the end of the 120-day redemption period. If your property was bought at a judicial sheriff sale auction, go to the IRS website and print IRS publication No. 487, "How to prepare an Application Requesting the United States to Release its Right to Redeem Property Secured by a Federal Tax Lien" and publication No. 4235, which contains the various remittance addresses for the technical services advisory group where you send your application. If you bought property at a non-judicial foreclosure sale, such as a trustee auction, then you would go to the website for the U.S Attorney's office, www.usdoj.gov, and print out Form OBD 225 and follow the instructions. There is a fee associated with doing this and filing the request does not guarantee the IRS *will* release the lien. And even if the IRS ultimately decides not to exercise their right of redemption, the lien will still remain a "cloud" on the title, preventing you from selling the property before the 120-day period ends. Releasing the lien from the property however does not relieve the former owner's responsibility of paying the tax debt. The bottom line on dealing with property that has IRS liens against it is this: if you are at all unsure of the IRS's status, hold off doing any rehab work until after the 120-day redemption period has passed.

Judgments: A judgment is a ruling from a court saying that one entity is indebted to another and fixing the amount of the debt. Judgment liens must be filed and recorded in the public records. A judgment can be for a variety of reasons, such as an unpaid utility, credit card, or just about any bill that the homeowner has not paid in a reasonable amount of time. The creditor that receives the judgment lien cannot force the foreclosure of the property with the lien; however, if the owner of the property decides to sell it, the judgment lien must be paid in full along with any applicable interest before the sale can go forth. If however the property ends up at a foreclosure sale, then the judgment lien ends up like any other lien and is subject to lien priority for payment.

Taxes: There are several taxes directly and indirectly connected to real estate. Property taxes such as county, local municipal and school are directly tied to the real estate by way of the properties assessed value. State and federal (IRS) taxes, while not directly connected with the property, can be liened against the property for non-payment. In fact, the IRS has tax delinquent sales where they auction off repossessed properties to satisfy their past due taxes. You can find more about past due real estate taxes at the county's tax assessment office, or sometimes that information is available online at the county's website. You will need the property's folio or equivalent identification number to access that information.

CHAPTER 11

RESEARCHING THE LIENS

If there is only one thing that you take from this book it is **NEVER, NEVER, NEVER** bid on any property at a foreclosure auction without having previously researched the liens, mortgages, and taxes against it. It doesn't matter how good of a deal it looks like from the outside at the sale, or who said what about the property, *never* bid without having done your due diligence title work prior to the sale. Not doing it is a recipe for possible financial disaster. And doing title search work yourself if you have never done it before can also produce that same recipe results. Just getting your feet wet in foreclosures is not the time to begin learning how to do title searches. You may have heard from someone who heard it from a friend's friend say it's easy. You just go online or down to the courthouse and look the stuff up.

Well, not so fast. First of all, you have to know *what* you are looking for, right? And then you have to know *where to look for it.* And then you have to know *how* to interpret what you found, providing you found all there is to find. And then finally, you have to have the *time* to spare to gather up all of that information. Sound confusing? It can be and is. Especially if you make a mistake by *miss reading, miss interpreting* or just plain *missing* something in your records search. And if that mistake is a big enough one, it could cost you dearly.

What I *strongly* recommend you do, at least in the beginning while you're getting your feet wet doing foreclosures, is have the title searches done by the title company you've chosen for your team. Once you become more familiar with reading and interpreting title searches, *then* go to your county courthouse and do the research yourself using search results done by the title company as a guide. See if you come up with the same information the title company did. If after doing several of these you begin to get the hang of it, then chances are you can probably do the simple title searches yourself, working your way up to the more complex ones. I do almost all of the title searches myself now, but it has taken me a long time and a lot of searches to get comfortable enough to get to that point. And even after you learn to do the searches yourself, you probably will still need the services of the title company from time to time for the really complicated ones. This is not to say that title companies don't ever make mistakes doing searches, they do. But their errors are few and far between. *However*, if you *really* feel compelled to do your own title work, I will give you a simplified view and some pointers on how to go about it. But no matter which route you decide to go, you want to have the search done as close to the sale date as possible. This is so your results are based on the most current information available. Searches that are three or four months old could have changed and are then worthless. I try to do them the week prior to the sale. If you're using a title company, be sure to ask them what their lead time is so you don't get stuck. After you receive the search back from the title company, or if you've done it yourself, you'll want to review it with your attorney.

USING A TITLE COMPANY TO RESEARCH LIENS

If you haven't already done so, you need to get on board with a title company. Your realtor or attorney may know of, or already works with, a title company, and that's fine. Some realtors may also do their own title work. If you joined a local real estate investing group, you can get recommendations from them too. But if not, look in the phone book under the listing "Title Companies" and you will find many to choose from. There are various types of title searches offered for different requirements. When you are in the preliminary stages and looking at a variety of properties, what you need is a quick way to evaluate how much the debt on a property is and which of those properties have enough equity to make them worth pursuing.

You can find this out by doing an inexpensive type of title search of the current owner called a "Last Owner Search." This type of search also goes by such names as "Judgment & Lien Search" or "Type I or II Basic Search," but they are all the same thing and usually cost about fifty dollars or less per search. These are not full-blown title searches, as they only research the mortgages, liens and judgments of the most recent or last owner and are as a rule accurate. From these searches you will be able to determine lien priority, whether the property has any equity in it, and which liens will stay with the property and which will probably be wiped out.

If you decide, after crunching the numbers from the last owner search, to pursue the property, you should now order what is called a "Full Title Search" or "Abstract of Title." The cost of a full title search runs about two hundred dollars. The main difference between the last owner search and a full title search is the last owner search looks at mortgages, liens, judgments, and anything else indexed only against the current owner. The full title search will uncover all of the same items that the last owner search did, however the full title search not only looks at what was indexed against the current owner, it looks at *all of the owners* in the chain of title. In most situations a last owner search will give you all of the proper data you need to make a correct decision on a property. However, if there are any mortgages, liens or judgments against the property that *predate* the current owner, they will not show up on a last owner search. For example, a second mortgage for "X" dollars that was taken back by the previous owner when the property was sold to the current owner would not show up on the last owner search since its scope of search is confined only to items with the current owner's name on it. It is possible that if the first mortgage holder were to foreclose and due to some error the second mortgage holder/previous owner was not notified of the foreclosure, that lien would stay attached to the property if it sold at foreclosure sale, and you would not know about it if you only did a last owner search. Only by checking the names on the full title search with the names on the 3129 affidavit (or similar document for your area) will you be sure of every lienholder. After you receive the search back from the title company or if you've done it yourself, you will want to have your attorney review it with you and check it for accuracy.

DOING YOUR OWN TITLE SEARCH

As it is true that not all states and counties have the same foreclosure rules, not all counties index their information exactly the same way. If you have decided to do your own title research work, I would recommend starting at your county courthouse. That is where most if not all of the information you are looking for will be found. And while many counties now have their public information available online, it may not be *the most up-to-date information available.* If you want to be *sure* you are getting the most current mortgage, lien, and judgment records out there, go to the courthouse. Below I've listed where specific information is typically found at the courthouse. Yours may be different. Check with the information clerk there.

- Mortgages and deeds are usually found in the Recorder of Deeds office.
- Liens and judgments are usually found in the Prothonotary's or County Recorder's Office, sometimes referred to as the Office of Judicial Support (OJS), or the Recorder of Deeds office.
- Tax information records are located in the Tax collection or Tax claims office.
- For liens resulting from non-payment on government backed loans such as SBA, student loans, FHA, VA or federal taxes, check with your local U.S court. Sometimes this information will show up on the records of OJS.

If these locations do not have the information you are looking for, ask where you can go to find it. Many times there is a lag period between the recording of the liens and when the liens are actually *posted* to the county's public records system, further complicating things. Do not automatically assume that all of the information contained in the notice of default or the lis-pendens is absolutely correct. Mistakes can happen. While the folks at the courthouse usually will not look up the information for you, they will show you how to use the computer or microfiche system to access the information. Your real estate attorney can also help guide you. Below is the form that I use to help me organize all of the information I am collecting when doing my title research work:

REAL ESTATE WORK UP SHEET

Ref #_____   Attorney: _____

Name:_____

Address:_____

_____

_____

Folio #_____   Foreclosing Debt $_____

Term & Number _____   Hand Money $ _____

Occupied:_____ Y _____ N _____ Unknown

Liens/Judgments: Plaintiff   Docket#   Filed   Amount

_____

_____

_____

_____

_____

_____

_____

_____

Mortgages   Book&Page Dated   Recorded   Amount

_____

_____

_____

_____

_____

_____

_____

_____

Taxes Past Due:_____

_____

_____

Comments: _____

_____

_____

_____

Once you have gathered all of the information—and this is the challenging part—you will need to separate what liens, mortgages, deeds of trust, or judgments are still valid against the debtor. To do this you need to match up the list of mortgages that have been satisfied against the ones that are still outstanding and put them in order of their recording dates. You will need to do this for the liens, judgments, and any other information you have obtained. Local real estate taxes come under the heading of superior liens, and these local taxes are not divested but actually added to the overall amount of debt to be included into the upset or minimum bid price.

Do not be as concerned about the recording dates of the real estate-based taxes, since they are not divested at the sale. The only exception is IRS tax liens, which in almost all instances are junior liens but because of the 120-day right of redemption that IRS liens enjoy they are not wiped and will go along with the property at the time of sale. You need to account for those liens.

LISTING ORDER FOR HOW THE MONEY COLLECTED FROM A FORECLOSURE SALE IS DISBURSED

Illustrated below is the typical order in which money collected from a sheriff sale of property in Pennsylvania distributed from first to last paid might look like:

1. Transfer Tax portion due the state.
2. Payment to the sheriff for their costs to conduct the sale.
3. Transfer Tax portion due the local municipality.
4. The superior lien(s) and/or the local real estate taxes and/or municipal services.
5. The entity that did the foreclosing.
6. The next lower priority lienholder(s) in line behind the foreclosing entity. These payment(s) continue until the money runs out.
7. If there is any money left at this point it goes to the former owner.

SAMPLE TITLE SEARCH

Let's look at and analyze a hypothetical last owner search by the numbers:

XYZ title Search Company

1   **Search Order #** 789   **Date:** 9/14/2007

2   **Name Given Current Owner:** John Q. Public
      Address Given: 123 Peach St.
      City: Mellontown   **County:** Apple   **State:** PA   **Zip:** 18888

3   **Type of Report Ordered:** Last owner Search

4   **Date of Deed:** 1/15/00   **Date recorded:** 1/25/00   **Book/Page:** 100/344

5 MORTGAGES

Book/Page	Mortgagee	Dated	Recorded	Amount
203/471	Happy Times Mortgage Co.	2/1/00	2/10/00	100,000
603/1525	Nickel & Dime Bank	10/20/05	10/25/05	30,000

6 LIENS

Plaintiff	Docket No.	Filed	Amount	Defendant
Happy Times Mortgage	06-1234	2/10/06	$60,000.00	John Q. Public
Mellontown School Dist.	06-3478	9/23/06	5,500.00	John Q. Public
Apple County Sewer Auth.	07-126	1/30/07	300.00	John Q. Public
Honest John Contractor	06-5178	11/20/06	12,000.00	John Q. Public
IRS	07-398	7/19/07	30,000.00	John Q. Public

This sample format for a title search is only an example. The one you receive back from your title company will look different. You will want the assistance of the title company clerk or your attorney to help you understand what all of this means. This is crucial. You must understand how all this information relates to the property you plan to bid on. This will allow you to determine if the property is even worth pursuing. Let's look at what the example is telling us:

1. This is the number you would use when inquiring about the search.
2. Who the search is for. Re-verify the person's name, address and zip; be sure it matches what you want.
3. The type of search requested, in this case a last owner search.
4. Indicates the date the deed for this house was drawn up on and when it was officially recorded in the county records. It also gives the book and page number that the deed was recorded in.
5. "Mortgages" shows a listing of all the active mortgages in effect on the property, the book and page they were recorded in, the date of the mortgage, when the mortgage was recorded in the county records, and lastly the amount of the mortgage. It is this recording date that is used in determining the superiority of a lien. This shows a first mortgage of $ 100,000 and a second mortgage of $ 30,000 in the form of a Home Equity Line Of Credit (HELOC).
6. "Liens" indicates what entities have filed liens against the property owner for uncollected monies due them. It shows Happy Times Mortgage filed their lien on February 10, 2006 for the amount of $ 60,000 against John Q. Public. It also shows Mr. Public did not pay his Mellontown school taxes or his municipal sewer bill to Apple County either. So the school district filed a lien on September 23, 2006 for $ 5,500 and the sewer authority filed on January 30 for $ 300.00. It looks like Mr. Public did not pay Honest John the Contractor for work done, as Mr. John has filed a mechanic's lien against Mr. Public for $ 12,000 on November 20, 2006. And finally, Mr. Public did not pay Uncle Sam his taxes, so the IRS has filed a lien in the amount of $ 30,000 on July 19, 2007. The docket numbers are chronological and indicate the year and the civil case number. Happy Times Mortgage's docket number shows that it was filed in **06** signifying **2006,** and it was the 1,234th civil case item filed so far that year at the courthouse. Docket numbers are very important. They are the key to accessing documents at the courthouse. Whenever you need to look up information at the court-house you will need the docket number.

CHAPTER 12
DETERMINING YOUR BID PRICE

EVALUATING THE LAST OWNER SEARCH

Now that you have the last owner search back from the title company you need to evaluate the information to determine if the property has any equity worth bidding on. If it has, you need to come up with a *maximum bid price*. Using the sample last owner search from the previous chapter, let's look at two possible scenarios. In each of these scenarios it is assumed we completed our due diligence and have comps showing that Mr. Public's house has a current value after rehab of $ 140,000. Mr. Public lives in Pennsylvania, a state that practices judicial foreclosure, meaning his property is going to sheriff sale.

MORTGAGES

Book/Page	Mortgagee	Dated	Recorded	Amount
203/471	Happy Times Mortgage Co.	2/1/00	2/10/00	100,000
603/1525	Nickel & Dime Bank	10/20/05	10/25/05	30,000

LIENS

Plaintiff	Docket No.	Filed	Amount	Defendant
Happy Times Mortgage	06-1234	2/10/06	60,000.00	John Q. Public
Mellontown School District	06-3478	9/23/06	5,500.00	John Q. Public
Apple County Sewer Auth.	07-126	1/30/07	300.00	John Q. Public
Honest John Contractor	06-5178	1/20/06	12,000.00	John Q. Public
IRS	07-398	7/19/07	30,000.00	John Q. Public

SCENARIO #1

In this example we find that Happy Times Mortgage is foreclosing for $ 60,000 and they have a judgment against Mr. Public. Nickel & Dime bank does not have a judgment, but the balance presently owed by Mr. Public is $ 20,000 as he is currently up to date with his payments. The total value of liens against the property is $ 107,800. The house's current value after rehab is $ 140,000. The house goes to foreclosure sale and is sold for $ 85,000.

For clarity, assume the two percent transfer tax will be calculated on the selling price. Here is how the money is disbursed:

1. Transfer Tax paid (2%) ....$ 1,700
2. Cost paid to sheriff for conducting sale (poundage) ....$ 1,300
3. Paid to Mellontown School District (superior lien) ....$ 5,500
4. Paid to Apple County Sewer Authority (superior lien).........$ 300
5. Paid to Happy Times Mortgage (senior lienholder)...............$ 60,000
6. Paid to Nickel & Dime Bank (junior lienholder)....................$ 16,200
7. Paid to Honest John Contractor (junior lienholder); ....$ 0
8. Paid to IRS (junior lienholder)...$ 0

TOTAL................ $ 85,000

Here is what happened:
1. The first paid is the two percent Pennsylvania transfer tax.
2. The second to get paid is the sheriff. The fee that the sheriff collects for conducting the sale is called "Poundage" and is a percentage of the price that the house sold for. There are other costs involved which will be explained later.
3. Mellontown School District tax lien is connected to real estate, so it is a **Superior Lien** in this state and it jumps to the head of the line and gets paid first.
4. Apple County Sewer Authority is also a **Superior Lien** connected to real estate and it also gets paid before the other liens.
5. Happy Times Mortgage, the **Senior Lienholder** and foreclosing entity, gets paid in full.
6. Nickel & Dime Bank, a junior lienholder, gets paid next, since their mortgage was **recorded** on 10/25/05 **before** Honest John and the IRS filed their liens. So due to that fact, they received almost all of their monies and their lien is considered satisfied and is divested.
7. Unfortunately, since at this point there are no monies left to distribute, Honest John is wiped out. His lien is divested and he loses any future ability to make claim against the property.
8. The IRS lien is not wiped out. Due to the right of redemption clause, the IRS has 120 days to exercise their lien if they decide to buy back the property from the successful bidder.

SCENARIO #2

In this scenario the second mortgage holder, Nickel & Dime bank has a judgment for $ 25,000 and is the one foreclosing. The mortgages and liens look like this:

MORTGAGES

Book/Page	Mortgagee	Dated	Recorded	Amount
203/471	Happy Times Mortgage Co.	2/1/00	2/10/00	100,000
603/1525	Nickel & Dime Bank	10/20/04	10/25/05	30,000

LIENS

Plaintiff	Docket No.	Filed	Amount	Defendant
Nickel & Dime Bank	06-1455	1/15/07	25,000	John Q. Public
Mellontown School District	06-3478	9/23/06	5,500	John Q. Public
Apple County Sewer Authority	07-126	1/30/07	300	John Q. Public
Honest John Contractor	06-5178	11/20/06	12,000	John Q. Public
IRS	07-398	7/19/07	30,000	John Q. Public

Mr. Public is up to date on his payments to Happy Times Mortgage, and has a current outstanding balance of $ 80,000. The total value of liens against the property is $ 72,800. The house's current value after rehab is $ 140,000. It goes to foreclosure and is sold for $ 85,000, subject to Happy Times' first mortgage.

Here is how the money is dispersed:
1. Transfer Tax paid (2%) ....$ 1,700
2. Cost paid to sheriff for conducting sale (poundage) ....$ 1,300
3. Paid to Mellontown School District (superior lien) ....$ 5,500
4. Paid to Apple County Sewer Authority (superior lien).........$ 300
5. Paid to Nickel & Dime Bank..$ 25,000
6. Paid to Honest John Contractor (junior lien) ....$ 12,000
7. Paid to IRS (junior lien) ....$ 30,000
8. Paid to former owner Mr. Public...$ 9,200

TOTAL................ $ 85,000

Here is what happened:

1. Once again the two percent PA transfer tax is paid first.
2. Sheriff is paid for conducting the sale.
3. Mellontown School District real estate connected tax lien is **superior** and gets paid next.
4. The Apple County Sewer Authority is also real estate connected and **superior,** so it gets paid now also.
5. Nickel & Dime Bank is the **foreclosing lienholder** and gets paid the full amount owed.
6. This time there was enough funds available, so **junior lienholder** Honest John gets paid the full amount owed to him.
7. Also, there were enough extra monies to satisfy the IRS's **junior lien**, so they get paid in full.
8. Any excess funds remaining go back to the former owner, in this case Mr. Public. In Pennsylvania it is the responsibility of the former owner to claim these funds, which are held for seven years and if unclaimed will revert back to the state.
9. Happy Times Mortgage does not receive any monies from the sale and retains its first lien position status. Not only is this first lien position status not wiped out, the new owner of the property, the high bidder, inherits the mortgage with the property and it is now their responsibility. Happy Times could demand immediate full payment of the loan or could even foreclose on the property from the new owner to get it. That is what happens and what is meant by the term "subject to a first lien." Bidding on properties with first liens is tricky. Depending, the amount of the lien and the value of the house after rehab will determine whether or not you should bid.

PROBLEMS

From the previous examples, what can go wrong before you bid? Well, several things. Let's look at what variables you need to check.

NOTIFICATION

Pennsylvania law requires all creditors or parties who may have an interest in a foreclosed property, be notified at least thirty days prior to the foreclosure sale. That law, included as part of the Pennsylvania Code known as "Rule 3129," contains the list of creditors and parties, the "Affidavit Pursuant to Rule 3129.1." If a creditor or party was not notified within the thirty-day period, then the lien, if one existed, will not be divested should the property sell at the sale. For example, referring back to scenario No. 1, Honest John Contracting was wiped out at the sale, since there were not enough monies to pay him.

Now, let's assume that the foreclosing attorney failed to notify Honest John of the sale. Since Honest John was a junior lienholder, he would have been wiped out at the sale. But because he was not properly notified and thereby denied the option of defending his lien at the sale, his lien stands and remains with the property. Honest John can now demand that his lien be paid, or he can foreclose on the property. You need to verify that all creditors have been notified so you don't unknowingly end up bidding on a property with a lienholder who wasn't properly notified and might not be divested. The Rule 3129.1 form is filed by the foreclosing creditor's attorney and contains the list of names and addresses of all of known creditors and persons with interest in the foreclosure. Ask your attorney if there is a form similar to the 3129 and the time frame for notification in your area.

In Pennsylvania, to view this and all of the other forms and filings relevant to the foreclosure, you need to go to the to the Prothonotary's office in the courthouse. The title **Prothonotary** derives from Greek and means "first scribe or officer." All civil litigation is filed with the Prothonotary and foreclosure is considered civil litigation. Within the Prothonotary's office is the records division, usually called the "Office of Judicial Support," or OJS for short. This is where information on civil cases is kept. To access this information you'll need the docket number that pertains to the entire foreclosure and not just the individual docket numbers of the judgments. Give that number to the clerk and they should hand you back a folder containing the information on the foreclosure. Depending on the extent of the foreclosure and how long it have been ongoing, you may find it chock full of papers. What you are looking for are the papers initially filed by the foreclosing attorney that will contain the Rule 3129 list. It may be stapled to a fairly thick bunch of other papers with the Rule 3129 list somewhere in it. Review the list against what you received in the last owner search. Chances are they will not match up exactly, as the Rule 3129 list has all *possible* creditors and persons, and your last owner search has all *actual* creditors, but you should see your creditors listed. When viewing the foreclosure's filing documents take note, as it names who (bank, lending institution, etc.) is foreclosing. This is typically on the first or cover page, and it reads "creditor vs. debtor" or "defendant vs. plaintiff." This is handy for identifying the correct foreclosing lender if there are several lenders listed on the last owner search.

SUBORDINATION

A rare twist that can occur with a lien is called subordination. Subordination is when a senior lienholder switches positions with a junior lienholder. The senior lienholder allows itself to be *subordinated* to junior lien status while the junior lien now assumes the senior lien's position. The danger in this is a junior lien may now be senior and still may need to be satisfied if you win the property at the sale. This happens for various reasons, such as the seller of a piece of land who held the first mortgage allowed their mortgage to be subordinated so that a construction loan to build the structure could be approved. While these instances do not crop up often, they can happen, and you need to review all mortgage documents carefully to see if this occurred. Check with your attorney if you think one of the liens might be subordinated.

PURCHASING DISCOUNTED JUNIOR LIENS

Purchasing discounted junior liens is a technique used by experienced bidders that in certain situations can turn a property that otherwise might not be profitable into a potentially profitable one. And you don't even have to be the winning bidder! As you know, when a senior lienholder is foreclosing, many of the junior lienholders ultimately end up getting wiped out at the sale if the property does not sell for enough and the monies received were insufficient to satisfy all of the debt. When purchasing junior liens, you negotiate with the junior lienholder(s) to buy their lien from them at a discount and then have the lien *assigned* to you. This procedure can be used to make money, even if you are *not* the successful bidder. Why then, you may ask, would a junior lienholder sell you their lien for less than they are owed? Because most junior lienholders have three options. First, if the final winning bid is not sufficient to pay all liens, they will either get wiped out completely or *possibly* receive a fraction of their lien amount. Their second option is to attend the sale and bid high enough to win the property. They then would need to resell it themselves to recoup their lien amount. Their third option is to sell their lien to you for less. Like the old saying goes, "A bird in the hand is worth two in the bush." You'll find many lienholders will accept the third option of *surety of cash today* rather than hope for *possible cash tomorrow*. You'll need to contact the lienholder. If that lienholder is a bank or mortgage company, ask to speak to someone in either the "loss mitigation" or "collections" department. If the lienholder is any other entity, ask for the person in charge of the financial or bookkeeping department.

Don't be surprised if they have no idea that the property is scheduled for sale or that they even have a lien against the property at all. While they should have been notified of the sale and probably were, many times the paperwork gets relegated to never-never land and is forgotten about. Explain that the house is scheduled to go to foreclosure sale on such and such date with a senior lienholder foreclosing and that their junior lien will most likely get wiped out at the sale, with them receiving nothing. Ask them if they would be interested in selling their lien to you. If their answer is yes, get the contact person's name, phone, and fax number and tell them you will present your offer to them via fax. If they say no or are unsure, give them your name and phone number anyway, so if they change their mind they can get back to you. But be sure to remind them that if the property sells at foreclosure sale and they do get wiped out, there is nothing you can do for them at that point, so time is of the essence.

You need to present your offer in the form of a letter. A sample of this type of letter is shown below. If this is your first time doing this and you are uncertain about how to go about it, this may be a good time to avail yourself of your real estate attorney's consulting services by asking them to review your offer letter. Should they accept your offer, your attorney can draw up the required paperwork and review the documents specific for your locale to complete the transaction.

SAMPLE DISCOUNTING JUNIOR LIENS LETTER

January 1, 2000

Mrs. Jane Smith
Loss Mitigation Officer
Small Bux Mortgage Company
123 Main St.
Anytown FL. 24578

    RE: Loan # 2345678901
    Mr. John Q. Public 123 Peach St. Mellontown, PA 18888

Dear Ms. Smith;

As per our conversation on 12/30/1999 in regards to the property referenced above and your mortgage loan of $ 20,000 against the property also referenced above, please accept this letter as my cash offer of $ 3,000 for an assignment of that loan on said property. As you are aware, the property is scheduled for sheriff sale on January 15, 2000 with a senior lien having a judgment of $ 75,000 foreclosing. I have personally visited the property which is vacant at this time and noted the following problems I could verify:

1. Roof has deteriorated and needs replacing. Gutters and down-spouts falling down.
2. Broken and rotted windows and frames.
3. Siding falling off and damaged in several areas.
4. Large tree down in backyard.
5. Woodwork on front porch rotted.

I estimate repairs to the exterior alone could total $ 15,000. Since the house is locked, I could not inspect the interior; however, in my opinion I would assume it to be in same state of disrepair as the exterior. Based on this, it would be very difficult to sell in its present state. My research estimates indicates the house as it sits currently to be worth no more than $ 80.000. If that is true, chances are your subordinate mortgage and any other junior liens will be wiped out at the sale.

Please let me know at your earliest convenience if this offer is acceptable to you. If so, my attorney will forward to you a list of any documentation required from you and necessary paperwork to be signed and returned by your company to complete the transaction as soon as possible. This offer is valid until 5 PM EST on January 10, 2000, after which it is withdrawn.

Please feel free to contact me at (123) 456-7890 should you have any questions. I look forward to hearing from you.

Sincerely,
Your Name

You should make your initial cash offer at no more than ten to fifteen percent of what the lender is owed. Remember, they will probably counteroffer you, and if you start low you can always go higher, but if you start high you can't go lower. Never go higher than thirty percent of the value of the lien. Offer to settle in as short a time as possible, five to seven days maximum, or less if the foreclosure sale is coming up fast. Make sure your offer contains a date and time after which it expires. When describing the condition of the property in your letter, call attention to all of the problems that you know to be wrong with the house. The idea here is to present the property in its most unfavorable light, but be honest and don't make up problems that you know don't exist. If you do lie and get caught, you could find yourself at the end of a lawsuit for deception and fraud. Once you complete the transaction have it recorded in the county records *right away*. You want the public records updated to show as soon as possible that you are now the owner of the lien, which would be reflected by that date.

Let's look to see what happens now that you own the lien. Using the above letter as our example, you purchased the $ 20,000 *2nd lien position* debt for $ 3,000. In other words, you bought something *potentially worth* $ 20,000 for only $ 3,000. And even though you paid $ 3,000 for it, it is still shown in the county records as a $ 20,000 lien.

While purchasing discounted junior liens can be a great secondary way to make money, there can be pitfalls. What can go wrong? First, the property *MUST* sell at the auction to a third party. It cannot end up being bought back by the bank via the attorney on the writ. If this happens, then the lien you purchased will be divested and *YOU* will be wiped out. Second, before offering to buy the discounted lien from the lienholder you'll want to have a pretty good idea that the property will sell and be bid up to a fairly higher price than the foreclosing amount. So before making the offer, be certain to go look at the property and do your due diligence research. If the property is a dog that no one would want to bid on, pass it and don't buy the lien.

Here are three sample scenarios and possible outcomes when buying discounted junior liens:

BEST: The property starts out at the sale with an upset price of $ 85,000 and the winning bid buys it for $ 110,000. The $ 75,000 senior lien is satisfied as well as the other costs included in the $ 85,000 upset price. Since there are enough additional monies left over you are paid your $ 20,000 for the lien. The remaining $ 5,000 goes to the debtor. **Your net profit is $ 17,000.** That is over a 500 percent return on your investment! Nice going!

GOOD: The property starts out at the foreclosure sale with an upset price of $ 85,000 and the winning bid buys it for $ 95,000. The $ 75,000 senior lien is satisfied as well as the other costs included in the $ 85,000 upset price. Since there is still additional monies left over you are paid $ 10,000 for the lien. Nothing goes to the debtor. **Your net profit is $ 7,000.** That is still over a 200 percent return on your investment. Not bad.

NOT SO GOOD: The property starts out at the foreclosure sale with an upset price of $ 85,000. No one bids over the upset price and it does not sell to a third party; it is bought back by the lender. The lien will then be divested, and unfortunately you'll lose the money you spent to buy the lien. In this case, your only other option to save your investment in the lien would be to bid slightly over the upset price and buy the property yourself. Then make any needed improvements or repairs enough to profitably resell or rent it. Unfortunately, this last outcome is the worst case scenario you will run into. That is one of the reasons you do not want to pay more than thirty percent for a lien, in case you get into trouble with this last situation.

CHAPTER 13
BID PRICING

Now comes the task of putting all the previous information together to determine your maximum bid price for the property. You need to have this price decided and written down *before* you get to the sale. If you don't, there is something that occurs at the sale known as auction fever, and it's easy to catch. Auction fever occurs when the bidding for a property starts and the participants bidding on the property get so caught up in it that the price reaches a ridiculous level. Before you know it the bidding is out of control and the property sells for far more than it's worth. People develop the mentality of "I don't care what it takes I am going to get that property no matter what" and just keep bidding it up and up. After the dust has settled, the winning bidder later realizes they paid far too much and the question of how much profit can be made is replaced with the realization of not making any profit or worse yet, a loss.

Never, Never, Ever take for granted the person or persons you are bidding against know more than you just because they keep bidding higher. They may have no idea what they're doing or some ulterior motive for doing it! What's more, you can't expect to get every property you bid on. Realize that there are people bidding on properties for various reasons. There are people bidding on properties that they plan to rent out. There are people who are bidding on properties to flip. And finally, people are there bidding on properties to live in as personal residences. The people who are there bidding on the properties to flip generally need to pay the least, since their rehab and holding costs are going to be the highest. Those who are planning to buy properties for rentals can afford to pay more than the flipper, since rehab costs for rentals are normally less. And the person who is bidding on the property to make it their personal residence can afford to pay the most, since they do not need to turn a profit on it. That is why you need to have your maximum bid price determined beforehand to suit your requirements for the property and not somebody else's.

Remember, this is a numbers game. What that means is after listing all of the costs required to purchase, rehab, hold, resell or rent the property, and if after determining your maximum bid price there is not a proper enough percentage of profit in it for you, then *do not bid on the property. Period.* The formula below illustrates how to determine this percentage of profit you need to make if you are planning to rehab and flip the property. Remember, if the numbers don't work, they don't work. Do not try to massage them so they will. Save your money for the next deal that does work. Now, let's review the formula that you will use to determine your bid price.

MAXIMUM BID FORMULA

<u>A</u>fter <u>R</u>epair <u>V</u>alue (ARV) x .70 (30%) – Repairs & Holding Costs =
Your Maximum Bid

Here is how it breaks down:

- **ARV,** or the After Repaired Value, is the price of what the property will be worth fixed up after the rehab is completed. You arrived at this figure by doing your homework and getting your comps for the property. Unless you are buying in an area where properties are literally "flying off the shelf" you always want to be conservative with this figure. Never set your ARV figure based on the assumption that "even though this isn't a great deal now, by the time I finish rehabbing it the values for this area should improve and so will my profits." **WRONG!!!** Assume nothing! If you are planning to flip the property, look at how many other properties similar to yours are up for sale and how long their **DOM** (Days on Market) is. You need to monitor price changes within your local market constantly so you can stay on track to have the rehab completed and up for sale while your comps are still good. If there are a lot of properties sitting for sale, it could be an indication of a slow market in that area and you might want to look at other properties in more robust locations. The same holds true for properties bought to be rentals. This amount of "holding time" will give you an indication of your carrying costs.

- The .70 or 30 percent is the average discount (many investors look for a 35-40 percent discount) below the ARV price that you need to buy the property at if you plan to rehab and flip it and still be profitable. While this number is not completely set in stone and is somewhat governed by how competitive your market place is, you should never go below a *minimum* 25 percent discount. If you will be bidding on a property that is currently occupied, use 40 percent as your discount figure, since it will probably take some time and extra expense to get the owners out. If you are bidding on a property to rent out, be sure that the maximum bid price will allow a positive cash flow of at least $ 150 to $ 200 per month after all expenses are paid.

- There will be temptation when you are bidding at the auction to go lower than the 25 percent just to get the property, but don't. *Stick to your Maximum Bid Price.*

This part, trying to estimate your repair and holding costs, is the trickiest. You really need to be as accurate as possible in both your cost of materials, labor to do the work, and the work itself that needs to be done. You might be saying, "If I can't get into the property to look at it, how can I be accurate?" Trying to figure out what needs to be done can be daunting. Here are some guidelines starting from the top of the property on down.

- Flat roofs normally cannot be seen and therefore make it impossible to tell their condition, unless a neighbor or an MLS listing tipped you off. I always figure on having to replace a flat roof. If after inspection it is determined that the roof is okay or only needs to be patched, you are ahead of the game cost-wise. Better to be ahead than behind. Standard asphalt shingle roofs are easier to predict. If you see a roof with shingles that are curling, have lost lots of their pebbly material, or are missing altogether the roof will probably need to be replaced. If you are lucky and the roof has no rotten wood underneath it, then you should be able to get away with putting another layer of shingles over the existing ones, which costs less that a complete tear off. Unfortunately, if there already is a failing second set of shingles over the first ones, you cannot put a third set on. It will have to be ripped off down to the wood and replaced, costing considerably more. Other types of roofing materials, such as cedar shingles, terracotta tiles or slate, can be very costly to repair or replace.
- Power washing can clean up an exterior nicely.
- Older properties with an overhead electric feed may need a new feed cable. This is the large wire that runs up the side of the building from the electrical box to the top of the roof line and ultimately connects to the pole. You do not need to replace it all the way out to the pole, just where it connects at the roofline and down to the meter and electrical breaker box. You may also need to upgrade the electric service at the same time, depending on the condition and age of the service box. This is a job that must be done by a licensed electrician. Do not try this yourself. Ask an electrician for their opinion and pricing.
- Windows, if they are the older single pane type, will probably need to be replaced with a more energy efficient kind. Tilt in vinyl replacements are great for this and come in a variety of styles, sizes, and prices. While we're talking windows, think about the doors in the front, side, rear, and garage as well.

- As was discussed in an earlier chapter, check your sidewalks and curbs for cracks and breaks.
- Does the driveway need to be replaced or will a coating of sealer make it look new?
- Check your landscaping for curb appeal.

Before moving on to the inside, here is a general rule of thumb to follow when you can't actually get into the property to see it: **"If the outside looks good, then the inside is probably good. If the outside looks bad, then the inside will probably be bad."** Hopefully, you were able to get a peek in the windows. Moving inside and keeping the rule of thumb in mind here are some more tips:

- Depending on the age of the property and if the previous owners smoked or had pets, if there is carpet you may need to replace it. Check with a flooring store for square foot prices on carpet. Hardwood flooring costs are similar per square foot as carpet and pad to refinish.
- Kitchens and bathrooms always can use some freshening up. Sometimes just updating the countertops, sinks and faucets can make a big difference. If the kitchen and bathrooms turn out to be really bad, a gut job might end up being needed, so refer back to the rule of thumb and figure accordingly.
- Assume you will be doing some drywall/spackle/patching work, if only at minimum to cover up dents and dings in the walls. Plan on repainting the entire interior of the property in a neutral color. New paint covers a lot of imperfections. Painting can be time-consuming, but you can save big on labor by doing it yourself. Grab some friends, pizza and "beverages," and depending on the size of the house you can usually have it painted in a weekend or so.
- Again, unless it is a relatively new place, presume updating many of the attached exterior and interior lighting fixtures—such as kitchen or bathroom—and budget accordingly.
- Mechanical systems for the building such as the plumbing, heating and air conditioning can be a tough call. Newer properties, such as those built within the last ten years or so, should have those systems in working order, needing little if any repairs or replacements. Older buildings, depending on whether or not the original mechanical systems were ever replaced at some point in time, may be fine and not need replacement. There really is no way of knowing this until you get inside. When you are crunching the numbers for your maximum bid you may want to figure in an allowance for mechanical system repairs.

Now let's address the costs of materials and labor. A great resource for this is *The Home Repair and Remodel Cost Guide* published by Marshall and Swift. The guide, which is updated yearly, contains cost tables, definitions of key terms, worksheets, and localized costs for cities in the U.S., Canada and more. Whereas the book won't completely replace having an estimate done by a contractor on site, it will allow you to closely estimate the costs for work on the property so you can prepare your bid price as accurately as possible. This is especially handy if you are just starting out and not familiar with the costs of materials and labor. While the book is not cheap (about $ 80.00), it will pay for itself in no time flat. You can order it directly from Marshall & Swift at 1-800-544-2678 or from their website, www.marshallswift.com.

Some of the larger building supply or home centers have construction calcula-tor tables on their website or at the center itself to help you estimate costs. While you are there, take a walk around through the aisles and take notes on the cost of various items in the plumbing, paint, wood, door, and kitchen departments, etc. so you have some idea of a basis from which to figure out what material costs are to do a project. If you possess the know-how and can do the project yourself, then you can save big on labor. If not, then you need to get an estimate from your contractor to do the job. Ask if he/she is okay with you supplying your own material to save money and just paying for the labor. Some contractors are and some are not okay with this setup, so it never hurts to ask.

After you get a few properties under your belt you will be able to "ballpark" the costs to redo certain things, like a powder room and such. I can look at a shingle roof on a house and determine from experience that that roof will cost about "X" dollars to replace without having to ask a roofer to come out and give me an exact price.

HOLDING COSTS

This can be one of the biggest expenses people starting out don't understand and mess up on. Holding or carrying costs are what you will be spending every month that you own the property up to the day you sell it or secure a tenant to rent it that are above and beyond the cost to purchase and rehab the property. Unfortunately, people either underestimate these costs or forget to account for them entirely. Holding costs can add up quick and be quite substantial. When estimating holding costs you need to be honest about how long you expect to own it before flipping or renting it. For example, say you bought a property at sheriff sale to rehab and flip. The rehab runs about sixty days to complete and it takes about ninety days or so till you get the sheriff's deed in your area. Properties are taking about sixty days or so to sell. You will need to add in the usual forty-five or more day wait from the signing of the agreement of sale with the buyer until actual settlement time. Adding up all this time means you need to figure your holding costs for *at least 8 months!* It's not a bad idea to err on the side of caution and allow yourself an extra month of holding costs just in case things don't go quite as planned. Below are a list of holding costs you will need to figure on:

1. Interest to be paid on monies borrowed until you sell the property or rent it out.

2. Insurance for property. You'll need to get special "builder's risk" or "unoccupied property insurance" for these projects while the rehab is under way, up to and until you sell the property or rent it. Check with your insurance agent. This type of insurance is much more expensive than the traditional occupied homeowner's insurance policy you may be familiar with.

3. Taxes. State, local, and school taxes that will be due after you receive the deed accruing during the selling process while you still own the property.

4. Principal, if required to be paid back on monies borrowed until the time you either sell the property or refinance it if it is to be rented out.

5. Utilities. Electric, gas, heat, trash, water, sewer, etc. required while you are working on the rehab and/or up to your either selling it or renting it out.

6. Condo fees. The monthly fees due, again, until you either sell or rent it.

SELLING COSTS

Selling costs are just that. Costs you will incur if you choose to sell the property. If you decide to hold on to the property as a rental, you will not have this expense. Two selling costs you need to be aware of are both taxes that you cannot completely avoid. The first is the local real estate transfer tax and the other is the federal capital gains tax. If you are selling the property yourself without the aid of a realtor, then you will have no realtor's commission to pay. But there will probably be various "fees" deducted from your check at the settlement table. Your attorney can advise you on these fees.

- Local Real Estate Transfer Taxes. Almost every locale has them and their percentage varies greatly. Traditionally they are split evenly between the buyer and seller. Your attorney or real estate agent can advise you on what is customary in your area.

- Commission to realtor and closing costs when you sell the property. This is a big one. It usually costs you a total of about seven to eight percent of the selling price when you go to settlement.

- Capital Gains Tax. While this is not actually paid at settlement it does have to be paid when you are calculating your federal income taxes. This is a tax on the profit you made on the sale of the property. How much you pay in capital gains tax is determined by your tax bracket and how much you spent on the rehabbing costs. Your accountant can give you more detailed information on this.

To illustrate what all of these assorted costs look like, let's look at and examine each of them:

1.	**ESTIMATED SELLING PRICE (ARV)**	$
2.	**ESTIMATED COST TO PURCHASE (max bid)**	- $
3.	**ESTIMATED FINANCE COSTS**	- $
4.	**ESTIMATED INSURANCE COSTS**	- $
5.	**ESTIMATED REAL ESTATE TAXES**	- $
6.	**ESTIMATED REPAIR COSTS**	- $
7.	**ESTIMATED FUDGE FACTOR: 15% of #6**	- $
8.	**ESTIMATED 8% REALTOR & CLOSING COSTS**	- $
	YOUR PROFIT (excluding capital gains tax)	$

1. **ESTIMATED SELLING PRICE (ARV):** This is what you estimate the value to be of the property after rehab and what you expect to sell it for.
2. **ESTIMATED COST TO PURCHASE (max bid):** This is the price you determined would be your **Maximum Bid Price**, or approximately the most you are prepared to pay for the property.
3. **ESTIMATED FINANCE COSTS:** This represents the approximate amount you expect to spend for the interest you will be paying on the money borrowed to finance the house until it sells or rents.
4. **ESTIMATED INSURANCE COSTS:** This is how much you expect to be paying for insurance on the property until it is sold or rented.
5. **ESTIMATED REAL ESTATE TAXES:** This covers real estate taxes that are *NOT* paid out in the distribution of funds *before* you receive the deed. These are taxes that you will be responsible to pay *after* you legally own the property and have received the deed. These will be paid until it sells or is rented
6. **ESTIMATED REPAIR COSTS:** Just what it sounds like. What you estimate it will cost to rehab the property.
7. **ESTIMATED FUDGE FACTOR: 15% of #6:** This covers things that you might have missed or could not have known about that crop up during rehab.
8. **ESTIMATED 8% REALTOR & CLOSING COSTS:** If there are realtors involved you will have some percentage of this deducted for commissions at the closing table. If not you won't have to deal with that expense, however in either case you'll need to account for the proper percent of transfer tax for your area, as well as any other miscellaneous settlement fees or expenses that crop up.
9. **YOUR PROFIT (excluding capital gains tax):** Finally a rough estimate of what you can expect to make as your gross profit. I say *rough* and *gross* because **A:** things will change as the rehab progresses so you need to adjust your costs as this occurs, and **B:** you need to keep in mind that

capital gains taxes will be due at some future date, so keep a portion of the profits in reserve to cover it.

Let's look at an example and plug some numbers in. The property you are looking to bid on has a ARV of $ 175,000 and you estimate repair and total holding and selling costs (3–8) of $ 35,000 figuring six months hold time for purchase, rehab and sell.

ARV x .70(30%)	- REPAIR & HOLDING	= MAXIMUM BID
$ 175,000 X .70 =$ 122,500	- $ 35,000	= $ 87,500

Your maximum bid price for this example would be $ 87,500. This is accomplished by taking the ARV of $ 175,000 and multiplying it by .70 to get the figure of $ 122,000, or 30 percent off of the $ 175,000. Next, subtract the repair and holding costs of $ 35,000 and come up with the maximum bid price of $ 87,500.

This example assumes a total transfer tax of 1 percent to be divided evenly at 1/2 percent between buyer and seller and is included in number 8.

1.	ESTIMATED SELLING PRICE (ARV)	$ 175,000
2.	ESTIMATED COST TO PURCHASE (max bid)	- $ 87,500
3.	ESTIMATED FINANCE COSTS	- $ 3,000
4.	ESTIMATED INSURANCE COSTS	- $ 1,200
5.	ESTIMATED REAL ESTATE TAXES	- $ 1,500
6.	ESTIMATED REPAIR COSTS	- $ 13,300
7.	ESTIMATED FUDGE FACTOR: 15% of #6	- $ 2,000
8.	ESTIMATED 8% REALTOR & CLOSING COSTS	- $ 14,000
	YOUR PROFIT (excluding capital gains tax)	$ 52,500

If we want to change things and have our discount off to be 35 percent, we would need to multiply by .65 and the results would look like this:

ARV x .65(35%)	- REPAIR & HOLDING	= MAXIMUM BID
$ 175,000 X .65= $ 113,750	- $ 35,000	= $ 78,750

As you can see, it is not that difficult to come up with your maximum bid price using the formula. Be realistic though when determining the percentage for your maximum bid price. Look at the comparable prices for properties in that area. Never go below the 25 percent minimum. If your area supports a 35 or 40 percent discount, by all means go for it. Just keep your wits about you when you are bidding. In rare instances when bidding, I will go over my maximum bid price, but I *never* allow myself to go more than $ 500 over it. If you do go higher, before you know it you are going $ 1,000, $ 2,000, $ 3,000 or more over, and then auction fever sets in and your bidding gets out of control. Don't fall victim to it.

Remember, every dollar you spend over your maximum bid price to acquire the property is ***potential profit out of your pocket.*** Let someone else pay too much for the property.

CHAPTER 14
PRIOR TO THE SALE

THE RULES

By now you should have completed all the last owner searches on properties you looked at. If you haven't done so yet, it is time again to narrow down the list and eliminate properties that are upside down and have more debt than they do equity with no profits to be made. These would also include properties that require excessive amounts of rehab work, driving up the cost beyond whatever profit you could make flipping or recoup renting it. Any properties with liens that the lienholder would not negotiate on, thereby making the property unprofitable—eliminate those also. Even if you are planning to live in the property as your personal residence, you still need to evaluate the cost to acquire the property, including fix-up costs versus what the value of the property will be worth over the span of time you expect to occupy it. Make sure you are getting the deal you expect and do not let this become emotional. Remember, it's still a numbers game.

SAMPLE LISTINGS of SALE RULES

Because the rules or conditions of sale governing sheriff, trustee, and real estate auction sales are as varied as the locations where they are conducted, it is very important for you to be absolutely familiar with the rules concerning the particular sale you will be attending. Below are examples of rules for a sheriff sale and a trustee auction.

SHERIFF SALE

CONDITIONS OF SALE

The deposit mentioned in the handbill where the bid shall be that amount or more, shall be deposited in cash with the Sheriff by each bidder when their bid is registered, and in any case, the deposit shall be sufficient to cover the Sheriff's fees, costs of advertising and the $ 300 debtors exemption, unless the purchase price shall be paid forthwith; otherwise, upon failure or refusal to make such deposit, the bidder shall lose all benefit of his bid, and the property may be immediately put up again and sold unless a deposit of the sum required be made by a second bidder willing to take the property at the highest price paid.

The balance of the purchase money must be paid in cash by the highest bidder to the Sheriff, at his office, within (10) days from the sale, without any demand for same being made by the Sheriff; otherwise, the Sheriff may settle with a second bidder who has made the required deposit, upon receipt of the highest sum bid, less the deposit already made, within (10) days after the first bidder's failure to settle, or in case no second bid be registered, the property may be sold again at the risk of the defaulting bidder, and in case of any deficiency on such resale, he shall make good the same to the person injured thereby, though the hand money required to be paid at the latter sale shall have been increased by any change in the condition of sale.

The deposit made by any bidder, who fails to comply with the above conditions shall be forfeited and applied on the purchase of the property by any second bidder, or if the property is resold, to any liens or equitable claims thereon discharged thereby but not satisfied out of the proceeds thereon, including the right of any real owners to have the highest bid first made realized.

No checks, drafts or promises to pay will be accepted in lieu of cash, except certified Checks to the Sheriff. As each property is called for sale, the attorney on the writ shall stand , identify themselves and open bidding by bidding one dollar to represent costs.

If the attorney on the writ is not present when their property is called for sale, and has authorized another person to represent the plaintiff, the representative shall produce a letter signed by the attorney on the writ authorizing the representative to act on behalf of the plaintiff.

If the attorney on the writ is not present when their property is called and no other representative has been properly authorized to act for the plaintiff, the property shall not be sold and shall immediately be removed from the list; the Sheriff shall then return the writ or execution to the Office of Judicial Support.

TRUSTEE AUCTION

CONDITIONS OF SALE

Bidding registration will be on site and commence one hour prior to the auction. You must be registered to bid. A driver's license or similar identification will be required at registration.

A deposit of 15% is due the day of sale for the winning bidder. Acceptable forms of deposit are CASH or CASHIERS CHECK. Trustee reserves the right to accept any other form of payment. Balance of sale amount due within 45 days of sale date.

Property is being sold As is/Where Is. It is the buyer's responsibility to verify all information pertaining to the property whether or not provided by the trustee or auction company. Auction company or trustee makes no claim to the accuracy of information provided.

ALL SALES ARE FINAL. If you are the winning bidder and for whatever reason you cannot complete the sale within the specified period of time your deposit will be forfeited.

Property is sold pursuant to terms contained in Deed of Trust. Transfer of property will be by Trustee Deed. Trustee has the right to reject any and all bids deemed inadequate before knockdown or to cancel sale.

Announcements made prior to the auction on the day of sale take precedence over any and all previous publications and notices either written or oral.

A buyers premium of ten (10) percent will be added to the winning bid to determine the sale price.

The auctioneer represents the **SELLER** and not the buyer.

Many times these rules can be found posted at the respective county or auctioneer's website. If you cannot find rules for the sale at the website, you'll need to go to the county courthouse if you are looking at a sheriff sale, or phone the person conducting the auction if it is a trustee or real estate auction. While most clerks at the sheriff's office are congenial, they may not be helpful answering all of your questions. Many times you will get the answer "We do not provide legal advice, consult an attorney"—and that is why you have an attorney on your team. Both the attorneys and the sheriff or auctioneer conducting the sale appreciate it when the bidders know the procedures. Nothing is more annoying to those bidding at a sale than the person slowing down the sale by having to have the procedures explained to them.

THE RIGHT OF REDEMPTION

Right of redemption is a procedure that allows the previous owner to legally reclaim their "right" to the property even from the successful bidder within a specified period of time by paying the bid price plus any taxes, interest, fees, etc. Right of Redemption applies to both occupied and unoccupied properties. Not all states have a right of redemption. In states that do not have right of redemption or where that redemption period ends prior to or at the sale, you do not have to worry that the former owner could try to reclaim the property. The following twenty-eight states allow the right of redemption in one form or another:

Alabama, Alaska, Arizona, Arkansas, California, Colorado, Connecticut, Idaho, Illinois, Iowa, Kansas, Kentucky, Maine, Maryland, Michigan, Minnesota, Missouri, New Jersey, New Mexico, North Dakota, Oklahoma, Oregon, South Carolina, South Dakota, Tennessee, Vermont, Wisconsin, Wyoming.

This redemption period can be as short as ten days in New Jersey and as long as 365 days in Missouri. In states with a large agricultural presence the redemption period is usually six months to allow farmers time to harvest and market their crops. Refer to the quick reference list in the Reference List and Resources section in the back of the book for a detailed list of each states right of redemption policy.

And remember, the IRS 120-day right of redemption is valid in all fifty states. If you do buy a property in a state that has a right of redemption period you must be cautious before proceeding with any rehab work or reselling the property. In most situations the original owners do not have the available financial resources to redeem the property. If they did, they probably would not have ended up in foreclosure in the first place then would they? But situations can change during the redemption period and the former owner might somehow raise the monies needed to do this. Also, in some situations a junior lienholder can also redeem the property if the former owner does not. What you want to do is strike an amicable deal with the owner right after you purchase the property at auction to buy out their redemption rights that they probably would never use anyway. Typically you should be able to do this for anywhere from a few hundred to a few thousand dollars. Most cash-starved former owners are happy to sell their rights. At this point they generally realize their likelihood of recovering the property is nil. By buying their rights you eliminate the possibility of any other lienholder attempting to take possession of the property. Once you eliminate the right of redemption, you can now proceed with the rehab of the property.

BEFORE THE SALE: SHERIFF SALES

The day before the sale there are several things that you need to do. First, you want to try to find out the upset price for the property. Knowing the upset price ahead of time can be helpful for several reasons. First, it will tell you what the minimum bid for the property will be set at and if there is an upset price ahead of time, which means chances are pretty good the property will be up for sale as scheduled. Second, if the property is going to be stayed or continued and thus not up for sale, you will know this ahead of time too. In almost all cases the upset price will be *higher* than the dollar figure shown on the foreclosure list because it includes all of the additional expenses that accumulated since the owners stopped paying their mortgage. In a few instances you will find the upset price will be *lower* than the foreclosing amount. This usually happens because the foreclosing creditor is, for whatever reason, accepting less than what is shown as owed for the property.

The advantage of knowing this information ahead of time is twofold. First, if you happen to have done your homework on that particular property, there may be even more money to be made if you win the bidding. Next, if you didn't do your homework on that property and you can get that information quickly, then this might be a very good deal. To get the upset price before the sale you need to call the foreclosing attorney. Their phone number should have been somewhere on the original foreclosure documents when you viewed the 3129 affidavit (or similar document) at your courthouse. If you cannot locate the phone number on those documents, try a web search online. Usually the attorneys are still calculating the upset price the day before the sale so you may not be able to get the exact dollar figure, but you can get close which will work. You'll want to phone them either late afternoon the day before, or early morning the day of the sale. When you call, ask for the paralegal who handles the foreclosures. Give the paralegal the address of the property you are planning to bid on and ask if they know what the upset price is. Do not ask to speak to the actual attorney handling the foreclosure, as they will probably not have this information.

If you cannot get the upset price before the sale, you will need to get it at the sale before it starts. To do this, arrive early, perhaps a half an hour or so before the sale is set to begin. Look for the people dressed in business suits or business attire. They are usually the attorneys handling the foreclosures. Find out which one is the attorney you're looking for and ask them what the upset price is for that property. Things can get a bit confusing the day of the sale, as you will probably not be the only one looking for this information. There are not a lot of attorneys that do foreclosure work, and many of the ones that do handle hundreds, if not thousands, of foreclosures per year, especially when larger lenders are involved. They are referred to as "foreclosure mills," cranking out a multitude of foreclosures with their staffs of paralegals and assistants handling paperwork and the attorneys attending the sales. Chances are that attorney at the sale was only given the property and upset price information that morning and might have a dozen or more properties scheduled for sale that day. As you attend more sales, you will see many of the same attorneys as well as bidders there over and over again. The attorney will either tell you the upset price or advise you that the property will not be going up for sale today and whether it is going to be rescheduled.

If your property is scheduled to be sold, you will need to get your **hand money.** This is the amount of money that you will give to the clerk after it is declared sold at knock down by the sheriff and you are the winning bidder. The amount of hand money, if it is a fixed amount, should be noted somewhere on the list of foreclosures that you obtained. In some cases though, hand money is not a fixed percentage of the foreclosure amount but rather a fixed percentage of your *winning bid,* so you will need to base that amount on the maximum bid price you calculated beforehand. If you are unsure about the hand money, contact the sheriff's office prior for clarification. You will need to have this money with you at the sale. Do not expect the sheriff to allow you time to run out to your bank or wherever to get it. They won't. If you cannot pay it immediately, the property will be put right back up for auction. Hand money and your final payment is almost always required to be paid in either *cash, bank or certified check, or money order.* Some sheriffs will accept a personal check with certain stipulations. And who knows, there may be a sheriff out there that accepts credit cards. If you are unsure about what your local sheriff accepts, check with their office before the sale. I generally carry a mix of bank checks made out to that particular sheriff and cash to make up the difference. You can also have the checks made out to you and endorse them over. Since I am usually bidding on several properties with different upset prices, I get the checks made out in even dollar amounts. I can then mix and match the checks and the cash to cover the upset price. Bring a bit more money with you than you think will be needed just in case. Don't worry if when you go to pay the clerk the price does not exactly match the funds you have and you end up giving them a bit more hand money than is called for. They will credit the extra money against the final balance due on the property.

I try to go out and look at the property(ies) one last time before the sale, just to see if anything has changed since I'd last seen it. Perhaps the property was occupied the first time and now the owners have left. Or maybe the previous night a severe storm bought down a large tree that now has to removed, or worse yet, damaged the structure. If you become the winning bidder, you would now have to add in that extra repair expense. If you find out the day before the sale that the property(ies) you were planning to bid on are for whatever reason (such as a stay or continuation) being taken off the sale list, by all means still plan to attend. I always recommend in the beginning when you are first starting out to just go to the sales, "sit on your hands" so to speak, and watch what happens.

BEFORE THE SALE: TRUSTEE & REAL ESTATE AUCTIONS

Trustee and RE (real estate) auctions are easier to prepare for than sheriff sales because there are fewer variables to be concerned about. But you still need to **read the terms of the sale very carefully.** Pay particular attention to anything concerning whether the property is being sold free and clear of all liens and encumbrances or if it is being sold subject to any existing liens and mortgages. Be sure you recheck all of your data about the property. In the case of sheriff sales you have the upset price which determines the minimum bid. Trustee and RE auctions, depending on the type of sale it is, may or may not have a minimum bid price. If it is an absolute auction, there is no minimum bid price. If there is a minimum bid price, it should be indicated in the published information for the sale.

You will still want to contact the person who is conducting the sale the day before, for several reasons. You'll want to check that the sale is still on at the time and place indicated. Also, you want to verify the deposit figure as well as their required form for it, should you be the successful bidder at knock down. One of the big differences between the sheriff, trustee, and RE auction sales is that in some cases with the latter two you are required to register and pay a "good faith" fee to bid. This fee can range from several hundred to thousands of dollars. Of course if you are not the successful bidder you get your money back, but you still have to "put it up" first. One thing you can do with most trustee and RE auctions that you cannot do with sheriff sales is pre-inspect the property. Again, you need to check with whoever is conducting the auction to see when this small window of opportunity is available. Most times, it is shortly before the auction is held, or possibly the day before. Be sure to be there with notepad and camera in hand, checking everything with the property that you can.

CHAPTER 15

AT THE SALE

Be certain of the location for the sale beforehand so you don't get lost going there and end up missing it altogether. Arrive there early, as sales start on time and happen very quickly. Sheriff sales are almost always held at the county courthouse. Depending on local custom, where the sale is *actually conducted* at the courthouse can be as varied as a meeting room, a hallway in the courthouse, or some sales are literally held on the courthouse steps. This is known as "sale by public outcry." Trustee and RE sales can be held at either the property location or a predetermined meeting location. You want to either sit or stand in the back of where the sale is being held. This is so you won't attract a lot of attention to yourself and you can observe the actions of the other bidders. In most cases bidding is done by raising your hand and calling out your bid. While the clerk has to record every bid, winning or not, the action moves rather quickly once it gets going and typically is over in a minute or two.

Before proceeding any further with the actual goings-on at an auction, I want to go over what you should expect as far as typical *initial* buying opportunities at the various auctions. For sheriff sales, only about ten percent or less of the properties on the sale list that are up for auction that day ultimately make it to bid. Most properties, for whatever reason, either get stayed, which means they are removed from the list and probably will not be put up for sale again, or continued, due to bankruptcy or any number of other reasons and will reappear for sale again at a later date. If the property you planned to bid on gets continued, you will need to follow the list of properties from month to month to see when your property has reappeared for sale. Sometimes it takes multiple continuations lasting several months or more until the owner runs out of options and the property finally makes it back to the sale list and ultimately sells. Each time the continued property you're following comes up for sale again, it's a good idea to recheck the current lien status on it, either by doing it yourself or having a new last owner search done. Most times the lien status stays the same, but just in case the lien situation has changed since the last search was done, you will want to be aware of it. If it has changed, you'll want to make any adjustments necessary to your buying strategy before bidding on it again. Buying property at the sheriff sales is a process, and it takes a bit of legwork on your part to follow it along.

Of the properties that do end up for sale, many are bought back by the foreclosing creditor because either their upset price is too high or just plain nobody wanted them. Most of those will likely end up at an REO realtor at some point. The rest of the properties are bought by investors like you and me, or folks looking for a new house to live in, so don't despair at this low percentage number. Sometimes you get lucky and the property you are planning to bid on *DOES* make it to sale the first time around, and hopefully you end up the winning bidder.

At trustee and real estate auctions, unlike a sheriff sale, there is little chance that a property will be stayed or continued for some reason. Properties that are up for sale, for the most part, do sell. That does not mean they always end up selling to an investor such as you or me. Just like at the sheriff sales, if the bid price was not satisfactory, the property goes back to the foreclosing creditor. Most if not all of the properties that are either no-reserve or no minimum bid end up selling. Properties that have a minimum bid or reserve price stand a better chance of possibly not selling.

I will be using the Philadelphia, Pennsylvania region as the reference point for explaining what takes place at an actual sheriff sale, since this is the area I buy in. Whereas the actual procedures and terms of your sale will in all probability be somewhat different, the fundamental idea is the same. Your attorney can advise you with regard to specific procedures for your area. Check the Reference Lists and Resources section in the back of the book to see sample rules of various counties across the country. For clarity, I have broken down describing the actual sales into two categories: "At the Sale-Sheriff Sales" and "At the Sale-Real Estate & Trustee Auctions." Now let's go to the sale!

SHERIFF SALES

THE PRELIMINARIES: The sale commences with the sheriff bringing down the gavel and calling the sale to order. Typically the sheriff asks if there are any announcements. These announcements usually concern a change in the status of a property and if so are made by the foreclosing attorneys. The sheriff begins by reading the list of current properties for sale that month and the list of properties that were continued from previous months, announcing their status of either for sale, stayed, or continued. If the properties being withdrawn from the list for that day's sale are to be continued at a future date, the sheriff will announce the date of the continuation. You will want to keep track of the status of all of the properties by noting it on your auction list of properties sheet. This will allow you to refer back to it at a later date if needed. Because all of this announcing status happens rather quickly, I find it easier to write abbreviations such as "S" for stayed, "C" for continued and "B" for bankruptcy when noting the status on my auction lists. Once the sheriff has finished running through both lists of current and continued properties, it's time for the bidding on properties to commence.

BIDDING STRATEGIES

There are as many different ways to "call out" your bid as there are bidders. Knowing "when" to bid is just as important as knowing "how" to bid. Here are several popular bid strategies that I have successfully used, or you can develop your own. Whatever strategy you decide upon, always call out your bid in a loud, clear and confident voice. Remember, the idea here is to out psych your competition.

1. **Bid the Upset Price:** You'll be able to tell who the neophytes are immediately after the foreclosing attorney announces the upset price as they begin bidding in one dollar or similar unacceptable increments. In almost *all* situations, bidding must progress in at least one hundred dollar increments. Because the sheriff must record all bids even though they may be well below the upset price, this really slows things down if you get clueless people bidding incorrectly. Raise your hand and bid straight to the upset price *plus* $ 100. By doing this you accomplish two things. First, it sends the message you *know* what you are doing by bidding straight to the upset price, thereby scaring off potential lower bidders. Second, it keeps things moving along quickly.

2. **Bid Big:** If the bidding is moving along slowly with bids only advancing by the minimum amount, announce your bid by "bidding big." By this I mean if everyone involved is bidding up the property in $ 100 increments, up your bid to $ 500 or $ 1,000 increments. Other bidders will think that to beat you they too will have to bid in the same increments or possibly more to best you, thus perhaps exceeding what they can afford to spend, thereby giving up and dropping out.

3. **Last Man in Bidding:** Now you wait until the last person has bid and the sheriff is down to "going once, going twice," and before the sheriff says "going three times," **then** quickly call out your bid of $ 500 or $ 1,000 greater than the last bidder. The ploy here is to make the last bidder think that they outlasted all the previous bidders. But here comes a new bidder (you) with a considerably higher starting bid, threatening to begin the bidding process again to an even greater amount and causing them to drop out.

4. **Look Like a Banker:** With this strategy, the idea is to fool other bidders into "thinking" you're from the bank, thereby lessening the chance they will challenge your bid when you call it out. To do this, you'll want to sit or stand as close as possible to the auctioneer and be properly dressed, so you look like a banker.

THE BIDDING BEGINS: The sheriff begins by announcing the property's term, writ number, location, property owner's name and foreclosing attorney. The foreclosing attorney announces the property's upset price and then calls out their opening bid, which may be $100 or less, and in many cases it is $1.00. Sometimes the attorney will say they bid "costs," which means the attorney is bidding the costs of their fees and expenses to perform the foreclosure for the bank. Since the bank won't bid against itself, and if there are no other bids higher than the upset price, the bank wins the bidding and becomes the owner of the property. While this opening bid is somewhat a formality on the part of the attorney (you cannot bid the same $1.00), the reason for this is that if you challenge the opening costs bid of the attorney by making a bid, you will now force the attorney to bid against you. And unless the bidding reaches the upset price at which point the attorney will stop bidding, the property will not sell to a third party bidder like you and will return to the bank.

For example, if a property has an upset price of $100,000 and the attorney bids $1.00, it is essentially the same as the attorney bidding $100,000. Unless someone bids over $100,000, the property does not change hands and is said to be "sold to the attorney on the writ." The attorney does not actually purchase the property. It means the property is ultimately "sold back to" the entity on the writ of execution in most cases the bank.

Sometimes when a second mortgage is foreclosing, the attorney when announcing the upset price will make known that the property is being sold "subject to a first mortgage of "X" dollars. This means that besides the costs contained in the upset price, the winning bidder will be responsible for satisfying the first mortgage also. However, if you did your due diligence and title search work you would have already known this little tidbit and it wouldn't come as a surprise to you.

WINNING THE BIDDING

Here is what happens when a winning bidder does not have the correct form of payment. Let's say for instance a property with an upset price of $ 100,000 has several bidders and the high bid of $ 105,000 wins. The hand money due is not the usual ten percent but a flat $ 2,000. The winning bidder strides up to the clerk and pulls out a personal check to pay with. The clerk informs them the court does not accept personal checks. Next, this person tries to pay with a credit card. The clerk reiterates that the court only accepts **cash** or **bank checks.** The high bidder then asks for twenty minutes to run to their bank to get the cash, but this too is denied and this person thereby loses the property. The sheriff then announces that the property will be sold to the previous high bidder, as long as that bid was over the upset price. Had that bid not been over the upset price, the sheriff would have started the bidding for the property all over again. If there were no satisfactory bids the second time around, the property would be returned to the foreclosing attorney.

The sheriff moves on to the next property. This just so happens to be the property that you came to bid on. You decide to use the "bid to upset price" strategy. The attorney reveals the upset price and you bid straight up to it, and to scare off any other potential bidders you best the upset price by $ 500. You encounter competition from another bidder and after going back and forth in $ 100 increments you decide to switch to the "bidding big" method. Being careful not to exceed your maximum bid figure, you increase your next bid by $ 750, causing the competitor to fold and you to win.

CONGRATULATIONS, you have bought a property! You get out your hand money and give it to the clerk. They in turn write you out a receipt for the money and that receipt, until you actually return within the correct number of days to pay the balance in full, will be your only proof of claim to the property. So put it in a safe place.

SAMPLE SHERIFF SALE RECIPT FOR HAND MONEY DEPOSIT

SHERIFF OF DELAWARE COUNTY

REAL ESTATE SALES RECIEPT

SALE NO:_____   NAME:_____

$ _____ Dollars is herewith paid to the Sheriff of Delaware County as a result of Sale, unless the purchase money shall be less than that sum, in which case only the purchase money shall be paid.

The balance of the purchase money must be paid to the Sheriff of Delaware County at his office, within 10 days from the time of Sale, without any demand being made therefore, or the property may be sold again at the expense and risk of the person to whom it struck off, who in case of any deficiency at said re-sale shall make good the same.

The purchaser complying with these conditions shall have a deed executed in due form on paying the legal fees.

SHERIFF_____

I do hereby acknowledge the Conditions of Sale and that the property was fairly struck off and bid at for the price or sum of $_____ dollars, which sum is hereby acknowledged.

IN TESTIMONEY WHEREOF, we have hereunto set our hand and seal this _____ day of _____, 20_____.

PURCHASER_____

ADDRESS _____

_____

After settling up with the clerk return to your seat, sit quietly and watch the rest of the auction. The sheriff continues down the list of properties for sale that day and the sale concludes. After you leave the sale you will have one more possible little known opportunity, if you wish, to purchase any of the properties that went back to the foreclosing creditor via the attorney on the writ. On the next business day, contact the foreclosing attorney and explain to them that you are familiar with the property and would like to make an offer to purchase it. Ask them if this is possible and how you would go about presenting your offer to the creditor. The idea here is to buy the property *before* the creditor turns it over to an REO realtor and incurs more expense, usually pushing up the price.

TRUSTEE & REAL ESTATE AUCTIONS

The progression of events at a trustee or real estate auction is fairly similar to what happens at the sheriff sale, with a few variations. Sometimes, instead of the sheriff conducting the sale, it could be the auctioneer from the company hired to handle the sale, or the trustee's authorized agent. Typically sales are held at the property being auctioned, many times on the front or back lawn. If a large collection of properties are to be auctioned at one time, then the sale is generally held in a large meeting or ballroom, hence the name Ballroom Auction. Don't be surprised to see neighbors and curiosity seekers looking on if held outdoors at the property. It is customary before the auction starts to have the property opened up for inspection. You will probably see folks milling about, looking over the building, asking questions while the auctioneer's staff gets set up, collecting good faith deposit money and registering the bidders. Unlike sheriff sales, where typically you only have to raise your hand to bid, most times at trustee and RE auctions you are issued a card with your registration number on it when you register. When bidding, hold the card up and call out your bid. Use the same bidding strategies from the sheriff sale for trustee and RE sales. Once the registration process is completed, the support personnel will assemble all the bidders while the auctioneer calls the sale to order.

In contrast to sheriff sales where the sheriff goes down the list of properties noting their status (stayed, continued, etc.), the auctioneer will describe the property, ask if there are any questions, and will then get things started. The type of auction it is (absolute, minimum bid, etc.) will determine how the auctioneer handles the bidding and the sale. If the auction is a minimum bid auction, the auctioneer will start the bidding at that point. If it is an absolute auction, then the auctioneer typically starts the bidding at some arbitrary point and it develops from there. Once the bidding gets started it moves fast and is typically over in a couple of minutes or less. As long as the high bidder meets the criteria for that particular type of auction then the going once, twice, three times knock down happens and the sale is over. The winning bidder gives the clerk any additional required deposit money and fills out the necessary paperwork. If the auction has a reserve price that is not met, then as in the sheriff sale when the bidding does not get to the upset price, the property is returned to the foreclosing creditor. If there are other properties to be auctioned, the sale continues. If not, it concludes.

CHAPTER 16

YOU WON THE BID AND GOT THE PROPERTY... NOW WHAT?

Well done, you were the successful bidder. While you have paid your hand money for the property, technically you own it and technically you don't own it. The terms of sale, including any laws or rules for your local area and whether or not the property is occupied or unoccupied, will determine what you need to do next. If you bought the property at a trustee or real estate auction and depending on the terms of sale, typically you can have from one to forty days to pay the balance due on the property. If you bought the property at sheriff sale, some sheriffs' departments call for payment that day by a specified hour. Others allow you up to thirty calendar days or more. In the areas where I buy, payment in full ranges between ten and thirty calendar days. If your terms of sale, whether it be sheriff, trustee or real estate sale, require full payment that day, then your first responsibility is to secure the funds and, as they say, go "pay the man or woman." If you have a longer lead time, then mark your calendar ahead so you are sure you don't miss making the final payment. If you don't make the final payment on time, you'll forfeit the property plus your hand or deposit money and you may possibly incur penalties. Once again, be certain of your local sheriff or auctioneer's terms and conditions of sale.

After you make the final payment for the property, this sets into motion a process which will eventually result in you receiving the deed. This will be discussed in the next chapter. As was mentioned in the previous chapter, in Pennsylvania and in most other states there is something known as the "Real Estate Transfer Tax." This is a tax assessed on all real estate when ownership is "transferred," meaning sold. There are some exceptions when the tax is not assessed, such as when it is transferred between family members. The Pennsylvania tax is normally two percent of the selling price, but some local municipalities add their own additional percentages on, raising the amount due even higher. Traditionally the cost of the transfer tax is split evenly between the buyer and the seller. However in Pennsylvania when you buy a property at sheriff sale, in effect you pay the full transfer tax. It was already figured into the upset price prior to the sale. For trustee and RE sales it depends once again on the terms of sale. In Pennsylvania when you return to pay the balance of money due on the property to the sheriff, you will be asked to complete a form called the "Realty Transfer Tax Statement of Value."

Pennsylvania "Realty Transfer Tax Statement of Value" Form

REV-183 EX (11-04)

COMMONWEALTH OF PENNSYLVANIA
DEPARTMENT OF REVENUE
BUREAU OF INDIVIDUAL TAXES
PO BOX 280603
HARRISBURG PA 17128-0603

REALTY TRANSFER TAX STATEMENT OF VALUE

See Reverse for Instructions

RECORDER'S USE ONLY
State Tax Paid
Book Number
Page Number
Date Recorded

Complete each section and file in duplicate with Recorder of Deeds when (1) the full value/consideration is not set forth in the deed, (2) when the deed is without consideration, or by gift, or (3) a tax exemption is claimed. A Statement of Value is not required if the transfer is wholly exempt from tax based on: (1) family relationship or (2) public utility easement. If more space is needed, attach additional sheet(s).

A. CORRESPONDENT – All inquiries may be directed to the following person:

Name   Telephone Number:
( )

Street Address	City		State	Zip Code

B. TRANSFER DATA   Date of Acceptance of Document

Grantor(s)/Lessor(s)	Grantee(s)/Lessee(s)			
Street Address	Street Address			

City	State	Zip Code	City	State	Zip Code

C. PROPERTY LOCATION

Street Address	City, Township, Borough	
County	School District	Tax Parcel Number

D. VALUATION DATA

1. Actual Cash Consideration	2. Other Consideration +	3. Total Consideration =
4. County Assessed Value	5. Common Level Ratio Factor X	6. Fair Market Value =

E. EXEMPTION DATA

1a. Amount of Exemption Claimed	1b. Percentage of Interest Conveyed

2. Check Appropriate Box Below for Exemption Claimed

☐ Will or intestate succession _____
(Name of Decedent)   (Estate File Number)

☐ Transfer to Industrial Development Agency.

☐ Transfer to a trust. (Attach complete copy of trust agreement identifying all beneficiaries.)

☐ Transfer between principal and agent. (Attach complete copy of agency/straw party agreement.)

☐ Transfers to the Commonwealth, the United States and Instrumentalities by gift, dedication, condemnation or in lieu of condemnation. (If condemnation or in lieu of condemnation, attach copy of resolution.)

☐ Transfer from mortgagor to a holder of a mortgage in default. Mortgage Book Number _____, Page Number _____.

☐ Corrective or confirmatory deed. (Attach complete copy of the prior deed being corrected or confirmed.)

☐ Statutory corporate consolidation, merger or division. (Attach copy of articles.)

☐ Other (Please explain exemption claimed, if other than listed above.) _____

_____

Under penalties of law, I declare that I have examined this Statement, including accompanying information, and to the best of my knowledge and belief, it is true, correct and complete.

Signature of Correspondent or Responsible Party	Date

FAILURE TO COMPLETE THIS FORM PROPERLY OR ATTACH APPLICABLE DOCUMENTATION MAY RESULT IN THE RECORDER'S REFUSAL TO RECORD THE DEED.

What this form does is establish a hypothetical fair market value of the property for the purpose of assessing the transfer tax. Payment of the transfer tax comes out of the proceeds from the sale of the property, in other words, out of the price you bid for it. Consult your attorney or title company if you have questions on the real estate transfer tax for your specific area. Finally, the sheriff's office will ask you for a letter stating the name you want the deed issued in and the address where you want it sent.

GETTING INSIDE: If you bought an unoccupied property at either sheriff, trustee, or RE sale that was not held at the property, the next step is go back to the property, check on its condition and secure it. Check if there are any rules for your area concerning the securing of an unoccupied property. Since the sheriff doesn't provide you with a key to unlock the door, you need to contact a locksmith and have them pick the lock so you can get inside. Once inside, you can ascertain the situation and secure the property. Look for a locksmith offering emergency lockout service that can meet you there as soon as possible. Explain that you just bought the property and you need to get inside. You might need to show the locksmith the sheriff's receipt as proof that the property is yours. Have the locksmith re-key all the locks on the exterior doors the same and cut you several spares. For trustee and RE properties you should be given a key by the auctioneer or representative at your settlement. If you are dealing with a property that is occupied you will not be able to get inside at this time. We will come back to dealing with occupied properties a little later on.

UNOCCUPIED PROPERTIES – ALL THAT STUFF: Once the locksmith gets you in, prepare yourself for a shock: all the previous owners' stuff they left behind. Depending on how much they left the first thing you might have to do after getting inside is to clean it out. As you purchase more properties at foreclosure you begin to "inherit" the leftovers of the previous owners. Sometimes you get lucky and they leave you some pretty good stuff that you can actually use. I have acquired quite a nice bundle of things courtesy of the prior owners. *TIP: If you have been left relatively decent items that you don't need, there are several ways to get rid of the stuff. You can have a garage sale at the property. Make sure you let everyone who attends the garage sale know that you are rehabbing the property and that it will be for sale soon. Free advertising never hurts. Or you can donate it to a charitable organization. Many will come out to pick- up and take away the stuff for free.* If they left you a bunch of junk though, throw it out. Just be sure to check before throwing anything away, as some locales require you to hold the prior occupants "stuff" for a certain period of time, usually 30 days, before disposing of it. Once the house is emptied out you can get a clean start and begin to get to work.

INSURING THE PROPERTY & THE TITLE: The next two calls you make will be to your insurance agent and title company. Whether the property is occupied or not, you still need to get insurance coverage bound as soon as possible. You will however need different types of insurance, depending on if the previous owners are still in it or not. If it is unoccupied and you are going to be doing any type of rehabbing work, you need what is known as a **builder's risk** or **vacant property** policy. This type of policy provides coverage for physical damage to the structure while renovations are being done up to the limit of coverage but usually does not cover liability. Liability means that if anyone is injured on the property, a builder's risk policy will not pay out for that, and they could sue you. If your builder's risk policy does not cover liability, you will need add a rider to it if possible, or take out a separate liability policy. Ask your agent.

Builder's risk policies do not come cheap. This is one of the items newbie's don't anticipate, or underestimate, when figuring out their holding costs. Insurance can run several hundred dollars a month or more, depending on the value of the property you are insuring. This is because there's an increased risk of vandalism and similar acts due to a decreased physical presence on the property, especially in the evenings. Do not be tempted to insure the property with the common and less expensive standard homeowner's policy. Insurance companies do follow up on what you tell them and if they find out you were not truthful when you purchased the policy, they will most likely cancel your coverage. If you had made any claims against them, they will most likely be denied and could hold you liable for any damages suffered by *them.* It's not worth the aggravation, so just be truthful. You'll sleep better at night.

If the property is occupied, you'll need to insure it for fire damage and liability. The fire part covers the structure in case the previous owners who are still there "accidentally" burn it down. The liability part covers you in case someone falls and decides to sue everyone even remotely connected to the property. As soon as the occupants vacate the premises, you can change the insurance to a builder's risk policy and commence with the rehab.

Next you need to contact your title company, as you *should* get title insurance. Here is why I say "should." Title insurance is one of those necessary evils, so to speak. Like any insurance, it's a crap shoot. Maybe I will need it, maybe I won't. The chances of having a problem with the title are only about one in ten. That means title insurance companies pay claims out only about ten percent of the time, so ninety percent of the insured have no problems. Unlike life and auto insurance which is paid on an ongoing basis, title insurance is a one-time, upfront payment. And unlike life and auto insurance that insures you against future events yet to happen, title insurance insures you against past events that *have* happened. Title insurance goes into effect when it is written and covers the title from that point on *back* through all of the owners, back to the beginning. What title insurance does is protect you in the event there was an error anywhere along the chain of title. More specifically, it protects you beyond the last owner portion of the search that you did. But keep in mind the lender or lenders previous to the foreclosure all did the same due diligence you are doing now before making the loan, including a full title search. If there was a problem when their search came back, you can bet they had the problem corrected before loaning the money. Lenders will always require title insurance when they loan money for a real estate purchase because it protects *their* interests. And besides, you are paying the cost for it anyway in your loan.

The biggest reason for title insurance in a foreclosure is to protect you from possibly some junior lienholder or such coming back at you saying, in some fashion, that they were not notified of the foreclosure sale and now they want to get paid for their lien or *they* will foreclose on *you*. But here is the catch. Depending on the number of creditors that came up on the title search report you ran, you will have some idea of how many possible chances there are that someone at some point will file a claim against you. For example, if the title report only came back with say two liens on it, one by the mortgage company and the other a municipal taxing authority for unpaid local taxes on it, chances are better than average you will have no future problems and really don't need title insurance. But if you get a title search back that has a laundry list of creditors and liens on it increasing the chances of a problem, then you should get title insurance. The cost of title insurance varies by company and area and can run into the thousands of dollars, depending on the cost of the property. Title insurance pricing is not government regulated, so shop around for the best deal.

NOTIFICATION: If the property is vacant, it's a good idea to introduce yourself to the next-door neighbors and the local police, advising them that you are the new owner of the property. Give them your phone number and tell them that if there are any problems or concerns to please call you at once. If the property is occupied, you should still notify the police that you are the new owner of the property, explain the situation to them and give them your contact information.

CONTACTING THE FORMER OWNERS

So what to do about those former owners who are now living in *your* house? Chances are if you bought a property at sheriff sale you may still have the former owners living there. There is less chance of this with trustee auction properties and no chance if you bought at a RE auction sale. The first thing you want to do is to contact them. They are aware their property went to foreclosure sale and sooner or later they will expect to hear from you. Whether you contact them by phone or go to see them personally (recommended unless they become hostile or threatening, in which case leave immediately), remember to be cordial and relaxed. If you do go to see them personally, wear casual clothes and be at ease. Don't try to intimidate them by showing up dressed in fancy clothes and flashy jewelry or by pulling up in a very expensive car. This will only serve to remind them of their misfortune and will definitely *not* get things off to a good start. Be pleasant. Tell them you are sorry for what happened to them; however, advise them they will need to vacate the premises as soon as possible. The idea here is to get them to agree to leave voluntarily, without having to spend money coaxing them to do so. Ask how long they need to vacate. You really want to have them out as soon as possible, preferably within a week or two.

GETTING THE FORMER OWNERS OUT
STATES WITH NO RIGHT OF REDEMPTION

If the owners do not voluntarily pick up and leave in a few days following the sale, then you will need to take steps to get them out. If your state has no right of redemption, then how do you go about getting these "squatters" to vacate the premises if they don't leave on their own? Well, there are several methods available to you before having to resort to getting the sheriff to eject them. Besides, hiring the sheriff or constable costs money. (You didn't think they did it for free, did you?) The idea here is to convince them to leave voluntarily. The reason you want to do it that way is this: the longer they stay, the more you're spending on holding costs, the longer the project drags out, and there is always the increased chance of them damaging the property. Your job is to get them out as soon as possible with the least amount of aggravation and damage. Bear in mind though, these people have just lost their property to foreclosure and are not happy, smiling campers. Think about that for a minute. Chances are this property was the biggest asset they had and now *you* own it. Being nasty and threatening them will only make them vindictive. What's to stop them from deciding to have a "let's destroy the house" party, smashing toilets, sinks, windows, damaging walls, and generally wreaking havoc to *your* house? Then they load up their car with whatever belongings they can carry and drive off into the night, never to return. You can vow revenge. Sue them maybe, if you can find them. What will you get? Their car and what few possessions they took including the clothes off their back perhaps. In the meantime they did thousands of dollars of damage to your property. Dealing with them tactfully and respectfully will lead to better results. There is a time, later on if necessary, to get nasty, but the beginning is not it.

As stated previously, you want them to leave voluntarily. If that does not work and they say they cannot afford to leave or something similar, then go to Step Two, which is paying them to leave, or what is sometimes referred to as **cash for keys.** Cash for keys can involve anything from paying them a flat sum to go away and get a fresh start to paying their moving expenses or the cost to rent an apartment for several months. This is where you test your negotiation skills. It is whatever you have to do to work this out with them. However, *never* agree to give them money up front or loan them money for any reason. Chances are excellent they will blow it on things not related to *your* end result. If moving them out involves renting a truck, you go and pay to rent the truck but put the rental agreement in their name. If you pay to rent them an apartment, you pay for it but have the lease put in their name. You only want to pay for the truck or apartment, not be responsible for it. Bear in mind when meeting with them, you must keep the situation under *your* control. If you find yourself losing control or the previous owners becoming belligerent with you, excuse yourself and just leave. Unless they contact you first, at this point, do not contact them. Most former owners in foreclosure are not familiar with all the rules and regulations governing foreclosure. At this point they may think that you are lining up the sheriff to throw them out, and leave anyway before that happens. If after a day or two it does not look like that's what's happening, then you will need to contact the sheriff's office to see how soon you can get the paperwork rolling to begin the ejectment process.

STATES WITH RIGHT OF REDEMPTION

To begin, you need to recheck the part of the "terms and conditions of sale" for your area that deals with an owner's "right of redemption" to be sure *when* you can legally have them thrown out. Getting the former owners to leave in a state with redemption rights is similar to getting the former owners to leave in a state without redemption rights, except for one small difference. *They have the legal right to stay.* So as discussed earlier what you want to do is convince them to sell you their right of redemption before the redemption period ends, and hopefully when it is just beginning. Start out by offering them a few hundred dollars and work your way up if you have to. You will find these people are starved for cash, so it shouldn't take long to strike a deal. Once you have acquired their right of redemption, then you can begin the process of getting them out. That process is the same as in states with no redemption rights. If you cannot cut a deal with them for their redemption rights, then you will just have to wait them out until the redemption period expires. You cannot get the sheriff to eject them until the redemption period has ended.

THE LEASE/PURCHASE OR RENTAL QUESTION

Sometimes the previous owners may try to persuade you to allow them to stay in the property and pay you rent or ask you to lease/purchase it to them with the intention of eventually buying it back from you. Many people who have had their properties sold out from under them will try almost anything to get it back. While you may be tempted to do this, *don't.* It's a big mistake. What makes you think if the previous owners could not pay the mortgage they will pay you the rent? They won't. That's how they ended up in foreclosure in the first place. And the longer they stay in the property, the harder it will be to get them out when they do default on you. What's more, lease/purchase agreements have been coming under increasing scrutiny as of late and, depending on how they are crafted, can open up a whole new set of legal problems for you with lending and usury laws. Just steer clear of the whole thing and get them out.

Once you have gotten them out you can begin to determine what needs to be done and get the rehab under way. The only other item you need to concern yourself with is whether there is an IRS lien against the property. Once again, remember the IRS has that 120-day right of redemption to buy back the property from you. So unless you have approached them and gotten them to release their right to redemption, you will need to be careful about doing any rehab work.

I'VE PAID FOR IT, SO WHEN DO I GET THE DEED?

Before beginning any rehab work it's a good idea to be familiar with the progression of how you will receive the deed to the property. In most cases if you bought the property at either a trustee or real estate auction, then receiving your deed as a rule is more straightforward than from a sheriff sale. If you purchased your property at a trustee auction, then you will most likely receive what is called a "trustee deed of sale." If you purchased your property at a real estate auction, in most instances the deed conveyed to you will be what is known as a "special warranty deed." Typically you will receive your deed within sixty days or less, depending on the settlement date of the property. Information on deeds and settlement is usually contained in the terms of sale and recommend you and your attorney review it.

The timeline for receiving your deed from the sheriff's office varies widely and is not as clear-cut as with the other two types of foreclosures. When returning to the sheriff's office to make the final payment for the property is a good time to ask how long the process takes. Remember, there is no standard set of rules governing when you get the deed, so you must check with your local sheriff's office for their timeline. Typically you can complete the rehab, but unless you can assign the deed, you cannot sell the property until you have the deed and it has been recorded, so this timeline is important. Most mortgage companies will not allow the buyer to go to settlement on an assignment of deed, sometimes referred to as a paper closing. On the other hand if you have a cash buyer, then you might be able to agree to an assignment of the deed. Once again, check with your attorney or title company to see what is customary for your local area or is workable in your situation.

Sample of a Sheriff Deed

Sheriff's Deed

Know all Men by these Presents

THAT, I,   Sheriff of the County of DELAWARE

In the Commonwealth of Pennsylvania, for and in consideration of the sum of

_____ (   )

dollars, to me in hand paid, **do** hereby grant and convey to   MARC SHERBY

DESCRIPTION

ALL THAT CERTAIN lot or piece of land with the buildings and improvements thereon erected, Situate in the   County of Delaware and State of Pennsylvania, described according to a Subdivision Plan of   made by   Registered Surveyor, Media, PA dated 7/25/1978 last revised 8/11/1978 as follows:

BEGINNING at a point on the Northwesterly side of   (50 feet wide) said point being 42.00 feet measured North 67 degrees 03 minutes East from the intersection of the Northwesterly side of   with the Northeasterly right of way line of the Southeastern Pennsylvania Transportation Authority; thence leaving the said side of   and extending along the Northeasterly side of Lot #1, North 22 degrees 57 minutes West passing through a party wall 115.00 feet to a point; thence extending North 67 degrees 03 minutes East 30.00 feet to a point; thence extending South 22 degrees 57 minutes East 115.00 feet to a point on the Northwesterly side of   thence extending along same South 67 degrees 03 minutes West 30.00 feet to the first mentioned point and place of beginning.

Being Folio #1

Sample of a Sheriff Deed page 2

The same having been sold by me to the said grantee, on the 18th day of March Anno Domini two

thousand and five after due advertisement, according to the law, under and by virtue of a writ of

Execution issued-Decree entered* on the 9th day of December two thousand and four

out of the Court of Common Pleas Delaware County as of Term, two thousand and four Number 7927

at the suit of

In Witness whereof, I have hereunto affixed by signature,

this 3rd day of   JUNE   Anno Domini two thousand and   FIVE.

SEALED AND DELIVERED
IN THE PRESENCE OF

Sheriff
OF DELAWARE COUNTY

*Eliminate which not applicable

The deed you receive from the sheriff is called, coincidentally, a "sheriff's deed." It is known as a "bargain and sale" deed and this type of deed implies that the grantor, in this case the sheriff, has the right to convey the title to the property but does not guarantee it against any encumbrances, such as liens. In other words, the deed is simply used to transfer the title of the property and nothing more. Remember, the sheriff does not actually *own* any of the properties. He is merely carrying out the court's orders to *auction* the properties. That means the sheriff does not warranty anything about the property other than basically the transfer of it and that you are the new owner. That's it. And that sheriff's deed is all you need when you go to sell the property. The explanation given below of progression from payment to receiving the sheriff's deed is from my local area. Your region will probably vary from this. Check with your sheriff's office for details in your location.

The area I buy in, suburban Philadelphia, Pennsylvania, requires on average 60 to 120 days plus or minus, to present you with the sheriff's deed. Once you've paid for the property, the process gets rolling. It consists of three segments. In the first segment the sheriff's office orders a title search and establishes the list of creditors and verifies the amounts of their liens. This segment also includes a 10-day waiting period from the date of the sale to allow any party who possibly may not have been served notice to contest the sale. The second segment has the sheriff's office preparing the schedule of distribution, which is a list of how the funds received from the sale are to be distributed. In other words, who gets paid what. For the last segment, the sheriff's office orders the payment checks cut and sends them out to the lienholders. Once the lienholders receive payment, they in turn notify the sheriff in writing stating that the lien was satisfied in full. After the sheriff receives the documentation that all the liens were satisfied then the deed is executed and delivered to you.

So you may ask, what can go wrong here? Well the lienholders not getting their paperwork back to the sheriff in a timely manner is one. If after a lienholder receives payment from the sheriff they do not immediately send out a satisfaction of payment on the lien, the sheriff cannot issue your deed. No deed, nothing happening. You should keep in touch with the clerks in the sheriff's office who are handling the paperwork. Keep in mind that not only are they doing your property but all of the properties sold at the foreclosure, and things can fall through the cracks. If some paperwork they're waiting for is getting hung up, ask if there is anything you can do—any phone calls you can make for them to help move things along. Remember, it's your deed you are waiting for, so sometimes you will need to make the extra effort.

CHAPTER 17
BEFORE THE REHAB STARTS

MAKING SURE YOU HAVE UTILITIES

Whether you purchased a sheriff, trustee, or RE auction property, assuming the previous owners have vacated the premises or the property was vacant to begin with, let's get down to what you need to know to rehab it. Do not be surprised if one or more of the utilities are shut off for non-payment when you finally gain possession. In my area if the electricity has been shut off to a property for more than six months, you are required to have a certified underwriter come out to the property and inspect the electrical panel to be certain it is in proper working order before the electric company will turn the power back on again. The underwriter can cost you anywhere from $ 50 to $ 200. Check with your local utility to see if they have the same requirements. If they do, be sure to figure this expense into your costs.

If the property was bought at a sheriff or trustee sale *and* the utility had a lien against the previous owners, you might run into resistance when you ask them to transfer service into your name. Remember, *only* municipal utilities are superior liens and are thereby always paid as part of the upset price. *When* they will receive the payment is another issue. When you contact the utility you will need to explain to them that the property you just acquired was bought at a sheriff sale. Tell them that they will get paid as proceeds from the sale are distributed. They should go along with you on this and turn whatever utility is theirs back on. If there were *not* enough monies collected and/or the utility did not have a judgment lien since non-municipal utility companies are junior lienholders, then you should not be responsible for paying the past due amount. That responsibility falls back on the utilities collection department to try to track down the former owner for payment. Don't let them try to strong arm you into paying it. It's not your responsibility. You'll need to tell them to change the billing address and to put the new account in your name. Sometimes doing all of this with a utility company can be quite a challenge before it all gets straightened out, so hang in there!

CHOOSING YOUR PROJECT

Before beginning the rehab it is assumed that you have the ultimate goal for the property in mind. By this I mean whether you plan to flip it, rent it, or have it become your personal residence. Since all three end results involve different degrees of rehab, I will address them separately. Let's start with the personal residence.

REHABBING FOR A PERSONAL RESIDENCE: This can be the easiest, in the sense that you can do whatever you wish without regard to how good it will look to prospective buyers or renters. You only have to please yourself, so I will not spend much time on this one. Depending on how long you intend to live in the property should have some bearing on the renovations that you do. If you only expect to live there for maybe five to seven years, plan the renovations with that in mind so that what you do will still be tasteful and in style when you sell five years from now. If you plan to live out the rest of your days there, what you do now won't matter much, since the renovations most likely will be out of style by the time your next-of-kin inherit the property upon your demise. After you get into the property, the first thing I would recommend you do is hire a home inspector to come out and do an inspection. This way you'll get an idea of what repairs need to be done. These types of projects can be a lot of fun, as you are only limited by your imagination. Let it run wild.

REHABBING FOR A FLIP: Here are the two credos you should always rehab by:

#1. Every dollar you save is a dollar you can put in your pocket.

As you begin to size up the rehab project, you need to think like a penny-pincher, if you don't already. I like to think of money in terms of *hard dollars* and *soft dollars.* Hard dollars are the actual currency you save by locating a bargain on materials or services. I've saved many hundreds of dollars by going to surplus materials auctions and buying items needed, such as sinks, faucets, lighting, and so on. When you go to the home centers, look for stuff that they have on sale or close out and work your design strategies around them if you can. Many times I've saved over fifty percent or more on closeouts just by altering my design requirements a little bit. Scratch and dent sales or slightly used appliances are another big source of savings. All of that money saved goes directly to increasing your bottom line profit.

Soft dollars is money saved by NOT spending it on replacing existing things that can be fixed or cleaned up to look acceptable, such as the stove or the kitchen cabinets. You actually did not put any money in your pocket, but you didn't lay it out either for new items. Oh, and one more very important money saving tip when purchasing at most big box home improvement centers. If you use their *in-house consumer credit card* to charge your purchase and it is over a predetermined dollar figure (usually $ 299) worth of material, depending on which promotion is going on at that time, they will allow you anywhere from six to twelve months to pay for your purchase *interest free.* How's that for letting *them* finance *your* project!

#2. Repair only what needs to be repaired, modernize only where you must, and avoid remodeling.

REPAIRS: Here is why you repair only what needs to be repaired. Anything that needs repair you can be sure will be picked up by the buyer's home inspector. And while a home inspection is not required, almost all buyers have one done. If this is your first rehab project and you are unfamiliar with all things building and mechanical, I recommend you hire a home inspector to come out and evaluate the property you bought. In fact, I would recommend you use a home inspector on every project you do. The home inspector will do a thorough evaluation of the structure, crawling into areas you wouldn't. Upon completion, the inspector will give you a detailed written report listing the condition of all the items checked. You can then make better decisions on what to repair and what to replace. The average cost for an inspection is about $ 400 to $ 500, but it is money very well spent.

MODERNIZING: There are basically two kinds of buyers: those looking for a deal on a fixer-upper that they will "fixer upper" themselves, and then there is everyone else. If you want to sell to the fixer uppers, that's fine. You would list the property for sale as "selling as is with seller making no repairs whatsoever, buyer responsible for U&O." Your profits will be smaller, as these people want a *deal* in exchange for them doing the rehab and repair work. You'll need to sell it as quickly as possible to minimize your holding costs. This is what basically is known as wholesaling, and there are lots of books out there showing you how to do this. I will be dealing here with the "everyone else," more commonly known as the "retail buyer." Most retail buyers just want to move in, with little or nothing to do in repairs or renovating. They do not have the time or desire to be bothered with that in the beginning. They just want to bring in their stuff, settle in and get on with their life. That is why there are certain things you should modernize if you want to minimize your time selling the property and maximize your opportunity and profits.

Windows are probably at the top of the list of the things buyers don't want to be bothered having to do. If your property has ratty-looking old single pane windows with cracked glass, you will probably need to replace them. Old, dirty kitchens with ugly, stained, cracked countertops and appliances that just barely work, in colors like avocado or harvest gold will need to go. Bathrooms will probably need similar attention. Attached interior light fixtures in rooms such as the kitchen, bathrooms, and dining room, as well as the exterior fixtures will need to be addressed if the existing ones are just plain ugly.

A great way to see what you need to do to modernize properly is to go look at some sample builder's homes in your area that are in the price range of your property after rehab. Take note of the colors they employ, fixture brands, etc. Builders use professionals to do the designing for them in their sample homes. They know what works, so why not learn from them. You want to make your property as good as or slightly better than the others for sale in the neighborhood. It is important to keep in mind that while the goal of modernizing is to do it as cost effectively and creatively as possible, you don't want to lose sight of the fact that you want to present the property as being worth more as a completed package than as the sum of the individual renovations. I will give you tips on ways to do this.

REMODELING: You want to stay away from remodeling as much as possible. The biggest reasons for not wanting to take on any major remodeling project are time and cost. Major remodeling typically takes more time by requiring permits and contractors or tradespeople, which all adds up to lots of extra money being spent. Do you see where I am going with this?

Which are the projects to avoid?

- Structural additions to the house
- Decks, porches, or patios
- Total redos of a kitchen or bath (modernize them for less)
- Finishing a basement or garage
- Replacing all the siding on the house (unless it is literally falling off)
- Adding a swimming pool

Major remodeling projects simply don't provide you with the return on investment you need. Some are just outright money losers. Leave the major remodeling projects to the buyer who purchases your house to do later on. Your job is to bring the property up to snuff and make it marketable.

CURB APPEAL: Probably the most critical and often overlooked item is curb appeal. Curb appeal is real estate lingo for how attractive or "appealing" your property looks when viewed from the street. It is said that most buyers decide in the *first ten seconds* of driving up to the property if they like it or not. But how can that be when they haven't even seen the inside yet? The answer is curb appeal. It is absolutely essential that you give your property curb appeal so it looks its best. Fortunately this is not all that expensive or difficult to do. Below is a list of some things you can do to make sure your property has curb appeal.

1. Add Flowerbeds. It's one of the easiest things to do and one of the best ways to call attention to your property, provided you are not selling it in the dead cold of winter. Create flower beds with edging or wooden landscape ties on sides that are visible from the street. Add mulch and use brightly colored flowers that will stay in bloom for a while. Marigolds,

available in a variety of colors, are perfect for this. Putting flowers around the base of trees and shrubs also works well.

2. Trim existing trees and bushes. Cut dead limbs off trees and trim back any bushes in front of the property that might be blocking windows or the view. Overgrown vegetation does nothing for a property's appearance.

3. Keep the grass cut, sidewalks and curbing edged, and pull out any stray weeds. This one should be a no-brainer.

4. If you have a front door that is painted, give it a fresh coat and the surrounding trim too. Pick a nice traditional color and add a brass kick plate to the outside bottom. A new polished brass door knocker and matching door knob/lock add a nice touch. If there are street numbers near the front door, replace them with decorative new ones.

5. If you have an asphalt driveway fill any cracks or potholes with patch and coat the entire driveway with sealer. If you have a concrete driveway and/or concrete walkways, sidewalks, or curb, fill in any cracks with concrete filler patch.

6. Be sure to remove all snow and ice from the driveway and walkways if you are selling the property in the winter.

7. Keep the yard free of trash and debris.

8. Add a nice new eye-catching mailbox with large street numbers on it.

9. Use clear light bulbs in your outside light fixtures. They look better than frosted ones, especially at night.

10. Make sure the glass in all the windows is clean.

11. Caulk any gaps around windows, siding or trim.

12. Put a nice welcome mat by the front door. If there is a front porch or landing step, add a few potted flowering plants there.

CREATING A BUDGET

What is a budget? Most people define "budget" as "A financial plan that you develop and vow to stick with but never seem able to." Okay, maybe that's not *your* meaning, and that's good if it isn't because you will need to create a budget to monitor your costs and work hard to stay within it. If you want to spend the money, there are lots of prepackaged computer programs you can buy to do this, but you don't have to. Here is how I easily do it. First, I size up what needs to be done by using the rehab estimation forms in the back of the book. I begin by going room to room through the entire structure, inside and out, making notes and writing down the areas that will need rehabbing and the approximate estimated costs. Next, I create my spreadsheet using the Windows spreadsheet program that is already on my computer. I set up the following columns as shown so that it looks like this.

Sample Spreadsheet

DATE	VENDOR	DESCRIPTION	AMOUNT	DATE PD.	PMT. TYPE

Now I begin entering the information. For example, let's just say the windows need to be replaced and the powder room needs modernizing. I had my window contractor stop by and he gave me a price to replace all twelve windows at a cost of $ 200 per window, for a total of $ 2,400. I put the total cost of that portion of the rehab into the spreadsheet. Next, I am also going to modernize the powder room. This is something I can do myself, as no permits are required for the work. On the rehab estimation charts I figured that will cost me about $ 500 for materials. So far, my total amount budgeted for this property is $ 2,900. As I do the work in the powder room, I enter every single purchase that I make, indicating the date, vendor (where I got whatever I purchased), description of items, cost, when and how I paid for it (cash, credit card, check).

DATE	VENDOR	DESCRIPTION	AMOUNT	DATE PD.	PMT. TYPE
1/18/05	Sheriff	Hand Money	4,000	1/18/05	Cash
1/18/05	Mr. Lock	pick locks/keys	175.00	1/18/05	ck. #105
1/19/05	Mr. Window	new windows	2,400	1/19/05	ch. # 106
1/19/05	Home Ctr.	toilet & seat	100.00	1/19/05	visa
1/21/05	home center	plumbing parts	45.96	1/21/05	visa
1/21/05	electric co.	turn on power	20.00	1/21/05	ck #107
1/22/05	ABC Tile	tile	225.00	1/22/05	mastercard
1/23/05	Penn Ins.	Property insurance	125.00	1/3/005	ck. # 108
1/24/05	BAM	paint	45.33	1/24/05	visa
1/25/05	easy $ lenders	interest payment	250.00	1/25/05	ck. # 109
1/28/05	Sheriff	final payment	40,000.00	1/28/05	bank check
1/28/05			47,386.29		

I prefer to enter every expense daily, including my holding costs (utilities, interest payments, insurance, etc.), on the same spreadsheet, as shown in the example below. This way, I keep track of *all* the expenditures on a daily basis as the rehab progresses to monitor if I am on track and on budget. If you prefer, you can set up separate spreadsheets to track rehab expenses and holding costs. At the end of every day if you highlight the cell at the bottom of the amount column and then double click the figure that looks like a sideways "M" (the auto-sum key) in the toolbar at the top, you will get a total of all the figures in the amount column. Total it out every day and you can keep a running balance of your expenses in the project. Just be certain to put *every single penny of expense on the spreadsheets*.

You can also do some creative "what if" scenarios by plugging in different items and their costs to see how far above or below what you projected the total rehab would run if you did things differently. A spreadsheet also makes life easier for your accountant when it comes time to figure out your expenditures and deductions for the project when calculating your capital gains tax.

CHAPTER 18
FINDING THE RIGHT CONTRACTORS

MAKING IT LOOK EASY

How many of you have ever watched those home improvement shows? Most, I'll bet. Isn't it amazing how those folks can remodel a kitchen or bathroom with no mistakes in only a thirty-minute episode? Well, having some really talented people both in front of and behind the camera doing the constructing and some creative film editing is good for a start. And having access to almost every power tool known to mankind is a big help. But even those trained professionals do make mistakes. Watch one of those episodes that features some of the "out-takes" you never see and you'll have a good laugh. What I am trying to say here is this: that just because you watch these shows does not make you a carpenter, a plumber, an electrician, or a whatever. Having the right tools is only the beginning. Having the talent, ability, knowledge and experience to do the job safely and correctly is another. Just because you're a weekend warrior handyman who can change the air filter in your gas-fired hot air furnace doesn't mean you are qualified to install one. You have to know where your abilities begin and end. If you do not have the talent or ability, then you need to hire it. Period.

FINDING THE RIGHT CONTRACTORS & TRADESMEN

Most locales require that for certain jobs only qualified, licensed and registered tradespeople can apply for the building permits and do the work. Permits are what local municipalities issue when specific construction work is to be done, such as plumbing, electrical and roofing. This insures that both the work and the people hired to do it are licensed, knowledgeable, and will adhere to and understand all applicable building codes. Some people try to save money by not pulling permits and doing the work themselves, hoping to not get caught. ***Don't do it***. Even though it might seem tempting, the penalties are simply not worth it. If you do get caught, the local code official will shut your job down immediately until the proper permits are pulled, further delaying the work. Then if you go to sell the property and it comes time for the local building code official to inspect it for a Certificate of Occupancy (CO), and it is discovered you did work without the proper permits, he could make you rip out all that you had done.

And then there are the possible insurance liability issues too. So save yourself a lot of aggravation and just pony up the money, hire the right people and pull the permits. Even though I have twenty-plus years of background in the plumbing and heating industry and I am fairly handy, I still hire a licensed plumber to do my work when needed. Why? Because he is knowledgeable and up to date on all the codes. He possesses all of the tools I don't, can pull permits and carries the proper insurance to protect both of us. If you want to save money, and say for instance you're gutting a really, really bad bathroom down to the studs to remodel it (yes, I know I told you not to do remodels, but this bathroom was really ugly with a capital U), do the rip-out and demolition work yourself. You don't need to pay a professional to do demo work, and most of the time they are glad to have you do the dirty part.

THE SCREENING PROCESS

It can be one of the hardest things to do—finding good, honest, licensed general contractors, "GCs" as they are known, or tradespeople such as plumbers and electricians. As with any industry, just as there are honest and competent GCs/tradespeople out there, there are just as many dishonest, unethical and incompetent ones simply waiting to take your money and run. The trick is to be able to tell the difference. There is an old saying: "If you find one good contractor, they will know all the others." It's true. Good, reputable tradespeople like to work with other good, reputable tradespeople and are respected within their industry. So how do you find them, the good ones? Good GCs and tradespeople are usually very busy, with work scheduled weeks or even months in advance. A good starting point is to ask a friend or neighbor who has had the same type of work you are looking for already done. Find out if they were happy with it and who did it.

Local real estate investment groups, again, are another good place to look. Investors there know who the good contractors and tradespeople are and can recommend them to you. Many times the local realtors know who the good contractors are. If you are having no luck finding someone via the previous methods, you can always fall back on either the phone book or the local newspaper, but be careful. Many of what I call "hackers" (people that only know enough to screw up the job) can lurk there. Once you have found someone, you need to find out the following information from them. When I use the word "contractor" I'm also referring to individual "tradespeople."

GETTING THEIR CARDS & INFORMATION

No, I don't mean just their business card, although you should get it and it should have their street address and phone number on it. Contractors whose business cards have just a post office box for an address don't want you to know where to find them when the job goes south. Ask to see their trade registration card that says they are a licensed plumber, electrician, or whatever their trade is. All "real" contractors will have a card or certificate that says they are licensed to work in that state or locale and they should have no problem showing it to you. If they can't produce one, that means they have not completed the proper training and passed local and/or state licensing examinations. If they don't have a license, then they can't pull permits. If they can't pull permits, don't hire them, no matter how cheaply they say can do the job. Here is other information you need to find out before hiring anyone:

- You want to see their certificates for workers' compensation and general liability insurance, and check that the dates on the policies are current. Again, any reputable contractor will be happy to show you these. Contact the insurer to verify that the policies are still in place. If their certificates are out of date, or they don't have insurance at all, get rid of them. They are a lawsuit waiting to happen.

- Ask how long they have been in business. The longer the better, but you want someone who has been in business at **least three years.** Besides knowing how to do the job, this indicates they also know how to run a business and should be around in the future to back up their work.

- Find out how they want to be paid. Most contractors will ask for a deposit up front. Ten to twenty percent when you sign the contract is typical with other payments made as the project progresses. The final payment, usually ten percent, is paid after completion and your approval. This ten percent final payment is your trump card. *Never* make the final payment before completely inspecting the job to your satisfaction. Beware of any contractors who require a very large up-front deposit (fifty percent or more) or worse, full payment before they will even begin work. Chances are excellent they are not reputable and will only run off with your money, never to be seen again. You don't want them.

- As silly as it sounds, look at the vehicle the contractor pulls up in. Are they and their truck clean and presentable? If the truck is a rusting, falling apart beat-up hulk and the clothes the person is wearing look like the only ones they own, that tells me this person is sloppy and doesn't care about themselves or the image their company projects. Do think their work is any different? Move on.

GETTING REFERENCES

Depending on how you found the contractor will determine the amount of references you should get. If the reference came from a friend who had similar work done before by this person and the results were always good, you probably need to look no further. But if this was someone you cold-called from the newspaper or phone book, then by all means ask for at least three references for work done in your area and check them out. Reputable contractors are proud of their work and should be happy to furnish them. Some even carry a photo album of previous jobs with them to show examples of their work. Find out if the work was completed on time and on budget, and if they would hire them again. You can check with your local Better Business Bureau to see if there are any complaints against them. Check as well with your local building/code enforcement department to see if there are any problems there also. Websites that allow people to share experiences they've had with contractors are another more recent source of information. One such site that comes to mind is "Angie's List."

FINDING THE RIGHT ONE

There are different contractors for the different types of work required. General contractors deal with most aspects of general remodeling and construction and can handle the entire project for you from soup to nuts. The GC reports to you and executes the project to your wishes. They will obtain all price quotes, hire and oversee all tradespeople, pull all permits, be responsible for scheduling and making sure all persons finish in a timely manner. When interviewing contractors for your job, be specific about what you expect from them. Explain your requirements as clearly and concisely as possible. Tell them all quotations *must* be in writing—nothing verbal—and *must* contain a detailed list of the materials, product specifications, warranties, timeline to complete, payment schedule, removal of trash, etc. What you don't want to get is a quotation that just says "Remodel powder room: $ 1,000.00" and nothing else. That leaves a lot of room for the contractor to do whatever and little room for you to take them to court if you need to. Match the correct contractor for the job. If you are going to do a rehab on a house that you plan to sell for $ 750,000 when finished, you will need a different quality of work than if you are doing a rehab that will sell for $ 100,000.

CHAPTER 19
DOING IT YOURSELF

If you are handy and *do* possess some of the skills needed and you have the time to commit for the rehab job, you can save yourself considerable money (hint: more profit) by acting as your own GC and hiring the tradespeople as needed to do what you cannot. This is what I do. Before beginning the sections on repairs and modernizing, look for the "tips," which are inexpensive tricks you can use to save money within these sections. ***Tips will be in bold italics.***

REPAIRS

Let's focus on the repairs first. If you hired a home inspector, you will have been given a list of all the defects in the property. You will need to address them on an item by item basis. If there are any leaks in the roof, they need to be addressed first. Depending on how long it has been leaking, it can wreak havoc on the interior of the building. An inspection by a qualified roofer will tell you the exact condition of the roof and what will need to be done. Sometimes a roof can be successfully patched, or if not, you may have to replace the roof. If the building has any structural or foundation issues, you will need to address those right away. They should be evaluated by a competent contractor or a structural engineer and corrective action taken.

Next, you'll need to check on the operation of the plumbing, heating and air conditioning, the so-called mechanical systems. Do they work properly? Chances are they will need at least a tune-up by a qualified technician. Some municipalities require proof that the heating and/or air conditioning system has been properly serviced within a certain time period before they will issue a U & O when you sell the property. Check with your local municipality's code enforcement division. What you want to do is make only the repairs necessary to get the systems up and running properly. Any leaks in the plumbing system will need to be fixed. Something to look for, particularly in older homes with cast-iron waste pipes that have been vacant for a long period of time, is water that sat in the pipes stagnating. Depending on the thickness of the pipe at that point, it can actually eat through it, producing a leak. If you find a leak, depending on the size and location of it, it can be quite expensive to fix, usually requiring the services of a plumber. If you have a property with an external electric feed from a utility pole, check the condition of the wire that is attached to the house that goes into the electrical breaker box. If the wire and/or the electrical box it feeds are in poor condition and will not pass inspection, one or both will need to be replaced. This *must* be done by a qualified, licensed and insured electrical contractor. This is not something to do yourself. Actually, any electrical work should be done by a licensed and insured electrical contractor. If there was ever a fire at the property during the rehab or after you sell it, and any investigation ultimately traces the fire to faulty electrical work done by you, you're setting yourself up for a possible lawsuit and more.

Obviously, any holes in the drywall/plaster will need to be fixed. If the previous owners were smokers and the place reeks of it, you'll need to repaint the interior, so make all the repairs to the walls and the ceilings first. Fill in any imperfections, such as holes from picture frame nails, with spackle or similar material. *TIP: Before you paint, if you have gaps between any trim and walls, get a tube of acrylic caulk (don't get the silicone type as paint will not adhere well to it). Fill in the gaps and smooth the caulk out with a wet finger. Let the caulk dry for 24 hours so that when you paint, it will be nice and smooth, with no ugly gaps visible, greatly improving the finished appearance.*

Repair any and all malfunctioning fixtures (faucets, toilets, etc.) in the bathrooms and kitchen. If the faucets are really gross-looking or so old you can't get the repair parts, replace them with new ones. Depending on whether the exterior is sided with vinyl, aluminum, stone, brick, or a similar maintenance-free product, if it is in relatively decent condition and just dirty, something as simple as power washing can make it look like new. You can rent a power washer for about $ 100 a day. If the exterior is wood or the old asbestos siding, you can power wash this too; just use caution when doing it so as not to damage the paint or underlying material. Contrary to popular belief, the asbestos siding attached to a structures exterior is not dangerous as it sits. It only becomes dangerous when you cut into the siding tile with a saw or similar device and the asbestos fibers become airborne and can be inhaled.

If the exterior of the house is painted, you want to try to just repaint the areas that are peeling or need touching up. What you don't want to end up doing, if possible, is repainting the whole exterior. Another thing to look for is any damage from wood destroying insects, such as termites and carpenter ants. Damage from these can be extensive and expensive to repair and treat. If you are unsure that you have or had them, or you did not have a home inspector look at the structure, then hire a licensed pest exterminator to check it out.

MODERNIZING

Think of modernizing as curb appeal for the inside. What you are trying to achieve here is to make the inside of the property as appealing as possible while still staying within budget. Now that you are in the house and you have the opportunity to better assess the situation, you can get an idea of what costs will be involved to do the rehab. More often than not this ends up going higher than what you budgeted for and that is why there is a "fudge factor" in your maximum bid calculations.

KITCHENS: The first areas to start the ball rolling are the kitchen and bathroom(s). Let's begin with the kitchen. Start by cleaning everything. Scrub the floor, walls, ceiling, cabinets, appliances—everything. Kitchens are notorious for oily films, so use a cleaner with a grease cutter. After cleaning, how do the cabinets and countertops look? Are the cabinets made of wood, laminate, porcelain coated steel, or some other type of material? Generally if the cabinets, doors and hinges are in decent shape with no major chips, dents, or gouges, they can probably just be cleaned up and will look fine. If your cabinets are wood, a nice furniture polish will make them really shine. Touch up worn spots on wooden cabinets with similar color touch-up sticks available at furniture and hardware stores. Painted cabinets can be touched up similarly with color touch-up or repainted entirely. *TIP: An easy and inexpensive way to dress up older cabinets is to replace the knobs, drawer pulls and hinges with new ones. There is a huge selection of styles available, and you would be amazed at the difference changing those pieces makes. Bring a sample of each with you to be sure of the size and dimensions.*

Kitchen countertops, sinks and faucets can take a beating. How do yours look? If they really look tired, consider replacing them. The kitchen is one of the first areas buyers look at. Replacing the countertops is an easy way to dress it up without replacing the entire kitchen. Unless you are doing a very high-end rehab or you know similar houses in the neighborhood have it, stay away from solid surface countertop materials such as marble, tile, stone such as granite or similar materials. All are very expensive and can take time to fabricate. Stick with less expensive laminated tops. *TIP: Made to order laminated countertops are available in "faux" granite finishes, and by adding a bevel to the front edge of it you will achieve an expensive granite look for a cheap price.*

When replacing the sink use a stainless steel one. They are much lighter in weight and easier to install than their porcelain coated cast-iron or similar counterparts; plus if you drop a glass in them, it won't break. Just be careful not to purchase one with a mirrored finish—it will show every fingerprint and look dirty. Get the brushed satin finish instead. There are a myriad of decorative kitchen faucets and finishes available for under $ 200. Pick one that matches the style of the kitchen. Also, if there wasn't a garbage disposer there previously, consider adding one. It is a convenience most people take for granted nowadays. Look at the overhead light fixture and any other light fixtures in the kitchen. If they look decent, consider just cleaning them up. If not, a new light fixture might be in order. They are fairly inexpensive and really help to dress up the room.

Next, let's turn out attention to the appliances. First of all, do they all work properly? If they do not work at all or are just plain outdated, you will have to replace them. If they only partially work, as in maybe only two burners on a four burner stove, you will have to determine if it is cost effective to repair the stove or replace it. Depending on the repair needed, many times it is more cost effective to replace it rather than fix it. Now you don't have to go and buy the most up-to-date stainless steel units out there (or maybe you do if you are doing a high-end rehab). Make them "comparable" with what you would expect to find in a property in the price range you intend to resell for. *TIP: If you do have to replace appliances, go to a store that sells scratch and dent units. They can be considerably cheaper than comparable "perfect" units. Damage is usually minimal and many times is hidden from view after installation anyway. In almost all cases the appliances are still covered by the full factory warranty.*

If you are lucky enough that all your appliances work properly, then just get out the gloves and give them a thorough cleaning and make them shine. One note: if there is a refrigerator and it's on its last leg or does not work at all, you do not necessarily have to replace it. Many times buyers will bring the fridge from their previous home with them and will not need yours, especially if theirs is a newer one full of fancy features.

BATHROOMS: Now let's turn our attention to the bathrooms. Right after the kitchen, bathrooms are the next most scrutinized room on a buyer's list. As with the kitchen, clean everything completely first. What type of sink is in the bathrooms? Is it the old hung-on-the-wall style lavatory with tubular metal legs and towel bars attached? Do you have a pedestal sink, or possibly a vanity cabinet with countertop? Are the sinks and/or countertops in decent condition or are they chipped, rusting, or have cigarette burns on them? If you have a vanity cabinet with countertop, and just the countertop is bad, do what you did in the kitchen—keep the base and replace the countertop. If your lavatory top is of the one piece variety with a molded sink, you are in luck. One-piece vanity tops come in many sizes and a variety of materials. One of most popular of these is made of a material called "cultured marble." Cultured marble vanity tops are made in a huge array of colors and styles, and are very reasonably priced. Once again, unless you are doing a very high-end rehab, stay away from the much pricier solid surface materials. Chances are you won't get the extra cost spent for these back when you sell. Pick out and install a nice new faucet and you are in business. *TIP: When purchasing a new faucet and lavatory, stick with faucets on 4" centers, known as "centersets." Although more elegant in appearance 8" center faucets, known as "widespreads," cost considerably more and are more complicated to install.*

If you have a powder room with a mirror on the wall that's in good condition, fine. If not, replace it with a new one. If your master bathroom does not have a mirror or a medicine cabinet, figure on installing one. Get one that is "surface mounted." That means it can be attached directly to the surface of the wall without having to cut out a new hole for the cabinet box or it can be mounted directly over an existing hole if the medicine cabinet you're replacing had a recessed box. Basic bevel-edged mirrored medicine cabinets are not expensive, and matching light fixtures can be obtained also. If you don't have one already, you need to check if your local code requires a bathroom ventilation fan.

Check if there are wall mounted electrical outlets in the bathroom and make sure that they are the GFI type that most building codes now require. A GFI (Ground Fault Interrupter) is a special type of electrical safety outlet with an internal circuit breaker. If an electrical appliance such as a hair dryer came into contact with water, the breaker in the GFI will instantaneously cut power to it, preventing a possible electrocution. GFIs are easy to identify as they have two small push buttons on the face for periodic testing. Check back in the kitchen also, as a GFI is required any time the electrical outlets are near a sink or water area, and most outdoor outlets need to be GFI protected too. As always, check with your local municipal code official on what is required for your area.

If your bathroom has a bathtub or shower, are the walls tiled? If so, look at the condition of those tiles as well as the grout between the tiles and the caulk between the bathtub and the bottom row of tile. Hopefully all they need is a good scrubbing to remove any built-up soap scum or mildew. If the caulk between the bathtub and the tile and the back corners of the walls is discolored or cracking, you will need to dig it out (home centers sell a tool for this) and replace it with new caulk. Once again, use an acrylic latex-type caulk. Don't use silicone caulk; it's a pain to work with and smells bad. If there are small pieces of grout that have come loose or fallen out, you can get a grout repair kit at most home centers or tile suppliers. Check the operation of the toilet and if it leaks or runs you need to fix it. Replace all the toilet seats with new ones. Don't neglect trim such as towel bars, toilet paper holders, soap dishes, and so on. Even though they may seem like little items they can make a big impression on buyers and are not expensive. Remember, the devil is in the details. Finally, if the bathroom needs it, repaint with paint designed for moist bathroom environments.

PAINTING: Any imperfections or problems in the walls or ceilings by this point you will have repaired already. If any of the rooms are wallpapered, you have a tough call. Because wallpaper is a real personal taste item and since everyone does not have the same taste, you will have to decide if it stays or goes.

Before we go any further you need to be aware of the lead paint issue. Federal Law states that any home built before 1978 may contain hazardous lead-based paint and you must disclose that fact to all potential buyers or tenants. If the property you bought is pre-1978 and has any peeling or chipped paint, you will need to take action. In most cases you do not need to have the all paint removed, which can be very expensive to do. You just have to "encapsulate" it, meaning you can simply paint over and cover it. Check with your local paint store for the specific paint to do this.

Unless the property is only several years old and the walls are clean and the paint looks like new, you'll need to give the entire interior a fresh coat of paint. If you are going to replace the carpet or refinish hardwood flooring, paint *before* you do this. Choose a neutral color of paint, like off-whites or neutral to light beige. Do not use dark, trendy or loud colors that are hard to decorate with and may turn buyers off. Use an *eggshell or satin* acrylic latex paint. Don't use flat (it shows dirt and is hard to clean) or gloss (it shows every imperfection in the wall). Don't be tempted to buy cheap, low quality off-brand paint. It's not worth the results. Buy high quality name-brand paint. Almost all good quality paint will cover in just one coat, which in itself is a major time, labor and cost savings. *TIP: If you choose an off-white color in eggshell finish, you can paint the walls and ceiling the same color instead of having to use one color for the walls and white for the ceiling. Saves time and will look just fine. If you have a ceiling that has a rough or irregular surface, save time and money by painting it with a textured paint instead of repairing or replacing it. These paints do a great job of hiding the imperfections. Textured paint comes in several degrees of texture, so just be sure to follow the directions so it does not end up looking like the surface of the moon.*

Paint the trim in a complimentary semi-gloss or gloss color. And one last thing to do after painting: replace all the switch and receptacle cover plates with ones that compliment the newly painted walls. This gives the whole room a look of continuity and really pulls it all together.

FLOOR COVERINGS: What sort of floor covering do you have in the living spaces in your home? If yours is like most homes, it's probably carpet. Many new high-end homes have hardwood or tile flooring primarily in areas such as the living and dining rooms, kitchens and dens. Carpet, however, is still the dominant floor covering, especially in bedroom areas, since that tends to be more comfortable in the cooler months on bare feet. When buyers first enter your house, what's the first thing they will probably notice? That's right, the flooring. It makes that first and lasting impression before the kitchen and the bathrooms are seen. New carpeting in a home has the same sensory effect as a new car's interior does—*it smells new.* It's that "new car smell" that turns people on, and they love it. Not only does new carpet feel plush under the buyer's feet, but also it makes the house smell new, and buyers like that.

If you have carpet, your first decision will be whether to clean it or replace it. If the carpeting looks and feels like it is of recent vintage, say five years old or less, and there are no major signs of wear and tear, then you can probably get away with just having the carpet cleaned. If your carpet is older and worn, or smells from smokers or pets that had "accidents," then you need to replace it. If after removing the old carpet and padding you find that pet urine has seeped into the wood sub-floor, it too will have to be cut out and replaced. If you don't do this, then the smell will remain, even after the new carpet and pad have been laid. *TIP: Save money when carpeting by removing the old carpet and padding yourself. Cut it into 4' to 6' wide strips and roll and tie them before putting them out for trash pickup.* If you're replacing the carpeting, then that is the last thing you do before the rehab is completed. You don't want workmen or anyone else tracking dirty footprints on it before you put the for sale sign out, do you?

Carpet and padding, like most other items, come in various grades of quality and color. When you go to pick out the carpet explain to the salesperson that this is for a rehab that you plan to resell. Ask them to show you their line of builder's grade carpet or the next grade up. Builder's grade carpet also meets FHA requirements for carpet. Do not buy below builder's grade. The colors in builder's grade are more limited than in the higher priced carpet, but that's okay. What you want to stick to once again is neutral colors. Bring along a color swatch of the paint you used on the walls to help choose the carpet color. When picking out the padding, use what is called 6-pound rebond padding. Do not go for the cheaper 3 or 4 pound rebond padding because using a denser padding underneath makes even inexpensive carpet feel plusher for a lower cost than buying more expensive carpet. In most cases it does not make sense to try to reuse old padding. *TIP: Save money on padding. Padding, unlike carpet, can be turned in any direction and even the smallest scraps can be used. Typically you need about 10% less padding than carpet (normally you don't pad inside closets and such). Don't let them sell you on extra padding you probably won't need and will only have to throw out.*

If you've removed the old carpet and pad and discovered that you have hardwood floors underneath and you plan to refinish them, you need to inspect them for damage. Problems to look for are stains from pet accidents that make the wood turn blackish in color or deep gouges and scrapes, both of which will usually require the replacement of the damaged wood. A qualified hardwood floor refinisher can advise you on this. Generally the cost to refinish a hardwood floor is comparable to the cost of new carpet and pad for the same area. If possible, check with other homeowners in the neighborhood to see which floor covering is typical for the neighborhood.

WINDOWS: Windows are one of those modernization items that can really help sell a property and will provide a return on your investment. Whether you actually *need* to replace the windows is a separate issue. Many local municipal codes pertaining to windows require that windows open easily and remain open in case of a fire for evacuation. If yours do not, then you should plan on replacing them or you might not be able to get a U & O when selling the property. If your property still has the original older single pane windows without storm sashes, *and* most importantly if the majority of other properties in the neighborhood have replaced their original windows, you should too. This is simply a job people don't want to do after moving in. Vinyl tilt-in replacement windows are pretty much the standard for rehabs these days and they come in a variety of designs and price ranges. Stick with a style that compliments the property, blends in with other properties in the neighborhood and does not stand out like a sore thumb.

Windows, in most cases, are made to fit the opening specified, so correct measurement is very important. Unless you have done this before, measurement and installation should only be done by a qualified installer. Permits are usually required for this if the replacement windows are different in size. When picking out replacement windows look for double pane glass. Do not opt for the more expensive triple pane. Ask the installer if a certain energy efficiency rating for the windows is required for your locale. After the windows have been installed, leave the specification stickers on the glass, as they show the energy efficiency ratings of the windows. Let the buyers remove them.

LIGHTING: Decorative replacement lighting fixtures are surprisingly inexpensive and add a warm elegant touch to your rehab. Your local home building center or discount lighting shop should have a large variety to choose from. As before, if you want to see examples of current trends and finishes in lighting go look at the local builder's sample in your area. Be sure to remove the existing fixtures from the walls and ceilings before you paint so that the old outlines of the base will be covered. *TIP: Use clear bulbs in fixtures that have clear globes and soft white bulbs in fixtures that have frosted globes. They will blend in with the fixture better and look nicer when lit. Use the highest wattage bulbs allowed for the fixture. This will make the room look bright and inviting.*

REHABBING FOR A RENTAL

Rehabbing for a rental is similar to rehabbing for a flip except that you do more repairing and less rehabbing. Based on where your rental is located and the type of tenant you wish to attract, researching rates on similar rental properties will give you some idea how much you need to spend to make your property rental ready. Obviously the components used for rehabbing a $ 50,000 property for rental will be different than those required in a $ 200,000 rental. As previously discussed, certain items will still need to be inspected and attended to no matter what. Any problems with the roof, structural concerns, or issues required to meet local building and rental codes will need to be take care of ASAP.

As for the mechanical systems in the property (heating, air conditioning, plumbing, electrical), they also need to be checked out for proper operation. The house heater and/or central air conditioning should be repaired if needed and given a "tune-up" by a qualified technician to ensure efficient operation. (This will help minimize calls from tenants that something is not working.) Any leaks in the plumbing fixtures (toilets, sinks, pipes, etc.) need to be fixed or replaced (especially since in all probability it is usually you, the landlord, paying for the water). If you need to replace faucets, stick to the same brand and style throughout so parts will be interchangeable and repairs will be easy. Replace all of the toilet seats with new ones. Any electrical switches, outlets or lighting that looks suspect should be replaced immediately. No one wants an injury, fire, or lawsuit. If there are any steps or railings outside the property that pose a safety or tripping hazard, repair or replace those also.

The entire interior should receive a fresh coat of paint. For this you can use a lesser grade of paint, again eggshell or semigloss for ease of cleaning. As for the flooring, if there are hardwood floors a cleaning should be all they need. If not, you may have to repair it as needed. If you have carpet and it is in relatively decent condition, you should just need to clean it. If the carpet is severely worn and beyond cleaning, or if there was a problem with previous pet odors, then you will need to replace it. When purchasing carpet this time, advise the salesperson that it is for a rental and ask to be shown appropriate carpets. In this case you **should** opt for the less expensive 3 or 4 pound padding.

Any kitchen appliances that do not operate properly will need to be repaired. As before, if everything works simply clean it up. Do not be as concerned about the style of the appliances if not up to date. Renters are more concerned that everything works rather than how it looks. Any windows with broken glass or damaged screens need to be repaired. As before, it does not matter if they are not the most up to date, as long as they are functional and meet local codes. The only time you might concern yourself with updating the windows is if you, the landlord, are responsible to pay for the heat, but I will leave those topics for the books on successful landlording. In the end, your job is to make the property as bright and as cheerful a place as your budget allows in order to attract the best tenant possible.

CHAPTER 20

SELLING THE PROPERTY

Remember, time is of the essence so you want to have your repairs and any modernization work completed as quickly as possible. Not only is every day you own the property adding to your holding costs and eating away at profits, it's also keeping you from using those profits to fund your next real estate deal. It's kind of a one–two punch. You don't want to lose out on other buying opportunities because your money is tied up in a property that has not yet sold. When you receive the deed you want to be able act quickly to sell or rent. Whether you plan to sell it yourself or list it with the realtor on your team (a good idea), start your advertising or have it listed on the MLS when the rehab is about three-quarters completed, noting that it is a rehab in progress and indicate your target completion date. This way, you start creating interest, so that by the time it is done and you receive your deed you will hopefully have a buyer all lined up and ready to go.

Certain times of the year are better than others for selling a house. Traditionally, the busiest time for real estate sales is in the spring and again in September, right before and right after the school year begins. Thanksgiving and the holiday season in December are tough periods to sell or rent a property. People's attention is elsewhere. The dead of winter in northern climates can be an especially slow time, and unless they have to, people don't like to move at that time of year. Buyers also realize that the housing market is typically slower then and will want to negotiate a better deal with you. Try to plan your sale when the advantage of market timing is in your favor.

MAKING SURE THE PROPERTY IS READY

There is an old adage in the real estate investment biz that says; "You make your profit when you buy and you get paid when you sell." Well, now it is time to get paid. Before you decide whether you are going to sell the property by yourself or through a realtor, here is a quick checklist to be sure it's ready:

- The carpet and floors are clean and vacuumed. There are no cobwebs anywhere.
- Windows have been washed.
- Countertops, fixtures, and appliances in kitchen and bathrooms are cleaned and shine.
- Grass is cut and edged where necessary.
- Any trash is picked up.

SELLING WITH A REALTOR

Are you planning to sell the property yourself or use a realtor? While it might seem tempting to want to save the commission paid to the realtor by selling it yourself, that is not always a good and *ultimately* profitable decision. Many beginners do not realize there is far more involved to selling a property than just finding someone to buy it. A realtor brings a wealth of knowledge and experience along with them that many times translate into a higher selling price realized for your property than you could have reaped selling it yourself.

A professional realtor makes sure you avoid any of the potential land mines out there, like legal issues such as the Federal and State fair housing laws, which if you violate can cause severe legal repercussions. Therefore if you have decided to sell your property with a realtor, you must first be sure that you have the right realtor for your property. Hopefully you did your homework, and the realtor you are using is the realtor you had originally chosen to be on your team. If not, and you have to go out and hire a realtor, remember this: be certain that the realtor you ultimately select sells property in your location and price range and is not just looking to sign you up to a long contract in the hope of making commission on a property they have no idea how to market. All that does is waste your time. Interview them carefully. Ask lots of questions. Find out how they plan to market your house. How often do they do open houses? What is their commission rate? Is it negotiable? Are they a full-time or part-time realtor? Stick to full-time realtors. They do it for a living, not as a sideline, and will probably work harder to sell the property.

Your realtor's responsibilities, besides listing the property on the MLS and doing open houses, include dealing with all of the paperwork for you, qualifying the buyers, handling the advertising, fielding the phone calls, and making sure the settlement goes smoothly, which is a job all by itself. When you do find an agent that meets your needs and with whom you feel comfortable, agree only to hire them for the minimum 90-day period. If the agent balks and says they will only sign a contract with you for at least 180 days, or even worse, one year, find another agent. The reason is the contract you sign is legally binding and very difficult to get out of if things turn bad between you and the agent. By signing for only the 90-day minimum, you only have 90 days until it terminates if the agent becomes lax in promoting your property. If you sign for a year, you are stuck with this dud for 365 days! Remember, the idea is you want this to develop into a long-term relationship as you buy and sell more properties, so be sure you are thorough before *you* sign on the dotted line and commit yourself.

SELLING IT YOURSELF – FSBO

Selling it yourself, also known as a FSBO (pronounced Fizz-Bow) in real estate jargon, stands for: **For Sale By Owner**. While FSBO saves you the realtor's commission, it may not be the best way to sell your property. Let's look at some advantages and some disadvantages of FSBOs.

The only real "advantage" to selling it yourself is not having to pay a commission and lock into a fixed-term contract with a realtor. And not having to pay the commission may only be half true. Unless they are specifically asked to, most realtors do not want to be bothered showing prospective buyers a FSBO property simply because there is no financial incentive for them to do it. If you want to have a buyer's agent show their customer your house, you will have to agree to give them some commission on the sale. Normally that commission is three percent of the selling price; but that figure can be negotiated. If you cut them out completely, they won't do it. So in the end you are really only saving about three percent by not having a realtor working for you to sell your property.

A relatively new approach to the old FSBO concept is a real estate service that has appeared in the last several years. These companies will, for a flat fee, list your property on the MLS (pretty much a requirement, especially if you want any buyer's agent to see and recommend it) and provide you with the materials and the support you need to sell it. This saves you money over the traditional realtor; however, you have to do most or all of the legwork. The flaw with this is that nowadays most buyers are represented by agents who possess the market knowledge and experience the FSBO seller lacks. And finally, buyers who are looking for FSBOs, in general, expect a better deal from you as opposed to someone selling through a realtor. Why? Because they know that by selling it yourself you are not paying a realtor's commission and they expect those savings, and more, to be passed on to them. If you do decide to go the FSBO route, here are some tips you'll need to know and do.

1. First you will need to establish your selling price. This involves getting comps for similar properties *currently for sale in your area.* You do this the same way you got comps for the property initially. If your property has amenities that add value to it above and beyond the comparables, then you should price it two to four percent higher than the other properties but no more. Pricing it substantially less than similar properties is not always a wise idea, as this can backfire into making buyers think there is something wrong with it or that you need to sell quickly, and then they look for an even lower price.

2. Get a professional-looking "For Sale By Owner" sign made. You can get one from a local sign company. Make it similar in size to the lawn signs you see realtors use. These are large enough so that they can be seen eas-

ily from the road. Make sure you put your phone number in large numerals and use a white background with blue or black letters and numbers. Purchase one of the literature holders that mount on the sign.

3. Make a flyer to put in the literature holder. The flyer should have at least six or more preferably color photos of the exterior and interior of the property. You want to give prospective buyers as much information as possible on the flyer. For ideas, pick up some flyers from other houses for sale in your area. Here is the type of information you should provide, and a sample flyer:

- Name, address, county, city, zip code and your phone number
- School district
- Approximate age of house
- Number of bedrooms and bathrooms
- Approximate taxes per year
- Size of lot
- Type of utilities: gas, electric, central air, public or private water, public or private sewer, etc.
- Information about the exterior of the house: vinyl siding, brick, stone, stucco, etc.
- Information about the interior of the house: fireplace, cable TV-wired, finished basement, w/w carpet, hardwood floors, etc.
- Information about kitchen: eat-in, gas or electric appliances, dishwasher, microwave, etc.
- Remarks: This is where you want to talk up all of your improvements, and anything and everything else you can think of to make the potential buyer fall in love with it.

4. Advertise! Advertise! Advertise! I can't put it more simply. You need to advertise and market as much as possible. Even if your property was put on the MLS, you should advertise in your local paper and on as many websites as possible, such as Craigslist. Most local newspapers have an expanded real estate section on the weekends. Be sure to advertise in it. Community bulletin boards at supermarkets, churches, hospitals, and so on are places you should put a copy of your flyer. You'll want to have open houses on the weekends. Promote! Promote! Promote! You want to sell that property as quickly as possible.

5. Home Warranties are one of the more recent marketing tools offered by sellers. A home warranty is a service contract sold by an independent provider that is purchased by the seller for the buyer. It covers, usually for a period of one year, the repair or replacement of certain major systems of the property such as plumbing, heating, electrical and major appliances that break down due to normal wear and tear. The idea of providing a home warranty is to give the buyer additional assurance that if any of the covered systems fail during the warranty period they will be taken care of. Doubly nice is that you are out of the loop. No one is going to be

calling you should their water heater fail. Costs for home warranties vary but are in the $ 400 to $ 600 range. Look under "Home Warranties" on the Internet or in the phone book and you will see a number of companies listed that provide this service.

Sample Flyer

FOR SALE
123 Main Street Anytown, PA 45678
$125,900

This beautiful 3 bedroom 2 bath home is located on a quiet street in the desirable Glen Valley neighborhood. Recently updated. Just unpack your bags and move in! Just look at all this house offers! Call today to make this house your home.

Maintenance free brick exterior	Full finished basement
Master bedroom has large walk in closet	Close to all shopping centers
Gas hot air heat	Prestigious Hill Valley School Dist.
Central air conditioning	Landscaped ¼ acre lot
New plush wall to wall carpet	Cable TV wired
Freshly painted interior	One year home warranty
Tilt in E-Z clean windows	Parking for 3 cars in driveway
Dining room with slider to deck	Newer roof
Eat -In-Kitchen with all new appliances	Taxes approx. $2,500 per year
Public water & sewer	And MUCH more!

CALL PETE SMITH AT (234) 567-8910 FOR COMPLETE DETAILS AND TO SCHEDULE AN APPOINTMENT

STAGING

Staging a property for sale is nothing new. If you have looked at a builder's sample house, then you have probably seen staging at its best. Staging is setting up the interior of the house with furniture, plants, knickknacks and some amenities so that prospective buyers can literally imagine themselves living there. And while builders have been staging properties for a long time, staging a property for sale by private individuals is definitely starting to catch on and gain acceptance. Studies have shown that staging a house helps to sell it quicker and usually for a higher price than a non-staged house. Why? Because it's a proven fact that people buy houses based on emotion. How many times have you heard the potential buyer looking at a house say "they just fell in love with it"? Sure sounds emotional to me. Showing a lot of empty, uninviting rooms doesn't really get people emotional, does it? It kind of leaves them cold. Have you ever noticed what happens when you remove all the furniture and objects from a room and then talk? You get echoes. Echoes don't quite convey warmth and coziness, do they? You want buyers to literally flop down on the bed and think "I'm home."

So if you want to give your rehab a definite advantage over the other properties for sale in the area, you really need to stage it. Many of the same professionals that builders use can be hired to stage your property. However, staging on the level that builders do can be quite expensive. If you look on the Internet, you can find names of individuals and companies that do staging in your area. Or better yet, check with your local real estate group; they will know who the good stagers are. The stager will supply, maintain, and remove all of the staging items. Prices vary, depending on what you want. If you do not wish to spend the money for a pro, you can do the staging on your own and still achieve desirable results. First, you will need furniture—at least enough to furnish a living room, dining room or kitchen, if eat-in, and minimum one bedroom, preferably two. You can get the furniture two ways. The least expensive is to use some of the furniture from your own house if it matches the style of the house you are selling. The problem with this is you're missing furniture at home to live with and you have to lug it all there and back again. Another way is to rent it from companies that rent furniture. Describe to them what you are doing and see what they have to show you that meets your criteria. They will normally deliver, set up, and remove the items when you are finished with them. Here are some other staging ideas that don't cost a lot of money but go a long way to making the rooms inviting:

- Put nice matching fluffy towels, a rug and a wastebasket in each bath and powder room. Be sure there is toilet paper in all the holders. If there is countertop space, put out a decorative pump-type soap dispenser or soap dish with fancy fragrant soaps in it. If it is a master bath, put out a nice toothbrush holder, fancy shower curtain, and anything else you can think of to give the bathroom a "homey" feel. Many of these items can be bought inexpensively at the local bed and bath shops.

- In the kitchen a nice standup paper towel holder on the countertop with a decorative roll of paper towels and a mild, twist-open air freshener in an unobtrusive corner of the kitchen is good. Several matching dish towels and potholders add a pleasant touch. A cookie jar also works well, to give the kitchen a "welcoming" feel. Remember, most people make up their minds about buying a house in the first five minutes they are there. Keep in mind that all these items you are using to stage the property don't go with it when it is sold. You keep them and use them again on your next one.

- Silk or artificial potted plants. Don't use real plants, as you will have to maintain them, and when buyers with bored young children come through, the kids have a tendency to want throw the dirt from the pots on your nice clean floor.

- While window treatments don't completely come under the heading of staging, I feel that they should be put on most if not all of the windows, and typically *do* go with the house at sale. Window treatments add much needed warmth to a room. There is nothing more uninviting to a prospective buyer than walking into room after room all with unattractive and undecorated windows. Plastic mini blinds, valances and curtains are relatively inexpensive and easy to install. Check with your local discount home goods store for a nice selection. Window treatments should be used on every house you do.

- If you decide not to stage the property, you should at least have a card or a small kitchen table on which to place your flyers and chairs for people to sit on. A few toys or coloring books to entertain young children while their parents are looking at the place is good idea.

OPEN HOUSES

If there is one necessary evil with selling a property it is having the open house. An open house will take up your time on the weekend and, unfortunately, a lot of the people you'll get coming through the front door are what I refer to as "tire kickers." These are people who have nothing better to do on a weekend than drive around looking at houses, taking up your time with no intentions of buying. But, you *will* also get people who *are* genuinely interested in your property, and that is why you need to do open houses. Traditionally open houses are done on weekends, either Saturday or Sunday for two to four hours in the middle of the afternoon. You can also do open houses in the summer for a few hours in the early evening before it gets dark out. A word of caution about Sunday open houses during football season: I know it sounds crazy, but it's true—you may see a lower turnout, so consider Saturdays instead.

Be sure you advertise the open house in your local newspapers and put a sign on the lawn announcing it. If your house is not easily visible or off the main road, see if you can put an open house sign with the address and an arrow on to direct potential buyers to you on a utility pole or on a lawn nearby. Some sellers swear that baking cookies helps by making the place smell nice, kind of like grandma's house did when you were little. I really don't know if it does or doesn't help sell a house, but freshly baked cookies on a plate for potential buyers to nibble on certainly can't hurt. It's your call. Make sure you are at the property at least 15 minutes before it is set to start so you can have everything ready, including the cookies if you are baking them. Be sure you have lots of flyers on hand.

DEALING WITH BUYERS and ANSWERING THEIR QUESTIONS

As you meet with potential buyers who are interested in your house you'll be bombarded with questions. Questions about the roof, the heating or air conditioning system, how long have you owned the house, are the windows new, and on and on. This is perfectly normal. A house is one of the biggest purchases most people make in their lifetime. They are bound to have questions and concerns. Your job is to put them at ease by answering those questions as *honestly* as possible. However, while you need to be truthful answering their questions you do not need to volunteer information that is not asked for. Unless you are specifically asked, do not tell the buyer or anyone connected with the buyer that the property was bought at a foreclosure auction. People get funny when they hear a property was bought at auction. They automatically assume you got a great deal and they should get a great deal in return. If asked the question, answer them honestly. Say, "Yes, the property was bought at auction" and explain that you do buy properties at auction, rehab them, making them better than before, and resell them for a profit. States have real estate disclosure laws that require the seller to disclose any *known* information they have about the property to the buyer. This is done on what is called the "Sellers Disclosure Statement," a multi-page form that typically covers all aspects of the property. Filling it out dishonestly is not only wrong it can get you sued by the buyer if it is found out later that you lied.

As any good salesperson knows, the best way to sell a product is to find out what the customer wants to buy. Once you know that, then point out all the aspects of your property that the buyer has indicated they desire in a home. Call attention to those features which your house offers but which the buyer may not be aware of as well. Talk up all of the improvements to the property that you have made. Emphasize any warranties on those improvements that would be a benefit to the buyer. Tell the buyer they are welcome to have a home inspector go through the property to evaluate it and check for any problems. You want to let the buyer know that you will do everything possible from your end to make their home buying experience as pleasant as you can.

QUALIFYING THE BUYERS

Not everybody that comes to look at your property will be able to afford to buy it. You need to be able to differentiate between the qualified buyers and the unqualified ones. What you need to do is pre-qualify prospective buyers. Unless they are going to be paying cash for the property, you should ask them if they have been pre-qualified for a mortgage and if they have a letter from their lender confirming this. If they answer no, nor have they begun to look for a mortgage, you should have the names handy of several mortgage brokers to recommend, with their phone numbers. Explain that to proceed with negotiations any further and before paperwork of any kind can be drawn up, you must be able to confirm their ability to afford to purchase the property.

Once you are able to confirm this, then you can proceed to have your attorney draw up what is called an Agreement of Sale, or AOS, and you get a good faith deposit from the buyer. The amount of the deposit can vary anywhere from a hundred to thousands of dollars. The agreement of sale is a legally binding, written contract. It states the buyer agrees to buy and the seller agrees to sell a particular piece of real estate, and it spells out the terms under which this will happen. Once it is signed by both parties, the clock is ticking and the terms of the agreement must be adhered to.

The hitch with signing most agreements of sale is that they contain what is called the "mortgage contingency." That contingency states that if after a specified period of time if the buyer cannot obtain a mortgage, they can call off the sale. However, while the property is under agreement or "contract," as it is called, it is essentially off the market. What this means for you is if the buyer reneges on the contract because they could not obtain a mortgage, not only have you lost that market time of thirty days or more, and possibly the chance to have sold it to a buyer that actually was qualified, but your holding costs keep accumulating as well. You lose all the way around. Agreements of sale can be written so as not to have a mortgage contingency clause but it is much easier to find someone who is *qualified* from the get go. Have them sign the AOS with a deposit and get them to the settlement table as soon as possible so you can get paid and move onto the next project.

NEW FHA LOAN RULES

In July 2006 the Federal Housing Authority (FHA) finalized their new anti-illegal flipping rules. These rules were put into place to make it more difficult for con artists who were using illegal practices flipping properties to scam both the seller and the lender. Flipping houses is perfectly legal, unless you are committing fraud when doing it. The FHA underwrites loans for buyers who cannot qualify for a conventional mortgage. The new rules governing the release of funds for FHA backed mortgages are as follows:

The seller of the property must have seasoned their title for at least 90 days before FHA will make those funds available. If the seasoning is less than 180 days and the sale is 100% higher than the original purchase price, then the seller will have to provide additional assurances and information to the FHA. Properties exempt from this are: Housing Authorities, HUD, Fannie Mae, Freddie Mac, REO, inherited properties, some HUD approved non-profits, and properties in federally declared disaster areas.

Seasoning refers to how long the seller has owned the property. What all this means is that if you want to sell your property before owning it for 90 days, you just can't sell it to a buyer who is using an FHA loan to purchase it. And the 90 days begins with the date the property is recorded in the public records, and not the date you purchased the property at the sale. FHA backed loans are normally for buyers who have less than the typical minimum twenty percent or less deposit money. If you're running into a problem with the seasoning issue then you would inform the buyer that they need to obtain conventional financing or make other arrangements. If you happen to have hit a home run and the selling price is double the initial purchase price, then you have to wait 180 days before you can sell to an FHA buyer, or jump through additional FHA documentation hoops. Bottom line: avoid FHA backed loans if possible and check with your accountant or realtor for other financing alternatives to offer.

WRAPPING UP THE SALE

By now you should either have a yes or no answer from your potential qualified buyer as to their intention to purchase your property. If yes, then congratulations! At this point you need to turn the completion of the sale and settlement over to your attorney and title company. Real estate transactions are complicated enough when everything goes right. There are many details that need to be taken care of and this is not the place for a beginner. As previously noted, the agreement of sale needs to be drawn up by your attorney and the deposit money put into the attorney's escrow account. This money will be returned to the buyer at settlement. The agreement will then be forwarded to the buyer's agent for signing. If the buyer has not retained anyone for this, you should recommend that they do so. Once all of the required documentation has been secured, inspections made, any problems or questions ironed out, and settlement date chosen, there is not much else to do except wait for the settlement. Typically, settlement is held at the offices of the title company. The closing agent will have all of the documentation ready and will go through each item before signing by the respective parties. Once all of that is completed, you will be given your payment check and then hand the keys to the new owner. Congratulations! Now, go out and celebrate for a job well done!

CHAPTER 21

SUMMARY

People buy books for different reasons, and I thank you for buying mine. Maybe the reason you bought this book was simply that you're curious about foreclosure auctions and want to know what the hubbub is all about. Perhaps you're looking for a way to make extra income to help pay the kid's college tuition or take a long overdue family vacation. It could be that you decided to finally enter the world of real estate investing, and foreclosures are the vehicle you plan to do it with. Whatever the reason, *congratulations!* You are taking the first step towards gaining greater financial success and independence in your life by obtaining the knowledge to do it with.

But knowledge by itself is not enough. Two of the most important attributes of success are commitment and persistence. You can't do it without them. This prospect holds even truer when buying foreclosures. Not only do you need commitment and persistence, but consistency as well. If you really want to be successful, you need to be diligent about looking at properties and attending the auctions on as regular a basis as possible, for the more properties you look at, the better your chances of getting one. Inconsistent efforts will only yield inconsistent results and frustration. And that is one of the biggest reasons most people give up and quit this. Don't be discouraged when you get outbid at the sales. It happens to everyone. It is better to wait it out for the right property to come along—and it will—and be the successful bidder on it than to just bid on any 'ol property just to get one. Never bid on a property just because you had a dry spell of not winning the bidding and you feel you need "to get a property." The successful real estate investor is not the one who *buys* a property at every sale, but rather the one who buys a *profitable* property at the sale.

Don't surround yourself with naysayers. They will give you every reason in the world to not do this, and you need to tune them out. Believe me, after they see you counting the cash from your first deal they'll be at your doorstep singing a different tune, wanting to find out how they can join you. Become a member of a local real estate group and you will find the emotional and practical support you need. The concepts and information presented in this book are not difficult to understand and master. Adding the key support people to your team will allow you to get started. Even though *you* may not have mastered all of the technical aspects or acquired the actual experience yet, ***they have.*** Let their knowledge work for you. I have no doubt that if you follow the procedures laid out in this book, you will find your success in foreclosures at the auctions.

AFTERWORD

I hope you enjoyed reading this book as much as I enjoyed writing it. I most certainly would like to hear from not only those people who have used this information to successfully buy property, but also from those of you who are hitting some ruts in the road and need advice. I don't have gatekeepers, so you can e-mail me direct at re4closureauctions@hotmail.com. I will do my best to answer you in a timely manner. I welcome any testimonials or comments about this book, or if you feel I may have overlooked or erred with regard to any of the contents, by all means please send them to me so I can change any subsequent printings.

PROPERTY REPAIR CHECKLISTS

EXTERIOR OF STRUCTURE

ITEM	GOOD	REPAIR	REPLACE	EST.COST	NOTES
Roof					
Ext. siding					
Gutters					
Downspouts					
Window Screens					
Doors					
Foundation					
Paint					
Deck/patio					
Chimney					
Screens					
Soffit					
Fascia boards					
Lighting					
GFI outlets					
Mailbox					
Electric service wire					
Porch/Steps					
Other					

PROPERTY REPAIR CHECKLISTS

PLUMBING/HEATING MECHANICAL SYSTEMS

ITEM	GOOD	REPAIR	REPLACE	EST.COST	NOTES
Main water supply					
Water Meter					
Well pump					
Main sewer line					
Septic system					
Sewer vent					
Hot water heater					
Interior water pipes					
Valves					
Interior drain pipes					
Floor drains					
Central heater Oil					
Central heater Gas					
Central heater Other					
Window air cond.					
Central A/C					
A/C condenser					
Solar heat					
Radiant heat					
Hot water radiators					
Hot water baseboard					
Hot air registers					
Water softener					
Water filters					
Other					

PROPERTY REPAIR CHECKLISTS

ELECTRICAL SYSTEMS

ITEM	GOOD	REPAIR	REPLACE	EST.COST	NOTES
Central service wire					
Electric meter					
Main breaker panel					
Electric outlets					
GFI outlets					
Electric switches					
Cable TV connections					
Phone jacks					
Interior lighting					
Exterior lighting					
Wiring condition					
Other					

PROPERTY REPAIR CHECKLISTS

ATTIC

ITEM	GOOD	REPAIR	REPLACE	EST.COST	NOTES
Insulation					
Vents					
Roof leakage					
Roof rafters					
Ceiling joists					
Mold					
Wiring					
Flooring					
Other					

PROPERTY REPAIR CHECKLISTS

KITCHEN

ITEM	GOOD	REPAIR	REPLACE	EST.COST	NOTES
Cabinets					
Cabinet hardware					
Countertops					
Sink					
Faucet					
Garbage disposer					
Electric switches					
GFI outlets					
Lighting					
Oven/Stove					
Range hood					
Refrigerator					
Dishwasher					
Microwave					
Trash compactor					
Flooring					
Windows					
Doors					
Paint					
Smoke detector					
Other					

PROPERTY REPAIR CHECKLISTS

BASEMENT

ITEM	GOOD	REPAIR	REPLACE	EST.COST	NOTES
Floors					
Walls					
Sump pump					
Moisture problems					
Windows					
Doors					
Lighting					
GFI outlets					
Wash mach. hook up					
Dryer vent					
Foundation cracks					
Termites etc.					
Mold					
Smoke detector					
Other					

PROPERTY REPAIR CHECKLISTS

GARAGE

ITEM	GOOD	REPAIR	REPLACE	EST.COST	NOTES
Floor					
Walls					
Windows					
Shelving					
Garage door					
Garage door tracks					
Exit door					
Lighting					
GFI outlets					
Other					

PROPERTY REPAIR CHECKLISTS

MASTER BATHROOM

ITEM	GOOD	REPAIR	REPLACE	EST.COST	NOTES
Lavatory sink					
Countertop					
Lavatory cabinet					
Lavatory faucets					
Bathtub					
Shower					
Bath/shower faucets					
Bath/shower door					
Towel bars etc.					
Lighting					
GFI outlets					
Switches					
Medicine cabinet					
Mirrors					
Walls					
Flooring					
Tile					
Toilet					
Water supply piping					
Drain pipes					
Mold					
Windows					
Exhaust fan					
Other					

PROPERTY REPAIR CHECKLISTS

ADDITIONAL BATHROOMS/POWDER ROOMS

ITEM	GOOD	REPAIR	REPLACE	EST.COST	NOTES
Lavatory sink					
Countertop					
Lavatory cabinet					
Lavatory faucets					
Bathtub					
Shower					
Bath/shower faucets					
Bath/shower door					
Towel bars etc.					
Lighting					
GFI outlets					
Switches					
Medicine cabinet					
Mirrors					
Walls					
Flooring					
Tile					
Toilet					
Water supply piping					
Drain pipes					
Mold					
Windows					
Exhaust fan					
Other					

PROPERTY REPAIR CHECKLISTS

BEDROOMS

ITEM	GOOD	REPAIR	REPLACE	EST.COST	NOTES
Flooring					
Walls					
Windows					
Ceiling					
Doors					
Closets					
Electric switches					
Electric outlets					
Door/window trim					
Lighting					
Ceiling fan					
Paint					
Smoke detector					
Other					

PROPERTY REPAIR CHECKLISTS

LIVING, DINING, DEN ROOMS

ITEM	GOOD	REPAIR	REPLACE	EST.COST	NOTES
Flooring					
Walls					
Windows					
Ceiling					
Doors					
Closets					
Electric switches					
Electric outlets					
Door/window trim					
Lighting					
Ceiling fan					
Paint					
Other					

PROPERTY REPAIR CHECKLISTS

HALLS & STAIRWAYS

ITEM	GOOD	REPAIR	REPLACE	EST.COST	NOTES
Flooring					
Walls					
Handrails					
Ceiling					
Smoke detector					
CO2 detector					
Electric switches					
Lighting					
Paint					
Other					

PROPERTY REPAIR CHECKLISTS

LAWN, LANDSCAPING & GROUNDS

ITEM	GOOD	REPAIR	REPLACE	EST.COST	NOTES
Driveway					
Sidewalk					
Walkways					
Curbs					
Sewer vent					
Pool					
Lawn					
Trees & shrubs					
Fences					
Outside pole light					
Lawn sprinklers					
Drainage issues					
Other					

QUICK REFERENCE LISTS

While every effort has been taken to make the following QUICK REFERENCE LISTS as accurate as possible, they are to be considered general in nature and the information contained in them intended as a guide only. Foreclosures and their related laws along with local customs are rewritten and change, so ask your attorney or check your local and state statues for the most current information.

QUICK REFERENCE LIST OF FORECLOSURES FOR ALL 50 STATES

Even though some states practice both methods of foreclosure this listing indicates the predominant method used in that state.

STATE	FORECLOSURE TYPE Judicial	Non-Judicial	SALE TYPE	PROCESS TIME	DEFICENCY DAYS	
ALABAMA		*	TRUSTEE	30 p98sible		
ALASKA		*	TRUSTEE	90-120		
ARIZONA		*	TRUSTEE	60-120		
ARKANSAS	*	*	TRUSTEE	120-150		
CALIFORNIA		*	TRUSTEE	120		
COLORADO		*	TRUSTEE	60-150	Y	
CONNECTICUT	*		COURT	60-150	Y	strict
DELAWARE	*		SHERIFF	90-210	Y	
DC		*	TRUSTEE	60-120	Y	
FLORIDA	*		COURT	135	Y	
GEORGIA		*	TRUSTEE	30-60	Y	
HAWAII	*	*	TRUSTEE	90-120	N	Both
IDAHO		*	TRUSTEE	150	Y	J
ILLINOIS	*		COURT	210-300	Y	
INDIANA	*		SHERIFF	150-210	Y	
IOWA	*	*	SHERIFF	160	N	I
KANSAS	*		SHERIFF	120	Y	
KENTUCKY	*		COURT	210	Y	
LOUISIANA	*		SHERIFF	60-180	Y	
MAINE	*		COURT	180-300	Y	Entry
MARYLAND	*		COURT	60	Y	
MASSACHUSETTS	*	*	COURT	120	Y	E
MICHIGAN	*		SHERIFF	60	Y	Jud
MINNESOTA	*		SHERIFF	90	N	J
MISSISSIPPI	*		TRUSTEE	60-90	Y	
MISSOURI	*		TRUSTEE	60	Y	
MONTANA	*		TRUSTEE	150	N	
NEBRASKA	*		SHERIFF	150	Y	
NEVADA	*		TRUSTEE	120	Y	
NEW HAMPSHIRE	*		COURT	60	Y	
NEW JERSEY	*		SHERIFF	90-300	Y	
NEW MEXICO	*		COURT	120-180	Y	
NEW YORK	*		COURT	120-450	Y	
N. CAROLINA		*	SHERIFF	110	Y	Ju
N. DAKOTA	*		SHERIFF	90-150	Y	
OHIO	*		SHERIFF	150-210	Y	
OKLAHOMA	*		SHERIFF	120-210	Y	Nor
OREGON		*	TRUSTEE	150	N	
PENNSYLVANIA	*		SHERIFF	270	N	
RHODE ISLAND		*	TRUSTEE	30-90	Y	
S. CAROLINA	*		COURT	180	N	
S. DAKOTA		*	SHERIFF	150	N	N
TENNESSEE		*	TRUSTEE	45-60	Y	
TEXAS		*	TRUSTEE	30-60	Y	
UTAH	*		TRUSTEE	140	Y	
VERMONT	*		COURT	30-90	Y	Stric
VIRGINIA		*	TRUSTEE	60	Y	
WASHINGTON		*	TRUSTEE	90-120		
W. VIRGINIA		*	TRUSTEE	60	Y	
WISCONSIN	*		SHERIFF	60-280	N	Judi
WYOMING		*	TRUSTEE	60	Y	

QUICK REFERENCE LIST RIGHT OF REDEMPTION FOR ALL 50 STATES

STATE	REDEMPTION Y/N	REDEMPTION PERIOD DAYS	MEMO
ALABAMA	Y	365	
ALASKA	Y	365	Applies to judicial foreclosure only
ARIZONA	Y	30-180	Applies to judicial foreclosure only
ARKANSAS	Y	365	Applies to judicial foreclosure only
CALIFORNIA	Y	365	Applies to judicial foreclosure only
COLORADO	Y	75	
CONNETICUT	Y	varies	Judge decides yes or no & redem. period
DELAWARE	N		
DC	N		
FLORIDA	N		
GEORGIA	N		
HAWAII	N		
IDAHO	Y	365	Redem. period judicial foreclosure only
ILLINOIS	Y	90	
INDIANA	N		
IOWA	Y	60-365	Depends on situation can be from 60-180 c
KANSAS	Y	365	If abandoned period can be eliminated
KENTUCKY	Y	365	Only if sale price is less than 2/3 appra
LOUISIANA	N		
MAINE	Y	90 or 365	Time frame depends on mortgage dates
MARYLAND	Y	varies	Court decides period
MASSACHUSETTS	N		
MICHIGAN	Y	30-365	Varies but 120+ days common
MINNESOTA	Y	180-365	Varies depending on mortgage
MISSISSIPPI	N		
MISSOURI	Y	365	Awkward process 365 days to judicial sales
MONTANA	N		
NEBRASKA	N		
NEVADA	N		
NEW HAMPSHIRE	N		
NEW JERSEY	Y	10	
NEW MEXICO	Y	30	For some properties can be to 270 days
NEW YORK	N		
N. CAROLINA	N		
N. DAKOTA	Y	180	Can be to 365 days for farm property
OHIO	N		
OKLAHOMA	N		
OREGON	Y	180	On Judicial foreclosures only
PENNSYLVANIA	N		
RHODE ISLAND	N		
S. CAROLINA	N		
S. DAKOTA	Y	60-365	180 days if occupied/60 days if vacant
TENNESSEE	Y	730	
TEXAS	N		
UTAH	Y	varies	Court decides
VERMONT	Y	180-365	Pre 1968 mortgages have 365 days
VIRGINIA	N		
WASHINGTON	N		
W. VIRGINIA	N		
WISCONSIN	Y	365	
WYOMING	Y	90	

QUICK REFERENCE LIST OF TAX LIEN STATUS FOR ALL 50 STATES

STATE	TAX LIEN CERTIFICATE	TAX SALE	INTEREST RATE	MEMO PAID
ALABAMA	*		12%	3yr. redemption period
ALASKA		*		
ARIZONA	*		16%	3yr. redemption period
ARKANSAS		*		
CALIFORNIA		*		
COLORADO	*		9%	plus interest
CONNECTICUT		*	18%	Tax deed sale w/6 mos. re(
DELAWARE		*		
DC	*		12%	
FLORIDA	*	*	18%	Both types w/2yr. right of re
GEORGIA		*	20%	Tax deed sales w/1 yr. rede
HAWAII		*		
IDAHO		*		
ILLINOIS	*		36%	24% on farm land & 2 yr. righ
INDIANA	*		25%	Redemption period varies
IOWA	*		24%	Redemption period 21 mos.
KANSAS		*		
KENTUCKY	*		12%	1 yr. redemption period
LOUISIANA	*		17%	3 yr. redemption period
MAINE		*		
MARYLAND	*		6-24%	Redemption period varies 6 m(
MASSACHUSETTS	*	*	16%	16% tax cert. sales less con
MICHIGAN		*		
MINNESOTA		*		
MISSISSIPPI	*		18%	2 yr. redemption period
MISSOURI		*	10%	Varies either 90 days or 1y(
MONTANA	*		10%	Redemption period up to 3 yrs
NEBRASKA	*		14%	Redemption period 3 yrs.
NEVADA	*	*	12%	Both but tax cert. sales less
N. HAMPSHIRE		*		5 yr. redemption period
NEW JERSEY	*		18%	2 yr. redemption period
NEW MEXICO		*		
NEW YORK	*	*	14%	14% on lien cert. only 1 yr.
N. CAROLINA		*		
N. CAROLINA		*		
OHIO	*		18%	Check avail. of interest paym(
OKLAHOMA	*	*	8%	2 yr. redemption period
OREGON		*		
PENNSYLVANIA		*		
RHODE ISLAND		*	16%	16% on right of redem., 1 y
S. CAROLINA	*		8-12%	Redemption period 12-18 mos.
S. DAKOTA	discontinued			
TENNESSEE		*		
TEXAS		*		
UTAH		*		
VERMONT	*		12%	1 yr. redemption period
VIRGINIA		*		
WASHINGTON		*		
W. VIRGINIA	*		12%	17 month redemption period
WISCONSIN		*		
WYOMING	*		18%	4 yr. redemption period

QUICK REFERENCE FORECLOSURE LAWS FOR ALL 50 STATES

ALABAMA:

Timeline for an uncontested foreclosure: 2-4 months

The preferred method of foreclosure is non-judicial. Judicial foreclosure is only used if there are problems with the title. The normal foreclosure period is about 3 months. Unless otherwise specified in the loan documents, notice of sale is advertised in a newspaper for 3 weeks or posted in 3 public places and on the courthouse door. Listed on the notice is the date and terms of the sale as well as a description of the property. Sales are held at the courthouse. A deed is presented to the winning bidder upon payment in full following the sale. Debtor has a 1 (one) year right of redemption following the sale.

ALASKA:

Timeline for an uncontested foreclosure: 3-5 months

Preferred method of foreclosure is non-judicial, taking about 4 months. Typically, Alaska deeds of trust contain a power of sale clause and the borrower must be at least 30 days or more in default before action is taken. A NOD (notice of default) is sent to all affected parties and is posted on the property. For judicial foreclosures, the borrower need not be 30 days in default to file Lis Pendens. For either method, a foreclosure notice of sale must be published in a local newspaper once a week for 4 weeks and posted in 3 public places at least 30 days before the sale, with one of the places being the closest U.S. post office. Judicial foreclosures are held at the courthouse, while non-judicial locations vary. Borrowers have a 12-month right of redemption for court foreclosures only, and must pay the sale price plus 8 percent and any other costs.

ARIZONA:

Timeline for an uncontested foreclosure: 3-4 months

Both judicial and non-judicial foreclosure methods practiced equally. Judicial method begins with filing of Lis Pendens, with borrower and all affected parties notified. Non-judicial sale can occur if deed of trust contains power of sale and takes place approximately 3 months after trustee records notice of sale at either the courthouse or trustee's location. Up to 5:00 p.m. the day before the sale, the debtor can stop the sale by paying amount owed plus any fees. The winning bidder has until 5:00 p.m. the day following the sale to pay in full. Trustee will transfer ownership within 7 days. There is no redemption period for non-judicial sales. Judicial foreclosures are conducted by the sheriff at public auction. Winning bidder has until 5:00 p.m. the day after the sale to pay in full, whereby a certificate of sale is given. If the property is occupied, the redemption period is 6 months. To redeem, the total amount owed plus any fees must be paid.

ARKANSAS:

Timeline for an uncontested foreclosure: 2-4 months

Both judicial and non-judicial foreclosure methods are used. Non-judicial fore-closures average about 3 months. In judicial foreclosures the court determines the default amount, and if the debtor fails to pay within the specified time, the property goes up for sale, usually within 30 days. The previous owner has 1 (one) year to redeem the property by paying the purchase price plus interest. If it's a non-judicial power of sale foreclosure, the NOD filed also serves as the notice of sale. Thirty days after the NOD is publicly recorded, a copy is sent to the debtor. A copy is also posted in the office of the county recorder, as well as in a local newspaper for 4 consecutive weeks, with the final notice being at least 10 days before the sale. The property must sell for no less than two-thirds of its appraised value. If this does not happen, the property is put up for sale a second time within 12 months of the original sale date and is sold to the highest bidder.

CALIFORNIA:

Timeline for an uncontested foreclosure: 4-5 months

Non-judicial is used most often and takes about 4 months. Judicial is rare and typically only if lender is seeking a deficiency judgment. Non-judicial foreclosure begins when NOD is filed with the county recorder. Notice is mailed to debtor and other affected parties stating the amount of the debt and cut-off date for full pay-ment to be made. If the debtor satisfies the default plus any fees up to 5 business days prior to the sale, it is stopped. The lender or trustee can schedule the foreclo-sure sale 3 months after the NOD is filed. Notice of the sale containing all of the details must be posted at the property as well as in 1 (one) public location, and also placed once a week for 3 weeks in a local newspaper a minimum of 20 days before the sale. Notice is also mailed to the debtor and anyone else who requests it 20 days before the sale. Additionally, the notice of sale must be recorded with the county at least 14 days prior to the sale. The trustee will conduct the auction on any business day between 9 a.m. and 5 p.m. at the location designated in the notice of sale. The debtor does not have redemption with a non-judicial foreclosure but has up to 1 (one) year redemption with judicial foreclosure.

COLORADO:

Timeline for an uncontested foreclosure: 6-7 months

Non-judicial is the process most commonly used, running about 6 months. Judicial foreclosures are rare. Sales are conducted by a public trustee for each county and begin when the public trustee receives the documents from the lender requesting the foreclosure sale. Once recorded, the sale can then be scheduled; however, the lender still needs to secure a separate court order allowing the sale to take place. After all affected parties are notified, a hearing is held and if no one contests the debtors default, the court then allows the sale to proceed. Notice of the sale is published in the local newspaper for 5 weeks prior to the sale as well as mailed to the debtor. The debtor can stop the sale by notifying the public trustee of this intention at least 15 days prior to the sale and satisfying the debt no later than noon the day before the sale. Sales are held at the courthouse by the public trustee, and the winning bidder must pay with cash or bank check and is then issued a certificate of sale. The redemption period is 75 days.

CONNETICUT:

Timeline for an uncontested foreclosure: 3-6 months

Connecticut is one of three states to use strict foreclosure. Judicial foreclosure can also be used and which method is decided by a judge. Depending on the process used, the timeline is about 3 to 5 months. Strict foreclosure is used when there is no equity in the property and thus no auction sale. A judicial foreclosure by sale occurs when there is equity and a public auction sale is held. The foreclosure process starts with the lender filing documents in court against the debtor as well as notifying them and other lienholders at least 12 days before the scheduled date that the debtor and lienholders are to appear in court. On that date the court will settle on the amount of the debt, including costs as well as the fair market value of the property, and decide if a strict foreclosure or foreclosure by sale will be used. If strict foreclosure is chosen, the debtor is given a date when the debt needs to be paid by. If the debtor does not pay, then the lienholders have the opportunity to pay the amount, thereby taking ownership of the property. If none of the lienholders pay the amount, then the lender takes ownership. If a judgment by foreclosure is decided, then a date for the sale is set by the court, typically 60 to 90 days from the initial ruling. An attorney assigned by the court publishes a sale notice and handles the sale. The court decides within 2 weeks after the sale whether to approve it or not. Until approved, the debtor still has the right to redeem the property by paying the amount owed plus any fees. If approved, the winning bidder has 30 days to pay the balance due.

DELAWARE:

Timeline for an uncontested foreclosure: 7-10 months

Judicial foreclosure is the only method used in Delaware. Typical foreclosure timeline is about 8-9 months from beginning to end. The process begins with the filing of the Lis Pendens in court. If the debtor does not appear within 20 days to show just cause why the foreclosure should not occur, then the court rules the debtor in default. Eleven days after the ruling the lender submits a request to the sheriff to carry out a sale. The sheriff will post notice of sale at the property as well as other public places 14 days before the sale date and will deliver notice to the debtor. The notice of sale is required to be published in two local newspapers no more than 3 times per week for 2 weeks prior to the sale. The auction sale is either held at the property or the courthouse. Conformation of the sale occurs within 2-3 months after, with the sheriff awarding ownership to the high bidder. The previous owner has no redemption rights after the sale.

FLORIDA:

Timeline for an uncontested foreclosure; 4-5 months

Florida uses judicial foreclosure only. A filing of the Lis Pendens starts the process. The lender notifies the debtor as well as any other affected parties of the foreclosure. If the debtor does not respond to the suit within the specified time, the county clerk finds the debtor in default and the lender asks for a final ruling. If the court rules against the debtor, then a foreclosure sale date is assigned. Typically, the sale date is about 30 days after the court ruling. The court clerk issues the notice of sale and publishes it once a week for 2 weeks prior to the sale, with the second notice appearing 5 days before the sale. The sale takes place in the courthouse and is conducted by the clerk. The winning bid requires 5 percent hand money with the balance due by the end of the business day. Upon payment in full, the clerk issues a certificate of sale to the winning bidder. There is no redemption period for the previous owner.

GEORGIA:

Timeline for an uncontested foreclosure: 2-3 months

Both judicial and non-judicial are available; however, judicial is used only when there are title problems or the loan documents lack power of sale. If judicial is pursued, then the lender petitions the court noting the property, amount and situation. The debtor has 30 days to cure the default. If not cured in the time period, a sale is scheduled. For non-judicial foreclosures, the process starts with the lender scheduling the foreclosure sale. Georgia law does not require the lender to notify the debtor that this process has been started. Depending on the loan documents, the debtor can stop the foreclosure by satisfying the default amount. The notice of sale is published once a week for 4 weeks prior to the sale. Notice is also sent to the debtor 15 days before the sale. Foreclosures are held at the county courthouse. The winning bidder is required to pay the full amount of the bid following the sale. There is no redemption period in Georgia.

HAWAII:

Timeline for an uncontested foreclosure: 6-12 months

Both judicial and non-judicial are used equally. Typical time frame for non-judicial foreclosure is 4 to 6 months, judicial, 10 to 12 months. Non-judicial foreclosures require the notice of foreclosure to be to be posted at the property and delivered to the debtor at least 21 days before the sale. The lender also publishes the notice of sale in a local newspaper once a week for 3 consecutive weeks with the last being at least 14 days prior to the sale. Judicial sales start with the filing of the Lis Pendens and delivers notice of same to the debtor. If the debtor does not respond to the suit within 20 days, they are considered in default. The lender then proceeds scheduling the foreclosure sale. Debtors can file an appeal within 30 days of the courts declaring the default. The debtor may cure the default by paying the debt, stopping the sale up to 3 days prior. For non-judicial sales, the winning bidder pays 10 percent hand money. Once full payment is made, ownership is transferred. In judicial foreclosures the court appoints a commissioner to sell the property and holds a hearing to confirm the sale. If the court finds the price fair and not undersold, then the sale is confirmed. If not, the court will order another sale with additional bidding to insure a high enough price and then confirm the sale. Hawaii has no redemption period.

IDAHO:

Timeline for an uncontested foreclosure: 5-6 months

While Idaho uses both types of foreclosures, judicial is rare. Foreclosure begins with the delivering of the NOD to the debtor and any persons who request it. The debtor then has 115 days to cure the default, thereby stopping the foreclosure process. If the debtor fails to cure the default, the lender files and records the NOD with the court and proceeds to schedule the foreclosure sale. At 120 days before the sale date the notice of sale is sent to the debtor. The lender also advertises the notice of sale in the local newspaper once a week for 4 weeks, with the final publication 30 days before the sale date. Typically, the trustee's attorney conducts the sale. After receiving full payment, the trustee transfers ownership of the property to the winning bidder who is entitled to possession of the property 10 days after the sale. The previous owner has a 1 (one) year right of redemption.

ILLINOIS:

Timeline for an uncontested foreclosure: 12 months

Judicial foreclosure is the only process used in Illinois. Foreclosure starts with the filing of the Lis Pendens and is distributed to the debtor and all other affected parties. All parties have 30 days to respond to the action. If there is no response, the lender continues with the foreclosure and if the court ruling is against the debtor for default, the lender will proceed to schedule a date for a public auction sale. The debtor, however, can stop the foreclosure within 3 months of notification by paying in full the default amount plus any fees. A notice of sale is sent to all affected parties and includes all details of the property and sale. The notice is published in the real estate and legal notice sections of the local newspaper once a week for 3 weeks, with the first listing no more than 45 days before the sale and the last listing no less than 7 days prior to the sale. If the sale is postponed more than 60 days from its original date, then a new notice will be published. The sale is conducted by the sheriff at the courthouse. Once the winning bidder has paid the full bid price, a certificate of sale subject to court conformation is issued. Once receiving conformation, the winning bidder takes ownership, and possession if the property is vacant. If occupied and eviction is needed, then possession is in 30 days. There is a 90-day right of redemption period in Illinois.

INDIANA:

Timeline for uncontested foreclosure: 8-10 months

All foreclosures in Indiana are judicial. The lender starts by filing a Lis Pendens against the debtor in court. While not required by Indiana law to send a default notice to the debtor prior to the filing, most lenders will. The date the mortgage was signed dictates the period between filing the Lis Pendens and the foreclosure sale. Typically it is 3 months but can be as great as 6 to 12 months for older mortgages. If the property is abandoned, there is no waiting period. Once the pre-foreclosure period has expired and the sheriff receives the court certified copy of the order of sale and judgment, then the sheriff appoints an auctioneer to conduct the sale. The notice of sale is published once a week for 3 weeks in the local newspaper, with the first publication being 30 days prior to the sale. In addition, the sheriff must post the notice at the courthouse as well as in 3 public places and deliver a copy to the debtor. Upon conclusion of the sale and full payment, the sheriff transfers ownership to the winning bidder. There is no redemption period.

IOWA:

Timeline for an uncontested foreclosure: 4-6 months

Iowa uses both judicial and non-judicial foreclosures, with trustee sales voluntary. Judicial foreclosures, at the lender's choice, may or may not include right of redemption. Debtors can also choose to agree to a non-judicial foreclosure, or the lender can opt for a non-judicial foreclosure without consent from the debtor. The debtor will receive the NOD containing the amount due and a deadline for payment to be received 30 days before the foreclosure process begins. If the debtor does not cure the default, then the lender starts the foreclosure process, with the court directing the property to be sold. While the sale usually takes place in 2 months if the lender is going for foreclosure without redemption, the sale could be delayed for 6 to 12 months at the debtor's request. The sheriff will publish the notice of sale in a local newspaper twice weekly, with the first notice at least 4 weeks prior to the sale. Also, the notice of sale must be posted in a least 3 public places and at the courthouse. If the property is still occupied, notice must be served at least 20 days before the sale. The sale is conducted by the sheriff, with debtors having a 1 (one) year redemption period if the lender chooses to pursue a deficiency judgment and a 6 month period if the lender chooses not to. The redemption period for unoccupied property can be as short as 60 days.

KANSAS:

Timeline for an uncontested foreclosure: 6-12+ months

Judicial foreclosures only are used in Kansas. The lender files a Lis Pendens, and the court filing is delivered to the debtor, who has 20 days to respond. If the debtor does not respond or the court rules for the lender, the debtor then has 10 days to cure the default or a foreclosure sale will be held. The notice of sale is published in a local newspaper once a week for 3 weeks, with the sale being held between 7 and 14 days after the final notice is published. The winning bidder, upon payment in full, receives a certificate of sale. The redemption period begins with the sales date and is 12 months if more than one-third of the principal has been paid. If less than that amount is paid, then the redemption period is shortened to 3 months. If the property is abandoned, a hearing is held and the redemption period can be further shortened or eliminated. With the expiration of the redemption period the winning bidder receives the deed.

KENTUCKY:

Timeline for an uncontested foreclosure: 5-6 months

Kentucky is a judicial foreclosure state, with one exception. The lender files the Lis Pendens to begin the foreclosure, except where the property is abandoned. The lender then takes possession once the borrower defaults. The sheriff delivers notice to the debtor, who has 20 days to respond. If the debtor fails to respond or the court rules against them, then a foreclosure date is set. Prior to the sale, the property must be appraised. Typically, the sale takes place 1 (one) month after the court ruling and a notice of sale is published in a local newspaper for 3 weeks. The sale is held at the courthouse and sold to the highest bidder, who must pay in cash or set up with the court to pay in installments. Following the sale, a deed is prepared by the clerk. If the sale price is less than two-thirds of the appraised value, the debtor has the right to redeem the property by paying the sale price plus 10 percent interest. The redemption period lasts 1 (one) year.

LOUISIANA:

Timeline for an uncontested foreclosure: 6-10 months

Louisiana is the only state that practices these two types of judicial foreclosure: executory and ordinary. Non-judicial is not used. The ordinary method, similar to a lawsuit, is more expensive and complicated, taking about 9 months to complete. The executory process is used when the mortgage includes a pre-existing "confession of judgment," which allows the foreclosure process to move quicker, with the timeline reduced to 6 months. State law does not require the lender to notify the debtor before commencing the foreclosure process; however, the mortgage documents may require it. Once served with the demand for payment of the defaulted amount, the debtor has 3 days to cure the default. If the debtor fails to do this, the sheriff serves notice to the debtor of the foreclosure sale. Notice of the sale is also published twice in a local newspaper. The sheriff conducts the sale, and the winning bidder must pay in cash on the day of the sale unless special arrangements are made with the court. The sheriff then issues the deed. There is no right of redemption in Louisiana.

MAINE:

Timeline for an uncontested foreclosure: 8-10 months

Only the judicial foreclosure method is used in Maine. The lender must send a default notice to the debtor, who has 30 days to cure the default in full plus interest. If the debtor fails to do this, then the lender files a Lis Pendens to begin foreclosure and sends notice to the debtor of this. If the debtor opposes the foreclosure, goes to court and loses, the debtor still has 90 days to retain the property and cure the default, thereby stopping the foreclosure. If debtor does not stop the foreclosure, the lender will publish a notice of sale in the local newspaper for 3 weeks. A sale is then held 4 to 6 weeks after the initial publication date. The sale can be held at the courthouse or at the foreclosing attorney's office who conducts the sale. The winning bidder, upon paying their hand money, has 30 days to make payment in full and is issued a deed. The redemption period varies from 3 to 12 months depending on the execution date of the mortgage.

MARYLAND:

Timeline for an uncontested foreclosure: 1-2 months

Judicial foreclosure is the method used in Maryland. To start the foreclosure process, the lender needs to file a complaint against the debtor. The court will then make a determination as to whether a default has occurred. If it finds that a default has happened, it then determines the amount of the debt as well as time frame for repayment. If repayment is not made within that time, the court will order the property sold and a date for the sale set. The lender is not required to give notice of the foreclosure to the debtor prior to the setting of the sale date. The notice of sale is published in a local newspaper for 3 consecutive weeks and must be sent to the debtor and any other lienholders 10 days before the sale date. The sale is held outside the courthouse by public outcry and is conducted by a licensed auctioneer. Once the bidding is completed, a notice of the sale is placed in a local newspaper. Any interested parties with objections to the sale must file them within 30 days. If there are none, then the sale is confirmed and a deed issued. There is no redemption period in Maryland.

MASSACHUSETTS:

Timeline for an uncontested foreclosure: 2-3 months

Massachusetts has two types of foreclosure: entry and possession, which is judicial and less common, and non-judicial, using power of sale. With entry and possession, there are two methods. The lender may file a lawsuit to gain possession for default. If awarded possession, the lender is then given permission to enter and evict the debtor. The debtor may redeem the property within 2 months by curing the default, and unless the debtor can pay off the mortgage within 3 years, the lender becomes the owner of the property. With the other entry and possession method, the lender openly and peaceably enters the property with two witnesses swearing that the entry was as stated. Once in possession, the lender waits 3 years for title. The more common non-judicial power of sale method is carried out in accordance with the terms in the mortgage and the power of sale. The lender publishes notice of sale in the local newspaper once a week for 3 weeks with the first notice 21 days before the sale. Notice of sale is also sent to the debtor and any other affected parties 14 days prior to the sale. A licensed auctioneer handles the sale, and the winning bidder must make final payment within 30 days. Following another 30-day period, the sale is recorded and the deed is issued. There is no right of redemption.

MICHIGAN:

Timeline for an uncontested foreclosure: 3-12+ months

Michigan allows both judicial and non-judicial foreclosures, but due to the fact that most Michigan mortgages contain a power of sale provision, non-judicial foreclosures are the preferred method. Michigan law does not require the lender to notify the debtor with a default notice before the foreclosure; however, the mortgage document might require it. The debtor can stop the foreclosure by curing the default. The sale is usually scheduled about 2 months after the foreclosure is started. The notice of sale is posted at the property and published once a week for 4 weeks in a local newspaper, with the sale not less than 28 days from the first publication. Typically, the sheriff or trustee conducts the auction at the county courthouse between the hours of 9:00 a.m. to 4:00 p.m. Ownership is transferred at the sale, with documentation stating the redemption period. This period can vary but is typically 6 months, during which time the debtor can redeem the property by paying the sale price plus interest.

MINNESOTA:

Timeline for an uncontested foreclosure: 3-8 months

Both judicial and non-judicial foreclosures are available in Minnesota, with non-judicial more common. If judicial foreclosure is used, the lender notifies the debtor of the default and then files the Lis Pendens. If the court rules against the debtor, a foreclosure sale is scheduled. The majority of foreclosures done are non-judicial, using the power of sale clause in the mortgage. The lender again notifies the debtor of the default, and if the debtor fails to cure it by paying the defaulted amount and any fees, then the lender proceeds with the foreclosure sale. The notice of sale is published for 6 weeks, and the debtor must be notified in person 4 weeks prior to the sale. The sheriff conducts the sale between 8:00 a.m. and sundown, typically at the courthouse. The winning bidder must pay the full amount at the sale and is issued a certificate of sale that transfers ownership after the redemption period of 6 to 12 months expires.

MISSISSIPPI:

Timeline for an uncontested foreclosure: 3-4 months

Both judicial and non-judicial foreclosures are available in Mississippi with non-judicial most common, using the power of sale provision contained in most deeds of trust. The lender sends the debtor a default notice 30 days prior to the foreclosure sale date. The debtor can stop the foreclosure prior to the sale at any time by curing the default plus any fees. The notice of sale is published once a week for 3 consecutive weeks in the local newspaper as well as posted at the county courthouse. Sale is typically conducted by the trustee on the courthouse steps by public outcry between 11:00 a.m. and 4:00 p.m. The winning bidder must pay the full amount due at the sale or it will be rescheduled. The deed is transferred by the trustee. There is no redemption period.

MISSOURI:

Timeline for an uncontested foreclosure: 2-3 months

Missouri allows both judicial and non-judicial foreclosures; however, judicial is rare and mainly used if there are problems with title or the deed of trust lacks a power of sale provision. Non-judicial foreclosure happens quickly, sometimes in as little as 60 days. Typically, the lender will send a NOD to the borrower upon default forewarning that the foreclosure is going to begin. As soon as the lender files the proper paperwork, the sale can be scheduled. At any time before the sale, the debtor can stop it by curing the default. Missouri law requires that notice of sale be published in a local newspaper, beginning 20 days before the sale and ending on the day of the sale if the city or county has a population above 50,000. In counties with less than 50,000 inhabitants, the trustee publishes the notice of sale in a local newspaper once a week for 4 weeks, with the last no more than 1 (one) week before the sale. In addition, notice must be served to the debtor and all affected parties 20 days before the sale. The trustee, or their representative, conducts the sale, usually at the courthouse. Only if the lender is the purchaser of the property does the buyer then have redemption rights. If it was purchased by a third party, such as an investor, then there is no right of redemption.

MONTANA:

Typical timeline for an uncontested foreclosure: 5-6 months

Montana allows both judicial and non-judicial foreclosure; however, non-judicial is the preferred method. With a judicial foreclosure, the court determines the amount due the lender and gives the debtor a period of time to pay. If the debtor does not pay in that time period, the lender then gives notice of the foreclosure sale. For non-judicial foreclosure, the lender follows the terms in the deed of trust and power of sale. The process begins with the lender filing the NOD with the county recorder and scheduling the sale at least 120 days after notice is filed. At any time before the sale the debtor may cure the default in full plus costs, thereby stopping the foreclosure. The notice of sale is posted in a prominent spot at the property at least 20 days prior to the sale as well as mailed to the debtor 120 days before the sale. The notice of sale is also required to be published once a week for three consecutive weeks in a local newspaper. Sales are by public auction at the county courthouse. There is no right of redemption.

NEBRASKA:

Typical timeline for an uncontested foreclosure: 3-6 months

Both judicial and non-judicial sales are allowed, with non-judicial the most common, taking about 4 months to complete. The process for a non-judicial foreclosure begins with the lender recording the NOD at the courthouse and also sending notice to the debtor and to all affected parties. The debtor has 35 days from the date on the default notice to cure the debt and stop the foreclosure. If this does not happen, then a notice of sale is published in the local newspaper once a week for 3 weeks and posted in 3 public places at least 20 days prior to the sale. The sale is usually held at the trustee's office and conducted by same. Once the winning bidder pays the full amount due at the sale, the trustee then transfers ownership and issues a deed. There is no redemption period for non-judicial sales. However if the foreclosure was judicial, then there is a 1 (one) year redemption period.

NEVADA:

Typical timeline for an uncontested foreclosure: 3-4 months

Nevada allows both judicial and non-judicial foreclosures; however, non-judicial foreclosures have no right of redemption for the debtor so that type of foreclosure is preferred. A non-judicial foreclosure commences with the lender recording the NOD with the county recorder and serving notice to the debtor. The debtor then has 35 days from the date on the notice to cure the default and stop the foreclosure. Ninety days after the recording date of the NOD the lender can schedule the sale. The notice of sale is sent to all affected parties, posted 20 days prior to the sale date in three public places, and published in a local newspaper once a week for 3 weeks. The sale is handled by the trustee named in the deed of trust and is typically held at their office. The full amount of the winning bid is payable at the sale, with the trustee transferring ownership after payment. If a judicial foreclosure was used, then there is a 1 (one) year redemption period.

NEW HAMPSHIRE:

Typical timeline for an uncontested foreclosure: 2-3 months

Non-judicial foreclosure is the only type of foreclosure available in New Hampshire. Two types of non-judicial are possible, power of sale being more common and strict foreclosure rarely used. With strict foreclosure, the lender must requisition the court to terminate the debtor's right to redeem the property; if granted, the debtor then has 1 (one) year to cure the default. If it is not cured in that time period, then ownership transfers to the lender. For power of sale foreclosures, the lender sends a NOD to the debtor with a 30-day grace period to cure the default. If this does not happen in that time period, then the lender will schedule a sale. The notice of sale is sent to the debtor at least 25 days prior to the sale date as well as published in a local newspaper once a week for 3 successive weeks. By curing the default, the debtor can stop the sale at any time. The sale is held at the property and typically is conducted by an auctioneer or the lender's attorney. Opening bid is usually set between 70 to 85 percent of the property's fair market value. The winning bidder must pay any balance due within 60 days of the sale, and upon completion of all paperwork, title to the property is transferred. There is no redemption period in New Hampshire

NEW JERSEY:

Typical Timeline for an uncontested foreclosure: 8-10 months

Judicial foreclosures only are used in New Jersey, with the process running about 9 months. Thirty days prior, the lender notifies the debtor in writing about the forthcoming foreclosure. During this period, the debtor can stop the process by curing the default. When filing the Lis Pendens to begin foreclosure, the lender can either sue for the past due payment amount or for the entire unpaid loan balance. The debtor is notified of the action and has 35 days to respond. If the court rules in favor of the lender, an auction sale date is scheduled. Notice of the sale is published in 2 local newspapers, one of which must be in either the county seat or the largest municipality in the county. In addition, notice must be posted in the county office as well as at the property at least 10 days before the sale. The auction is conducted by the sheriff at the county courthouse, with the sheriff transferring ownership of the property 10 days following the sale. The debtor has redemption rights during that 10-day period.

NEW MEXICO:

Typical timeline for an uncontested foreclosure: 6-8 months

In New Mexico judicial foreclosure is the method used for residential property, while non-judicial is only allowed in some cases for commercial and business loans above a certain dollar figure, with stipulations. Foreclosure in New Mexico begins with the lender filing a foreclosure complaint against the debtor and any other parties who have an interest in the property. After filing the complaint, a Lis Pendens is entered in the county courthouse where the property is located and the lender serves notice to the debtor, who has 30 days to respond. If there is no response, the court makes a ruling, and if not agreed upon, then a hearing is scheduled. If the court rules for the lender, then the sale is scheduled a minimum of 30 days after the court's ruling. A notice of sale is published once a week for 4 subsequent weeks in a local newspaper, with the last ad 3 days before the sale. The debtor can at any time stop the sale by curing the debt in full plus fees. The property is sold to the highest bidder whose bid is at least 80 percent of the fair market value. Once the sale is approved by the court, a deed is issued. Redemption period varies from 1 (one) to 9 months, with the debtor paying the sale price plus 10 percent interest and any fees.

NEW YORK:

Typical timeline for an uncontested foreclosure: 10-15 months

Judicial foreclosures are the primary method used in New York and can take as long as 15 months, the longest of all the states. Foreclosure begins with the lender suing for the amount of the default and serving notice, requiring the debtor to appear in court. A Lis Pendens is also filed. If the debtor fails to appear or does appear and the court rules in favor of the lender, then a foreclosure sale is scheduled. On average, the sale occurs about 4 months after the court ruling. The notice of sale is published in a local newspaper once a week for 4 weeks prior to the sale. Auction sales are held at the county courthouse. The highest bidder normally pays 10 percent hand money, with the balance due in 30 days. Ownership transfers with the final payment made, with no right of redemption for the debtor after the sale.

NORTH CAROLINA:

Typical timeline for an uncontested foreclosure: 3-5 months

Both judicial and non-judicial foreclosures are available in North Carolina; however, judicial foreclosures are rare. If judicial foreclosure is desired, the lender must first secure a court order for the foreclosure. It then proceeds under the direction of the court and is sold at a sale carried out by the sheriff. For non-judicial foreclosures through power of sale in a mortgage or deed of trust, a preliminary hearing is first held, conducted by the clerk of the court to determine if a sale will take place, with notice served to the debtor no less than 10 days prior to the hearing. If the clerk rules to allow a foreclosure sale to take place, then a notice of sale containing names of all affected parties, legal description and location of the property, and date and time of the sale is mailed to the debtor as well as to all affected parties and posted on the door of the county courthouse no less than 20 days prior to the sale. Additionally, the notice of sale is published in a local newspaper once a week for 2 weeks, with the last publication no more than 10 days before the sale date. The sale, conducted by the trustee, is held at the courthouse between 10:00 a.m. and 4:00 p.m., never on Sunday, and is sold to the highest bidder. A 10-day redemption period exists after the sale for the debtor by paying what the lender is owed plus any fees. One unusual feature of North Carolina foreclosure is that even after the sale a potential buyer can come in and purchase it through what is called an "upset bid" by placing a deposit and a bid of at least 5 percent over the previous winning bid with the clerk during the 10-day redemption period. The clerk will then order a re-sale of the property for as many times as there are upset bids submitted. Final sale occurs when there are no longer any upset bids submitted.

NORTH DAKOTA:

Typical timeline for an uncontested foreclosure: 4-6 months

Only judicial foreclosures are used in North Dakota. The procedure begins with the lender serving notice to the debtor of their intent to foreclose by either registered or certified mail, with no less than 30 and no more than 90 days before the start of the foreclosure process. After notice is given, the lender files the proper paperwork and the court determines the amount of debt and sets up a time frame for payment. If the debtor does not pay within those terms, then the property is set up for foreclosure sale. Notice of sale is sent to the debtor as well as published in the county newspaper 60 to 90 days prior to the sale. The sale is held at the county courthouse by the sheriff and is sold to the highest bidder, who receives a certificate of sale which can be redeemed after the debtor's redemption period has expired. The redemption period is normally 6 months but up to 12 months for agricultural property.

OHIO:

Typical timeline for an uncontested foreclosure: 7-8 months

Judicial is the only foreclosure process used in Ohio. The foreclosure begins with the lender bringing suit against the debtor, who is served notice of the suit personally or by certified mail. The debtor then has 28 days to respond or be in default. If found in default, the court orders a sale and instructs the sheriff to obtain 3 impartial appraisals and to publish a notice of sale ad in the local newspaper for 3 consecutive weeks on the same day each week. The debtor may stop the foreclosure at any time prior to the sale by curing the default. The auction sale is held at the county courthouse by the sheriff and sold to the highest bidder whose bid is at least two-thirds of the appraised value. The winning bidder, after conformation of the sale, receives the deed. The debtor's right of redemption period ends with the sale and has no right afterwards.

OKLAHOMA:

Typical timeline for an uncontested foreclosure: 5-7 months

Oklahoma allows both judicial and non-judicial foreclosures, but due to the complexity and limitations under Okalahoma law, non-judicial power of sale foreclosures are rarely used. With a judicial foreclosure, the lender would first serve notification to the debtor of the default. The lender would next file a Lis Pendens and serve notice to the debtor, who has 20 days to respond. If the court rules in favor of the lender, then the property is scheduled for sheriff sale. Notice of the sale is published in a local newspaper in the county where the property is located, each day for 4 subsequent weeks, not less than 30 days before the sale. The sale is conducted by the sheriff and sold to the highest bidder whose bid is no less than two-thirds of the appraised value. The winning bidder must post cash or certified check equal to 10 percent of their bid. Once the sale is confirmed by the court, in about 15 days, the redemption period ends.

OREGON:

Typical timeline for an uncontested foreclosure: 5-6 months

In Oregon both judicial and non-judicial foreclosures are allowed, with non-judicial more common. If there is a power of sale clause in the mortgage or deed of trust, the lender will record the NOD and at least 120 days prior to the property being scheduled for sale notify the debtor as well as any affected parties. The lender publishes the notice of sale in a local newspaper once a week for 4 weeks, with the last notice being published 20 days prior to the sale. If the lender is pursuing a judicial foreclosure, then a Lis Pendens is filed and goes through a court foreclosure. If the decision is in favor of the lender, then the property is scheduled and sold as part of a public sale. The debtor can stop the sale by curing the debt plus any fees. Auction sales are held at the location specified on the notice of sale between the hours of 9:00 a.m. and 4:00 p.m., with the winning bid paid in cash at the time of sale. Ownership is transferred within 10 days of the sale, with the winning bidder taking possession. Non-judicial foreclosures have no redemption, but judicial foreclosures have a 180-day redemption period after the sale by submitting notice to the sheriff and payment in full of the outstanding unpaid loan balance plus costs.

PENNSYLVANIA:

Typical timeline for an uncontested foreclosure: 9-10 months

Judicial sales are the only foreclosures carried out in Pennsylvania. Once the borrower is 60 days behind in payments, depending on the mortgage, the lender sends out notices advising the debtor of PA Act 6 and PA Act 91 relevant to the foreclosure. If after a 2 to 4 month period the debtor does not act to prevent the foreclosure, the lender then files a Lis Pendens and notifies the debtor that a foreclosure action has begun. The debtor has 30 days to respond to the action or the court issues an order to sell the property at auction. Thirty days before sale the sheriff personally serves notice of the sale to the debtor and posts a handbill at the property. The sale is advertised in a local newspaper as well as in the local legal newspaper once a week for 3 weeks. The debtor can stop the sale up to 1 (one) hour before by curing the full amount of the debt. The auction is conducted by the sheriff about 45 to 60 days after the court issued order and is sold to the highest bidder, with a deed being issued in about 90 days. There is no right of redemption.

RHODE ISLAND:

Typical timeline for an uncontested foreclosure: 2-3 months

Rhode Island has one of the shortest foreclosure periods, about 2 months. Both judicial and non-judicial foreclosures are allowed, with non-judicial preferred. Judicial foreclosures happen mainly because of issues with the title, or if there is no power of sale provision in the mortgage. A lender can choose to proceed with a judicial foreclosure by filing a Lis Pendens or by entry and possession. In some judicial foreclosures the right of redemption can be up to 3 years. In a non-judicial power of sale foreclosure, the lender would send notice to the debtor warning of foreclosure if the default is not cured. The lender forwards all documents to their attorney and accelerates the loan but must still give the debtor 20 days notice before advertising the sale. The notice of sale is published in a local newspaper once a week for 3 weeks, with the first notice appearing 3 weeks prior to the sale. An auctioneer conducts the sale at the property, with the winning bidder receiving a certificate of sale and a deed transferring ownership. There is no redemption period on non-judicial sales.

SOUTH CAROLINA:

Typical timeline for an uncontested foreclosure: 5-6 months

Judicial foreclosure is the only method used in South Carolina. Foreclosure begins with the filing of the Lis Pendens and within 20 days the lender personally serves foreclosure notice to the debtor. The debtor then has 30 days to respond. If the debtor does not resolve the default, notice is then sent to all affected parties and a hearing officer orders the property to be sold. A notice of sale with all relevant information is published in the local newspaper 3 weeks before the sale date and posted at the courthouse. The sheriff conducts the sale, which is held at the courthouse between 11:00 a.m. and 5:00 p.m., with the winning bidder paying 5 percent hand money at the sale and the balance within 30 days. If the lender waives their right to a deficiency judgment, then the debtor has no right of redemption after the sale. If the lender chooses to retain the right of a deficiency judgment, then the sale will continue for 30 additional days for anyone placing an upset bid of at least 5 percent over the previous bid plus a refundable deposit with the property going to the highest bidder. Once the winning bidder pays the balance due, the court confirms the sale and issues a deed.

SOUTH DAKOTA:

Typical timeline for an uncontested foreclosure: 6-12 months

Both judicial and non-judicial foreclosures are available in South Dakota, with judicial foreclosure more popular. If the property is to be foreclosed non-judicially through power of sale, the NOD is issued, with the debtor having 30 days to respond. If there is no response, then a foreclosure sale is scheduled. In judicial foreclosure, a Lis Pendens is filed and if the debtor does not respond in 30 days, the court rules in favor of the lender. A foreclosure sale is then scheduled. The lender publishes the notice of sale in a local newspaper for 4 consecutive weeks at least 21 days prior to the sale and serves notice to the debtor and any other affected parties. Once notification requirements are met, the sheriff conducts the sale between the hours of 9:00 a.m. and 5:00 p.m., with the winning bidder issued a certificate of sale with a deed given, transferring ownership after any redemption period expires. Depending on the situation, the redemption period can be as long as 1 (one) year to as short as 60 days if the property is vacant.

TENNESSEE:

Typical timeline for an uncontested foreclosure: 2-3 months

Even though Tennessee allows both judicial and non-judicial foreclosures, judicial foreclosure is very uncommon. As long as a power of sale clause is in the mortgage or deed of trust, non-judicial foreclosure is used. Once there is a default on the payments, the trustee begins the foreclosure and advertises the property for sale by publishing the notice of sale 3 times in a local newspaper at least 20 days prior to the sale date. While state law does not require notification to the debtor, in most cases the trustee usually does. The debtor may at any time stop the foreclosure by paying the full amount owed plus any fees. The sale is conducted by the trustee at the location specified or at the courthouse between 10:00 a.m. and 4:00 p.m., with the winning bid due in cash. The trustee then transfers ownership. The redemption period is 2 years; however, that can be waived in the original loan documents.

TEXAS:

Typical timeline for an uncontested foreclosure: 3-4 months

Texas allows for both judicial and non-judicial foreclosures. Judicial is used only when there is no power of sale clause in the loan documents, with the lender then having to file a Lis Pendens and proceed through the court process. Before beginning a non-judicial foreclosure, the lender notifies the debtor of a 20-day period to cure the default. Following the 20-day period, the lender sends a second notification letter saying that the full balance of the loan is now due and a foreclosure sale has been scheduled. While Texas does not require notice of the sale to be published in a newspaper, the lender must file a foreclosure notice with the county clerk, post notice of the sale at the courthouse, and send a copy of the notice to the debtor 21 days before the sale. The public foreclosure auction is held on the courthouse steps by public outcry between 10:00 a.m. and 4:00 p.m. on the first Tuesday of each month, with the winning bid due in cash on the same day. Upon payment the trustee transfers ownership. There is no redemption in Texas.

UTAH:

Typical timeline for an uncontested foreclosure: 4-5 months

In Utah both judicial and non-judicial foreclosures are available; however, judicial foreclosures are rare. If a lender pursues a judicial foreclosure, a Lis Pendens is filed and if the court rules that a default has occurred, then it establishes an amount due and sets a time for the debtor to repay. If the debtor fails to do so, then a public sale would happen in the same manner as when a non-judicial foreclosure is scheduled. For a non-judicial foreclosure, the lender records the NOD and sends a copy to the debtor. The debtor then has 90 days to stop the sale by curing the default or the property will be sold at public auction. The notice of sale must be posted in a prominent spot on the property and also at the county records office 20 days prior to the sale. In addition, the sale must be advertised once a week for 3 consecutive weeks in the local newspaper with the last advertisement 10 days but no more than 30 days before the sale. Public auction sales are held at the county courthouse between 9:00 a.m. and 5:00 p.m. with the property selling to the highest bidder. There is no redemption on non-judicial foreclosures. Redemption time for judicial foreclosures is decided by the court.

VERMONT:

Typical timeline for an uncontested foreclosure: 4-9 months

Vermont is a judicial foreclosure state, with settlement happening either in or out of court. Strict foreclosure is one type of judicial foreclosure used. With this type of foreclosure, upon default, the lender formally requisitions the court to terminate the debtor's right to possess the property. If the court rules in favor of the lender, then it takes possession of the property and title reverts to the lender.

The debtor's right of redemption period varies. For post-1968 mortgages it is 6 months; for pre-1968 mortgages it is one year. Another more common foreclosure occurs when the mortgage allows the lender to sell the property in the event of a default, which can happen either in or out of court, depending on the property. For court foreclosures, the court can decide to allow for the sale of the property. If it chooses to be done out of court, then the lender serves notice to the debtor of the default and imminent foreclosure with a time limit of at least 30 days before the notice of sale is published. The debtor may stop the sale at any time on out-of-court foreclosures by curing the default and any fees. If a public auction is held, it is at the property and sold to the highest bidder. In court foreclosures, the court will either confirm the sale or, if denied, order a resale. For out-of-court sales within 90 days after the sale, ownership of the property is transferred to the winning bidder.

VIRGINIA:

Typical timeline for an uncontested foreclosure: 1-2 months

Virginia allows both judicial and non-judicial foreclosures; however, judicial foreclosures are rare. If a judicial foreclosure is pursued, then the lender files suit and a court order is issued spelling out the terms and conditions of the sale. Once the court pronounces the foreclosure, the sale is held and the property is auctioned. For non-judicial sales, the trustee uses the power of sale clause to affect foreclosure without going through the courts. Before scheduling the sale, the lender sends the NOD to the debtor advising they have 30 days to cure the default and stop the sale. Once the sale has been scheduled, there are strict rules for notice of sale advertising based on the state law and the deed of trust. The newspaper where the notice of sale is advertised in requires court approval to guarantee it has adequate circulation for the area. If the deed of trust provides for advertising, then the notice of sale ad must be published for a minimum of once a day for 3 days in the newspaper. If there is no provision for advertising, then the notice of sale shall be published once a week for 4 weeks. However if the property is located near a city, advertising on 5 different days is sufficient. The debtor must receive a copy of the notice of sale at least 14 days prior to the sale. The sale must be held no less than 8 days after the first ad and no greater than 30 days after the last ad. The sale is held at the courthouse by the trustee between 9 a.m. and 5 p.m. Written, single price bids may be submitted to the trustee to be read aloud at the sale along with traditional bidding. The winning bidder pays a 10 percent deposit at sale and upon full payment a deed is given to the buyer. Depending on circumstances, in a judicial foreclosure only the court may grant redemption rights, otherwise there are none.

WASHINGTON:

Typical timeline for an uncontested foreclosure: 4-6 months

Washington uses both judicial and non-judicial foreclosures, with non-judicial more common. For judicial foreclosure, once the lender files suit there is a 30-day lead time for a court ruling. If the court rules against the debtor, then a sheriff sale is scheduled about 2 months following the ruling. If a non-judicial foreclosure is being used, the lender would send or deliver an NOD to the debtor. The debtor then has 30 days to respond before scheduling the property for auction. Up to 11 days prior to the sale the debtor can stop the sale by paying the past due amount plus any fees. If the debtor does not cure the default within the 30-day period following receipt of the NOD, the lender then records a notice of sale at least 90 days prior to the sale date. The county recorder then sends a copy to the debtor and to any affected parties and posts notice at the property. The notice of sale is also published in the local newspaper twice, once between the 32nd and 28th days before the sale and once between the 11th and 7th days before the sale. The sale must be held within 190 days after the date of the default and can be extended by 120 days at the discretion of the trustee. Public auction sales are held on Fridays between 9 a.m. and 4 p.m.

WASHINGTON DC:

Typical timeline for an uncontested foreclosure: 1-2 months

Non-judicial is the foreclosure method used in Washington DC. The lender using the power of sale will notify the borrower that the loan is in default. The debtor can reinstate the loan and stop the sale up to 5 days prior to the sale by paying the defaulted amount plus fees. This can happen only once in a given year. If the debtor fails to cure the default, then the lender mails the notice of sale to the debtor, the mayor or the mayor's representative, and to any other affected parties at least 30 days before the sale date. Unless specified otherwise in the mortgage or deed of trust, the sale is usually advertised in a major Washington DC newspaper 5 times before the sale. Likewise, if there is no specific location indicated for the sale, then it usually is held at the office of the licensed auctioneer who is conducting it and sold to the highest bidder. There is no redemption period after the sale.

WEST VIRGINIA:

Typical timeline for an uncontested foreclosure: 2-4 months

Although West Virginia allows both judicial and non-judicial foreclosure sales, judicial foreclosures are very rarely used. In a non-judicial deed of trust foreclosure, the lender initially notifies the borrower of the default and possible foreclosure, explaining that to stop the foreclosure they need to cure the default. If the debtor does not cure the default, the lender then schedules a foreclosure sale. The notice of sale is sent to the debtor and to all affected parties as well as posted on the courthouse door, at the property, and at two other public places at least 20 days prior to the sale date. Additionally, the notice of sale is advertised in a local newspaper once a week for 2 weeks unless other arrangements are called for in the deed of trust. Auction sales are open to the public and held at the time and place specified in the foreclosure notice, and are sold to the highest bidder with payment of one-third in cash due at the sale with a trustee's deed recorded within 30 days of the sale. There is no redemption period after the sale.

WISCONSIN:

Typical timeline for an uncontested foreclosure: 9-10 months

Both judicial and non-judicial foreclosures are practiced in Wisconsin, with judicial being more common. If there is a power of sale clause in the mortgage, then a non-judicial foreclosure is used based upon terms contained in the mortgage. If there is no power of sale, then judicial foreclosure will be sought. Judicial begins with the lender filing a Lis Pendens in court and the lender delivering notice of the filing to the debtor as well as to other affected parties. Once the lender obtains a judgment of the foreclosure, the debtor has, depending on the property and mortgage terms, a reinstatement period of from 6 to 12 months or, if the property is abandoned, 2 months to cure the default. The notice of sale must be advertised once a week for 6 consecutive weeks in a local newspaper, and while this can be done during the reinstatement period, the first time it is advertised must be at least 10 months after the court's ruling date. Also, the notice of sale must be hand delivered to the debtor or, if unable to locate them, then posted at a conspicuous spot on the property. If agreed to, the affected parties can decide on an earlier date. The sale is held at the location specified in the notice and is usually conducted by the sheriff between the hours of 9 a.m. and sunset, with the winning bidder responsible for 10 percent hand money at sale. Full payment is due 10 days following, whereupon the clerk confirms the sale and the deed is transferred. Once the sale is confirmed, there is no redemption period. If the property sells for less than the default amount plus costs, then it is not confirmed and the debtor has a 1 (one) year redemption period to pay the highest bid received at the sale plus any costs to redeem and may retain possession during that period.

WYOMING:

Typical timeline for an uncontested foreclosure: 2-4 months

Wyoming allows both non-judicial and judicial foreclosure sales, with non-judicial used more often. If there is no power of sale clause in the mortgage, a judicial foreclosure will be used. For judicial foreclosure, the lender files necessary papers and once the court approves the foreclosure a sale date is scheduled. For non-judicial foreclosures, terms contained in the mortgage or deed of trust dictate the procedure for foreclosure. Notice of intent is served to the debtor 10 days before the first publication of the notice of sale. The notice of sale is advertised in a local newspaper once a week for 4 subsequent weeks. Auction sales by public outcry are held at the front door of the county courthouse by the sheriff or deputy sheriff between 10 a.m. and 5 p.m. and sold to the highest bidder, who then receives a certificate of sale. The borrower has a 90-day redemption period after the sale to pay the winning bid price from the auction plus 10 percent interest and any other fees or taxes due. If the borrower does not redeem in the 90 days, then ownership transfers to the winning bidder.

GLOSSARY OF COMMON FORECLOSURE TERMS

Auction: The process conducted by an auctioneer whereby property is sold to the highest bidder.

Bankruptcy: An action with a specific chapter (7, 11, or13) filed in a federal bankruptcy court that effectively stops foreclosure proceedings.

Bid: The amount that is pledged to purchase a property at a foreclosure auction.

Certificate of Sale: Document that is given to the winning bidder at a foreclosure sale, describing their rights to the property upon the end of the previous owner's redemption period.

Clear Title: Title to a property that has no defects. Also referred to as clean title.

Deficiency: Amount of money the borrower still owes the creditor, since the sale of their property at foreclosure did not generate enough funds to pay off the loan.

Deficiency Judgment: A court order stating that the borrower still owes money to the creditor and allowing the creditor to recover the balance due.

Deed: Document that is signed and delivered conveying title and ownership to real property.

Deed of Trust: Used in many states instead of a mortgage as the security instrument to purchase a property. Whereas a mortgage involves two parties, the borrower and the lender, a deed of trust involves three: the borrower, the lender, and the trustee, who holds legal title to the property until paid in full.

Default: Occurs when the borrower fails to make payments in accordance with the terms of the original loan documents.

Divest: A giving up of one's right or claim to a property or monies owed against a property.

Equity: Value the owner has in a property less all outstanding debt owed against it.

Fair Market Value: What a property is worth on the open market.

FHA: Federal Housing Administration. An agency within the U.S Department of Housing and Urban Development that administers many types of loans and loan guarantee programs to make housing more affordable.

Hard Money: Term for a source of higher cost funds generally aimed at individuals who cannot acquire them from standard or traditional sources.

Foreclosure Sale: The forced public sale of a property to satisfy a foreclosure of the loan secured by that property.

Judicial Foreclosure: A foreclosure ordered by the courts.

Legal Description: A method of formally describing and identifying a property on government surveys and maps.

Lien: A charge put against property as security for the payment of a debt.

Lis Pendens: Latin for "suit pending." A recorded notice of the filing of a law suit in the public records.

Loss Mitigation: A department within a lender that handles delinquent loans.

Mortgage: A written document that a borrower gives as a security for repayment of a loan.

Non-Judicial Foreclosure: A foreclosure that does not go through the courts.

Notice of Default: Or NOD as it is known, serves notice that the borrower has missed their scheduled loan payments and is required by law to initiate a non-judicial foreclosure involving the sale of a property. The NOD is recorded in the public records.

Notice of Sale: Notice that gives specific information about the defaulted loan and the proceedings to take place. The notice is recorded in the county where the default has occurred and is advertised as required by law or as stated in the loan documents.

Power of Sale: A clause in a deed of trust or mortgage that gives the lender or trustee the right to sell the property if the borrower defaults.

REO: Stands for Real Estate Owned. A department within the lender where property that is acquired by foreclosure is held. Also applies to a type of realtor that markets and sells said properties for the lenders.

Right of Redemption: A borrower's right to redeem their property due to loss from foreclosure.

Sheriff Deed: The type of deed issued to the purchaser of a property at sheriff sale.

Short Sale: A process whereby the lender agrees to accept a shortage, or less than the full amount due for a defaulted loan thereby avoiding the time and expense of foreclosure. This allows the debtor to pay off the property for less than what would have been otherwise owed.

Title: The evidence (deed) that the owner of a property is in rightful possession of it.

Trustee: A neutral third party who holds legal title to a property for the lender until the debt is repaid. If the borrower defaults on the loan the trustee auctions the property at a foreclosure sale.

Trustee Deed: The type of deed issued to the purchaser of a property at a trustee auction.

Sample Sheriff Sale Terms & Conditions For Selected Counties

　　While the sample sale terms and conditions illustrated are accurate as of this writing, they can and do change and are to be considered as examples only. It is recommended if you plan to buy in any of the counties listed, you re-check with the local sheriffs department for their most up to date terms and conditions.

Dane County, Wisconsin

Dane County Sheriff's Office
Madison, Wisconsin

○ Conditions of
Sale

FORECLOSURE SALES

GENERAL INFORMATION

Are you looking for information on Sheriff's Foreclosure Sales? We don't post the notices here, but you can try searching the notices posted at madison.com or in one of the Madison newspapers. All foreclosure sales are advertised in the classified section for 6 weeks prior to the sale. Search the Classifieds at Madison.com

Sales are conducted Tuesdays at 10:00 a.m. in Room 2002, Public Safety Building, 115 West Doty Street, Madison, WI.

The Sheriff is a ministerial officer of the Court and is without power to make any terms except those authorized and prescribed by the Court. The Sheriff sells only the judgment debtor's title. If there is no title, the purchaser acquires none. The rule of Caveat Emptor (let the buyer beware) is fully applicable to sales made under execution.

Foreclosure sales are for real property only. The Sheriff's Office does not know whether or not persons occupy the property. Further, we cannot give permission for any prospective bidders to enter and inspect any structure that may be located on the property to be sold.

Properties sold at auction by the Sheriff's Office are generally advertised in The Wisconsin State Journal and Capital Times. Notices appear once for each of the six weeks prior to the date of sale.

In addition to newspaper advertising, written notice describing the real estate to be sold will be posted in three public places in the town or municipality where the real estate is to be sold at least three weeks prior to the date of the sale and also in three public places of the town or municipality where the real estate is situated if it is not in the City of Madison.

The Sheriff's Office does not have a list of properties for general distribution. Persons interested in following up on these properties must make their own lists by checking the legal advertisements in the newspapers or the postings.

Sales of property are "open-type" auction sales (no sealed bids). A minimum bid is normally bid in the first round by the Plaintiff.

The successful bidder, upon full payment of the bid, will receive a Sheriff's Deed. This deed may not give clear title to the property. In order to obtain a clear title one must satisfy all superior liens and encumbrances. If a purchaser does not complete the sale, he can be held liable for his deposit, and for all losses and expenses.

If you are interested in a particular piece of property, we recommend a title search before you actually bid.

Private firms conduct title searches. Their telephone numbers may be found in the

Dane County, Wisconsin page 2

yellow pages of the telephone directory. A fee is charged.

Should you have a legal question, we recommend you consult an attorney.

If the property you purchase is occupied, it is your responsibility to have the occupants removed.

In most cases the owner can redeem the property, even after the sale, for a period of 10 calendar days from the date of sale. By law the owner can declare bankruptcy within that same period.

CONDITIONS OF SALE

- Each property is sold subject to restrictions of record which are unknown to the Sheriff and subject to any unpaid taxes and water bills or assessments, and such state of facts as an accurate survey and physical inspection of the premises may reveal.
- The highest bidder at the sale shall be the Purchaser. If any dispute arises as to who may be the highest bidder, the property will be resold.
- If you are the successful bidder on a property, you are required to post a deposit of 10% of the total bid price in cash, certified check, or money order immediately after the close of that sale. **Certified checks MUST be made payable to: Dane County Clerk of Courts.** NO COMPANY, AGENCY OR PERSONAL CHECKS WILL BE ACCEPTED.
- The PURCHASER must pay recording fees and Real Estate Transfer Fees.

SOME ADDITIONAL CONDITIONS OF SALE ARE LISTED BELOW THAT MAY BE ANNOUNCED AT THE TIME OF SALE. THIS IS NOT A COMPLETE LIST AND IS PROVIDED AS INFORMATION ONLY.

- Subject to any unpaid municipal liens, unpaid taxes and assessments.
- Subject to such facts as an accurate survey and physical inspection of the premises will disclose.
- Subject to restrictions, reversions, reservations, easements and right of way of record, if any.
- Subject to rights of tenants and occupants, if any.
- Subject to Federal, State, County and Municipal ordinances, statutes and regulations, including zoning ordinances.
- Sold in an "as is" condition.
- Subject to the right of the plaintiff to apply to the Court for surplus moneys for sums advanced, with interest thereon since the entry of final judgment, additional advances for taxes and other items have been made by plaintiff. (Amount to be announced.)
- The right of redemption of the United States of America as a result of Federal Liens.
- If the subject premises is a Condominium, the sale is subject to any unpaid assessments, which may be a lien on the premises, and subject to all applicable provisions of the Master Deed and by-laws of Condominium Association.

There are times when the sale of property is not completed on the date advertised because of adjournments, settlements or bankruptcies. We recommend you call the Sheriff's Office, Civil Process Section on the scheduled date of the sale to determine the status of the sale.

Greene County, Pennsylvania

Greene County Sheriff's Office

10 E. High Street, Room 106
Courthouse
Waynesburg, PA 15370
Phones: 724-627-7207
724-852-5213
724-852-5218

Fax: 724-852-8318

Office Hours:
8:00 am – 4:30 pm

TERMS AND CONDITIONS OF SHERIFF'S SALE

Sheriff's Sales are held in the Greene County Courthouse, Waynesburg, Pennsylvania, at 10:00 A.M. on their scheduled dates of sale.

If an individual would like to bid on a property, they must appear in person on the date and time of the sale. The amount of the debt on individual properties can be obtained from the Real Estate Department in the Sheriff's Office.

All sales are posted in the Sheriff's Office at least thirty (30) days prior to the day of the sale. Sheriff's Sales are published for three consecutive weeks in the Thursday edition of the Observer Reporter and three consecutive weeks on Fridays in the Greene County Messenger. The same sales are not advertised in both newspapers. The sheriff's sales are published by the Greene County Bar Association in their legal journal, The Greene Reports.

The successful bidder must immediately pay ten (10) percent of the bid price or sheriff's costs, whichever is higher, by a certified check or cash. The balance of the bid price is payable twenty (20) days from the date of sale, and a deed will be recorded no earlier than thirty (30) days from the date of sale. Sheriff's poundage will be added to the purchase price and is paid by the purchaser. Sheriff's poundage is 2% of the bid price up to $100,000.00 and .05% of any amount above $100,000.00.

The opening bid for all sales will be the amount of taxes, municipal liens and costs. If you have any further questions, please contact the Sheriff's Office Real Estate Department at 724-852-5218.

Allen County, Ohio

Allen County
Sheriff's Office

Sheriff's Office Divisions

HOME

LINKS

REPORT A CRIME

CONTACT US

Sheriff's Real Estate Sales

The Sheriff's Sale Section is charged with the responsibility of appraising, advertising and selling foreclosure properties. This sale can be court ordered for either a bank foreclosure or a tax delinquency. After the sale, if necessary, this section will also enforce a Writ of Possession.

Check the list of properties for sale for the exact sale date. The list is updated weekly. Click here to view the list.

Sales are normally advertised in the legal section of the classified ads in the Sunday edition of the Lima News (http://www.limanews.com). The ads run once per week for a minimum of three consecutive weeks prior to the date of sale.

The Sheriff's Office does not mail a list of properties or information about purchasing foreclosed property.

The property is not available for tour or inspection. The buyer gets the property "as is," caveat emptor (let the buyer beware). The Sheriff's Office does not have information on liens or taxes.
- Real estate tax information can be found on the Allen County Treasurer's website.
- You can view the entire case file by going to the Allen County Clerk of Court's website.
- Property description information can be found on the Allen County Auditor's website.

Terms of Sale

- An initial deposit of 10% of the successful bid is due at the Sheriff's Office – Civil Division, by 4:00pm on the day of the sale. The balance of the amount bid is due and payable upon confirmation of sale and delivery of deed. All payments are payable in cash, certified check or bank money order only. NO PERSONAL CHECKS, COMPANY CHECKS, LETTERS OF CREDIT, CREDIT CARDS OR DEBIT CARDS ACCEPTED. Failure to pay for a property bid at the auction will result in contempt of court charges being filed against the purchaser.

- The only Real Estate taxes, which shall be paid from the proceeds of the sale of the subject real property, are those which are due and payable as of the date of the sale and are not pro-rated. Notice is given that such taxes and special

Allen County, Ohio page 2

assessments, or installments of special assessments, and any other assessments, which are not legally due and payable according to the law at the confirmation of sale shall remain a first and best lien on the parcels and the purchaser shall taken such premises subject to all such taxes and assessments. Any delinquent water and sewer bills may be the responsibility of the purchaser.

- The successful bidder must present proper identification at the time their bid is accepted by the officer in charge of the sale.

- All property sold at Sheriff's sale is sold on an "as is" basis and there is no warranty or guarantee. The Allen County Sheriff's Office is not responsible to determine and makes no representations regarding whether utility bills, such as water, gas, electric, sewer, etc. are paid or whether the property is free of liens. The Allen County Sheriff's Office and the appraisers make no representations, assume no responsibility and are not liable, for any condition of the property including any environmental or hazardous conditions that may exist within, under, around or near the subject property. The appraisal may or may not have been an inside inspection of the property.

All Sales Are Classified as"CAVEAT EMPTOR" (buyer beware)
Individuals who are attending a Sheriff's sale for the first time with the intent to purchase a property are advised top proceed with extreme caution. The law in Ohio relative to real estate is "caveat emptor" which means "buyer beware". It is expected that all purchasers at the sale have contacted their own real estate attorney and title company prior to the sale.

ENTERING THE PROPERTY WITHOUT THE PERMISSION OF THE OWNER OR OCCUPANTS IS A VIOLATION OF OHIO REVISED CODE SECTION 2911.21, CRIMINAL TRESPASSING, PUNISHABLE UP TO 30 DAYS IN JAIL AND $250.00 FINE.
Note: Property still belongs to the original owner even though the order of sale has been issued from the court. If you purchase a property at sheriff's sale, and have paid your deposit, it still belongs to the original owner until the Common Pleas Judge has signed the confirmation of sale. This process can take up to 30 days or more. This is hard for people to understand, and can be very risky in terms of money and other concerns. If you have any questions regarding this, you should consult your personal attorney before any real estate purchase from a sheriff sale. We cannot advise you of any legal questions you may have.

The successful bidder for the purchase of the real estate being sold will have approximately 30 days from the date of sale to obtain an examination of title to the real estate at their expense, if they desire one. Should such examination disclose the title to be unmarketable by reason of any defect in the court proceedings or the existence of any outstanding interest rendering the title unmarketable, the purchaser may, within the 30 day period, file a written motion requesting that the sale be set aside. If the court finds that the title is unmarketable, the court will refuse to confirm the sale or fix a reasonable time, not to exceed 90 days, within which the defect of title may be corrected.

Any questions about the utilities should be directed to the company or the municipality that provides the service.

Whatcom County, Washington State

Sheriff's Office

REAL PROPERTY

Sheriff's sales of real property are held on Friday mornings at 9:30 a.m. in the rotunda (main entrance) area of the Whatcom County Courthouse. If the time set for sale is other than 9:30 a.m., it will not be conducted by the Sheriff and you should contact your information source for questions. Other persons also conduct real property sales in this manner, and they may take place at the same time(s) in the lobby of the Whatcom County Courthouse.

Sheriff's Sales are "judicial foreclosures" and the order to sell comes from the Superior Court Clerk. We are selling only the judgment debtor's interest in the real estate. It is subject to all existing liens and encumbrances. To find out any lien information, you may need to do a title search though a company authorized to do this. We have limited information about the sale property since we do not need to know any information other than the address and legal description to conduct our sales. It is not possible for potential purchasers to view the interior of the structure prior to the sale.

The property sold may have a redemption period from eight months to one year. Redemption means that the owner may pay back the amount bid at the sale plus interest, taxes, etc. in order to "redeem" his property and become the owner again. If you have legal questions about this procedure, you should contact your attorney for direction, or read the Revised Code of the State of Washington pertaining to Redemption.

The sales of real property conducted by the Sheriff are published in one of three newspapers in Whatcom County, The Bellingham Herald, The Lynden Tribune or the Record Journal. It is the choice of the judgment creditor as to which newspaper they wish to use for publication. The Sheriff's Notice of Sale will be published once a week for four consecutive weeks prior to any sale.

If you bid at the sale, you must provide cash or cashier's check made payable to the Superior Court Clerk's Office issuing the Writ of Execution or Order of Sale by 2:00 p.m. that day or the sale will go to the next highest bidder. **NO EXCEPTIONS**. There is usually an opening bid from the judgment creditor; however this figure is not available until a day or two before the sale date.

Oklahoma County, Oklahoma

Oklahoma County Sheriff's Office

SHERIFF JOHN WHETSEL ★ "Serving the Citizens of Oklahoma County"

| | | | | | |

Oklahoma County Sheriff's Office -- Sheriff Sales

The Oklahoma County Sheriff's Foreclosure Sale is published one time each month, for two consecutive weeks, at least thirty days prior to date of sale. The foreclosed properties are published in area newspapers in which the property is located.

The Sheriff's Foreclosure Sales are located in the Oklahoma County Courthouse Annex Building at 320 Robert S. Kerr, Room 513, and start promptly at 2:00 p.m. every other Thursday.

To purchase a property you must meet the following requirements:

• Minimum bid must be at least two-thirds of the appraised price of the property.
• Down payment of at least 10 percent of the purchase price is due within 24 hours of sale. The remaining 90% of the purchase price is due within 9 days of the sale date, before the confirmation of sale hearing.

Certified funds are required, made payable to   Court Clerk. Any sale is subject to cancellation by the plaintiff.

Kent County, Delaware

NAVIGATION

Kent County Sheriff Department

THERE ARE THREE TYPES OF SHERIFF SALES:

1. TAX SALES.................PROPERTIES ARE BEING SOLD FOR NONPAYMENT OF COUNTY TAXES AND OR COUNTY WATER & SEWER FEES FOR NO LESS THAN A TWO YEAR PERIOD. THESE SALES ARE HELD APPROXIMATELY EVERY THREE MONTHS.

2. CITY OR TOWN TAX SALES.............PROPERTIES ARE BEING SOLD FOR NON- PAYMENT OF TOWN TAXES. ALL PROPERTIES ARE LOCATED WITHIN A TOWN OR CITY LIMITS AND TAXES HAVE NOT BEEN PAID FOR NO LESS THAN A TWO YEAR PERIOD.

PLEASE DO YOUR OWN LEG WORK, AS TO RESEARCHING THE PROPERTY TO MAKE SURE THERE ARE NO HIDDEN LIENS THAT YOU WOULD BE RESPONSIBLE FOR IF YOU ARE THE SUCCESSFUL BIDDER

THESE SALES ARE VERBAL BIDDING, PROPERTY GOING TO THE HIGHEST BIDDER.
NO MATTER WHAT IS OWED IN TAXES, THE PROPERTY IS GOING TO THE HIGHEST BIDDER.
THE FULL AMOUNT OF THE BID PRICE IS DUE DAY OF THE SALE. CASH, CERTIFIED CHECK AND CASHIER'S CHECK IS THE ONLY FORM OF PAYMENT THAT WILL BE ACCEPTED. YOU WILL BE GIVEN A COUPLE OF HOURS TO GO TO THE BANK TO SECURE FUNDS. THE ORIGINAL OWNER OF THE PROPERTY HAS APPROXIMATELY 60 DAYS TO PAY THEIR DELINQUENT TAXES PLUS 15% OF THE HIGHEST BID TO REDEEM THEIR PROPERTY. IF FOR SOME REASON THE SALE IS OVERTURNED BY THE COURT, THE HIGHEST BIDDER WILL ONLY RECEIVE BACK THEIR BID, BUT NO 15%. WITHIN THIS 60 DAY PERIOD, YOU WILL ONLY HEAR FROM THIS OFFICE IF THE PROPERTY IS REDEEMED OR IF THE SALE HAS BEEN OVERTURNED BY THE COURT. IF YOU DO NOT HEAR FROM THIS OFFICE, PROCEED TO YOUR ATTORNEY'S OFFICE TO HAVE YOUR DEED PREPARED. YOUR DEED WILL BE SENT OVER TO THIS OFFICE FOR THE SHERIFF'S SIGNATURE. AT THIS TIME A CHECK WILL BE MADE OUT FOR OUR 1 1/2% OF THE TRANSFER FEE.
THE SIGNED DEED AND CHECKS WILL BE RETURNED TO YOUR ATTORNEY FOR RECORDING.

3. MORTGAGE FORECLOSURES:.......................MORTGAGE FORECLOSURES ARE USUALLY HELD THE FIRST TUESDAY OR THURSDAY OF EVERY MONTH. PROPERTIES ARE BEING SOLD FOR NONPAYMENT OF MORTGAGE. THIS SALE IS ALSO VERBAL BIDDING. PROPERTY GOING TO THE HIGHEST BIDDER. THE ATTORNEY FOR THE MORTGAGE COMPANY GIVES THE OPENING BID AND THE BIDDING STARTS FROM THERE. PRIOR TO THE SALE, WE HAVE NO IDEA WHERE THE BIDDING IS GOING TO START OR STOP. THERE IS NO REDEMPTION PERIOD FOR THIS TYPE OF SALE. IF YOU ARE THE SUCCESSFUL BIDDER, WE REQUIRE 20% OF YOUR BID PRICE THAT DAY. PAYMENT AGAIN IS CASH, CASHIER OR CERTIFIED CHECK. YOU WILL BE GIVEN A COUPLE OF HOURS TO GO TO THE BANK TO SECURE FUNDS. THE BALANCE OF YOUR BID IS DUE IN APPROXIMATELY 30 DAYS, IN THE SAME TYPE OF FORM. AFTER THE SALE IS CONFIRMED BY SUPERIOR COURT, YOU THEN GO TO YOUR ATTORNEY TO HAVE A DEED DRAWN UP. THE DEED IS SENT TO THE SHERIFF'S OFFICE TO BE SIGNED BY THE SHERIFF, AT WHICH TIME A CHECK IS CUT FOR 1 1/2% OF THE TRANSFER FEE. THE DEED ALONG WITH THE CHECK

Kent County, Delaware page 2

FOR THE TRANSFER FEE IS RETURNED TO YOUR ATTORNEY TO BE RECORDED. IF FOR SOME REASON THE SALE IS NOT CONFIRMED BY THE COURT, YOU WILL BE NOTIFIED.

IT IS VERY IMPORTANT FOR YOU, THE BUYER, TO RESEARCH THESE PROPERTIES AS TO WHETHER THERE ARE ANY OTHER MORTGAGES OR LIENS AGAINST THE PROPERTY THAT YOU COULD BE RESPONSIBLE FOR IF YOU ARE THE SUCCESSFUL BIDDER. THIS OFFICE DOES NOT GUARANTEE CLEAR TITLES.....
RESEARCH CAN BE DONE AT THE RECORDER OF DEEDS OFFICE, WHICH IS LOCATED IN THE O'BRIEN BUILDING ON FEDERAL STREET, DOVER, ALSO AT THE PROTHONOTARY'S OFFICE, WHICH IS LOCATED IN THE COURTHOUSE ON THE GREEN.

IF YOU PAY YOUR 20% ON THE DAY OF SALE, AND DO NOT COME BACK WITH THE BALANCE OF THE MONIES ON THE ASSIGNED DATE, YOU WILL FORFEIT YOUR 20% DOWN PAYMENT. IF YOU ARE THE SUCCESSFUL BIDDER AND YOU DO NOT COME BACK WITH THE 20% DOWN PAYMENT, OR YOU FOR SOME REASON CHANGE YOUR MIND ABOUT PURCHASING THE PROPERTY, YOU WILL BE BARRED FROM ALL FUTURE SALES.

ALL SALES ARE ADVERTISED IN THE DOVER POST AND THE DELAWARE STATE NEWS ON WEDNESDAYS. WE HAVE SALE PACKETS IN THIS OFFICE FOR THE PUBLIC TO COME BY AND PICK UP. THERE IS ALSO A COUNTY WEB SITE, WHERE SALES ARE LISTED. http://www.co.kent.de.us/sheriff_na.htm

AS OF OCTOBER 1, 2003, A $2,000 CERTIFIED CHECK IS REQUIRED AT THE TIME YOUR WINNING BID IS ACCEPTED. THE BALANCE OF YOUR 20% MAY BE PAID WITH A PERSONAL CHECK.

210 •

Tippecanoe County, Indiana

Guidelines for the Sale

These sales are the result of lending institution foreclosures and interested individuals are not permitted to enter the pending sale residences to view the interiors of the properties. The Sheriff's Office cannot act as Realtor and does not have detailed property descriptions available (with the exception of legal description listed in the Notice of Sale.)

It is the responsibility of the potential buyer to FULLY research any outstanding taxes, liens and title searches. **It is also the responsibility of the buyer to have the FULL AMOUNT OF PAYMENT (BID) secured prior to placing their bid. The Sheriff's Office cannot allow additional time after the sale in order to secure a loan for the bid amount. All bids are due and payable the day of the Sheriff Sale.**

Any costs for the sale and any county assessed taxes outstanding will be deducted from the total bid amount and will be disbursed by the Sheriff's Office. Bid money must be submitted in the form of a certified cashiers check by 2:00 on the day of the sale. No personal checks will be accepted.

Individual sale notices are posted on the Information Board located at the Clerks office, 2nd floor of the Courthouse and advertised in the Journal & Courier Legal section. Sales are published for a period of three (3) consecutive weeks beginning approximately seven weeks prior to the sale.

In addition to these properties being advertised in the newspaper, listing are posted at various locations within the township where property is located. These listings are posted within 30 days of the sale.

Notification & Addresses

The Sheriff does not warrant the accuracy of the street address published on the Notice of Sheriff's Sale. All properties are sold by the Sheriff's Office "as is" and no express or implied warranties are to be construed to be given by the Sheriff's Office. All bids are final and irrevocable.

Notices are served to the Defendant(s) by personal or copy service and by mail and to the Attorney for the Plaintiff. The persons being served are listed on the Notice of Sale.

Most individuals residing in these properties have moved by the day of the sale, however, it is the responsibility of the purchasing party to file proper eviction papers with the Courts if the residents have not vacated the property.

The Treasurer's office can advise you if there are any taxes owed currently on the property. These taxes may include real estate taxes, sewer liens, weed liens, ditch assessments and unsafe building liens.

The Assessor's office can give you assessment information concerning lot size, square footage, room sizes, building materials, past ownership, yearly taxes due and etc.

The Recorder's Office and the County Clerk's Office may also have a record of any other liens against the property. A realtor may be able to advise if the property has been listed before and can give you a profile of the home if it has been listed for sale in the past.

The searches are the responsibility of the interested purchasing parties. All buyers should be aware that any Federal or State liens become the responsibility of the new purchaser. While the Sheriff's sale and issuance of Sheriff's deed to the purchaser will eliminate or clear claims of lien holders specifically named in the complaint

against the original mortgage holder, the IRS has 120 days from the date of the sale to redeem the property if they hold interest in it.

Sale Day and Afterwards

All bids must be submitted in person. Mailed or faxed bids are not accepted. Bidding begins at 10:00 a.m. Anyone can bid during oral bidding.

All properties must be paid in full by 2:00 p.m. on the day of the sale.

The Sheriff's Office does not act as a Realtor and cannot provide keys for the purchased properties. It is the responsibility of the purchaser to make the necessary entry provisions.

You can expect to receive a Sheriff's Deed within a few weeks of the sale. It is your responsibility to file this paperwork with the appropriate agencies and offices. If you have questions concerning these legal documents, please consult an attorney for clarifications and filing procedures.

Union County, New Jersey

UNION COUNTY
SHERIFF'S OFFICE

Sheriff's Sales Information

THE SHERIFF IS AN OFFICER OF THE COURT. HE CONDUCTS OR ADJOURNS SALES IN ACCORDANCE WITH STATE STATUTES OR COURT RULES.

IT IS RECOMMENDED THAT YOU TALK TO AN ATTORNEY BEFORE BIDDING ON PROPERTIES AT THE SHERIFF'S FORECLOSURE SALE.

Sales in foreclosure are for real property only, not structures. We cannot authorize persons to enter or inspect any property that may be offered for sale. The rule of caveat emptor (let the buyer beware) is applicable to all foreclosure sales.

All property to be sold at an auction is advertised in the "Star Ledger" four Monday's prior to the sale. Property is also advertised in a paper serving the sale community.

In addition to this advertising, notices of sales are also posted at the sheriff's business office located at the Union County Administration Building, and on the property to be sold.

The Sheriff's Office also offers printed listings of sale properties at a cost of $1.00 a page. Persons interested in properties may copy from the master list, which is available at our business office, or they should save advertisements printed in the "Star Ledger" or local newspapers.

We recommend calling the sheriff's foreclosure unit the late morning of the sale at 908-527-4478 or 527-4479 to determine if the sale will be held. Adjournments, settlements or bankruptcies may cause a sale to be canceled. This may occur at any time prior to the sale. In most cases, property will not be re-advertised. To speed your inquiry, refer to the "ch" number that appears in the legal notice or newspaper advertisement.

Sheriffs' sales of property are open type auction sales (sealed or mailed bids are not accepted). The plaintiff opens with a bid of $100.00 and all subsequent bids are in multiples of at least $100.00. Property is sold to the highest bidder.

The successful bidder must post a deposit of at least 20% of the total bid price immediately at the close of the sales. The balance, and a deed preparation cost of $35.00, is due within 30 days from the date of the sale. **Interest will accrue until the balance is paid.**

If the balance is not paid within 30 days, the buyer may lose his or her deposit. Additional time is **not** granted to the buyer to obtain a mortgage.

The purchaser will receive a sheriff's deed when full payment of the purchase price is received by the sheriff's office. This deed may not give clear title to the property. In order to obtain clear title, all liens, taxes or

Union County, New Jersey page 2

encumbrances must be satisfied. We recommend a title search before you bid on sale property.

Title searches are conducted by private firms. They may be found in the yellow pages of the telephone directory. They charge a fee for title searches.

To determine how much will be needed as a deposit; you must determine how much you intend to bid for the sale property. A certified check for 20% of the highest amount you intend to bid should be made payable to yourself. If you were the successful highest bidder, you would then endorse the check to "Sheriff of Union County."

In most cases, the property can be redeemed by the former owner within ten days of the sale. In some cases, the owner can also declare bankruptcy within this same time period. If this is done, the sale is put on hold until the court makes its decision.

Sheriffs' foreclosure sales are held every Wednesday at 2:00pm at the Union County Sheriff's Office, Union County Administration Building, Elizabethtown Plaza, Elizabeth, NJ.

All persons bidding on property must identify themselves when entering a bid.

The total amount due will not be given at the sale. You must obtain this information prior to the sale.

If the property is occupied, it will be your responsibility to have any occupants *legally* removed.

Eviction proceedings are only done by Superior Court order. There is a fee for this order and a fee for the sheriff to evict persons from property purchased at a sheriff's sale.

New Orleans, Louisiana

Office of the Civil Sheriff
Real Estate

Where is the Real Estate auction held?
In the lobby of the Civil District Courthouse located at 421 Loyola Avenue at Poydras Street.

When is the auction held?
Every Thursday at noon unless otherwise advertised. Each property and its auction date is advertised in the Times Picayune, the official newspaper of record, thirty (30) days before the auction and again on Monday, the week of the auction. Properties are also advertised in a second publication like The Louisiana Weekly newspaper to run concurrently with those ads run in the Times Picayune. Upcoming lists of properties for sale are available in the Real Estate Division of the Sheriffs Office three (3) weeks prior to the actual auction of a piece of property and on this website under the heading, "Real Estate Sales Lists."

How many days does it take before a foreclosed property goes to auction?
It takes a minimum of forty-five (45) days from receipt of the writ to advertisement for the auction. During this time the foreclosure may be stopped for reasons such as bankruptcy or payment of the balance owed.

What are the usual costs of foreclosure?
Advertising, appraisals, mortgage, conveyance and tax certificates, curators fees, deed, docket and a three (3) percent sales commission on the sales price to the Office of the Civil Sheriff. These costs and fees are not paid by a successful bidder. A successful bidder only pays the amount of his or her bid.

What is the minimum opening bid?
There are two categories for the minimum opening bid:
1. When the sale is with appraisal the bid must open at two thirds (2/3) of the appraisal and must satisfy any superior claims. If 2/3 of the appraisal results in an opening bid insufficient to cover the costs and commission, then the opening bid will be raised to reflect those expenses.
2. When the sale is "without" appraisal the bid must cover any superior claims plus the costs and commission. Usually this is a relatively low amount between two and five thousand dollars.

Can I enter the property before I bid?
No access is allowed prior to the auction. The sale is not officially

completed until the entire purchase price is paid in full.. Therefore it is only then that access to the property is legally permissible. All property is sold "As Is Where Is" and the deeds are not warranted.

Must I bring the entire cash amount to the auction?
Upon successfully bidding on the property, the successful bidder must immediately provide the Sheriff ten percent (10%) of the purchase price paid in cash, money order, official, cashiers or certified check (no personal checks are accepted), plus their name, address, phone number, marital status and social security number. With some properties the entire amount must be paid in cash and this will be specified in the advertisement prior to the auction.

When must I pay the balance due?

The balance must be paid within thirty (30) days after the sale unless the terms of the sale require the full purchase price at the time of the successful bid. Failure to meet this deadline may result in the property being reset for a second auction. Should the second auction result in a lesser sales price, the first bidder may lose all or part of his deposit.

When will I receive the property deed?

Not less than fifteen (15) days after paying the balance of the purchase price. Payment of the balance by certified funds results in delivery of the deed sooner.

Why are pictures shown on some properties and not on others?

In order to avoid confusion, pictures are not taken of condominium units, time share units, or vacant lots. Since condominium buildings consist of many units in various buildings, and since usually only the individual units are being sold, it would be impossible to properly depict in a photograph the specific premises being sold. Vacant lots bear no defined municipal number therefore it is most difficult to depict the property to be sold in a photograph. Certain properties which are otherwise suitable for pictures are not photographed for a number of reasons including but not limited to time constraints, weather conditions, remoteness of locale, and the availability of personnel to perform the service. The Sheriff reserves the right to make determinations relative to the publication of photographs of properties to be sold. No inferences should be drawn relative to the value or condition of property based upon the presence or absence of a photograph.

What does it mean when a property is sold with appraisal?

Under the law, both the plaintiff (the creditor) and the defendant (the debtor) have the right to appoint an appraiser to value the property which is being foreclosed upon if that right was not previously waived by the defendant. Each party who names an appraiser shall deliver the appraisal to the to the sheriff at least two days, exclusive of holidays, prior to the time of the sale. If the parties do not appoint an appraiser the Sheriff appoints the appraisers. Appraisals are posted on the internet, but because of the 48 hour opportunity the appraise, the amounts are usually posted immediately before the sale.

In a Sheriff's Sale can I rely on the appraisal supplied by the plaintiff, defendant or the Sheriff?

Pictures are not a substitute for viewing the property, and should not be used as the basis for purchasing any property offered for public auction. Pictures only depict the condition of property at the moment the photo is taken. It is possible that fire, vandalism, acts of God and other damage may

occur to property after pictures have been taken. It is even possible that due to error the picture shown may not be the correct photo of the premises to be auctioned. THE CIVIL SHERIFF'S OFFICE DOES NOT GUARANTEE OR WARRANT THE CONDITION OR THE TITLE TO PROPERTY AUCTIONED, NOR THE ACCURACY OF PICTURES SHOWN ON THIS BOARD.

Riverside County, California

RIVERSIDE COUNTY SHERIFF
COURT SERVICES

SHERIFF'S SALES

GENERAL INFORMATION

Sheriff's sales are the means used to satisfy a money judgment out of the personal or real property of the judgment debtor, to protect the value of perishable property under levy of writ of attachment by converting it to cash, or to enforce a lien against property under foreclosure proceedings.

Prospective bidders should refer to Sections 701.510 to 701.680, inclusive, of the California Code of Civil Procedure for provisions governing the terms, conditions, and effect of the sale and the liability of defaulting bidders.

The date, time and location of the Sheriff's sales will be stated on the Notice of Sale. The Notice of Sale will also contain a general description of the property to be sold. The Sheriff is selling only the right, title and interest of the judgment debtor(s) in the property. It is the responsibility of any potential buyer to conduct the appropriate research to determine what the debtor's interest is in the property being sold. Private firms, that conduct title searches for a fee, can be found in the Yellow Pages to help provide a prospective buyer with full property information such as liens, unpaid taxes, and encumbrances. The Sheriff's Office makes no guarantee or warranty regarding the condition, value, or functionality of any item sold. Every item is sold as-is.

Sheriff's sales are made at public auction to the highest bidder for cash in lawful money of the United States. The purchaser at a sale shall pay in cash or by certified check or cashier's check, made out to the Riverside County Sheriff. Bidders must have the cash, certified check or cashier's check with them at the time of the sale to cover the full amount of their bid or the amount of the deposit required for a credit bid pursuant to CCP 701.590.

The Court Services' Division conducting the sale will be indicated at the top of the sale notice. It is recommended that you call the Court Services' office conducting the sale, the day prior to the sale, to confirm that the sale has not been cancelled or postponed.

Riverside County, California page 2

CREDIT BIDS

This code section outlines the details for making a credit bid at a Sheriff's sale. Please note, the deposit is forfeited if the balance due, plus costs and interest, is not paid within 10 days after the date of the sale.

CCP 701.590

(a) Except as otherwise provided in this section, the purchaser at a sale shall pay in cash or by certified check or cashier's check.

(b) The judgment creditor may bid by giving the levying officer a written receipt crediting all or part of the amount required to satisfy the judgment, except that the levying officer's costs remaining unsatisfied and the amount of preferred labor claims, exempt proceeds, and any other claim that is required by statute to be satisfied, shall be paid in cash or by certified check or cashier's check.

(c) If the highest bid for an interest in real property sold exceeds five thousand dollars ($5,000), the highest bidder may elect to treat the sale as a credit transaction. A person who makes the election shall deposit at least five thousand dollars ($5,000) or 10 percent of the amount bid, whichever is greater, and within 10 days after the date of the sale shall pay the balance due plus costs accruing with regard to the property sold and interest accruing at the rate on money judgments on the balance of the amount bid from the date of sale until the date of payment.

(d) If the highest bid for an item, group, or lot of personal property sold exceeds two thousand five hundred dollars ($2,500), the highest bidder may elect to treat the sale as a credit transaction. A person who makes the election shall deposit at least two thousand five hundred dollars ($2,500) or 10 percent of the amount bid, whichever is greater, and within 10 days after the date of the sale shall pay the balance due plus costs accruing with regard to the property sold and interest accruing at the rate on money judgments on the balance of the amount bid from the date of sale until the date of payment.

(e) A person who makes the election under subdivision (c) or (d) is not entitled to possession of the property sold until the amount bid, plus accruing costs and interest, have been paid.

REAL PROPERTY SALES

DOCUMENTARY TRANSFER TAX: The purchaser of any real property at a Sheriff's sale is responsible for paying the Documentary Transfer Tax required by the County Recorder. The tax is $0.55 cents per every $500 of the total amount paid for the property. If the property is located within the City of Riverside, the tax is $1.10 per $500. Prior to recording the deed, the purchaser of the real property will need to provide the Sheriff with a check made out to the County Recorder for the amount of the Documentary Transfer Tax.

LIST OF REAL ESTATE INVESTMENT GROUPS

Listed below by state are various real estate groups located throughout the country. This is by no means a complete list and is meant to be a starting point. By going online and doing a search for "Real Estate Investment Clubs" or "Real Estate Investment Group" you will bring up many more of these throughout the country. Many of the groups listed here are associated with the national Real Estate Investors Association. The national REIA is a trade association and a federation consisting of local real estate investing clubs throughout the country. You can get more information on National REIA at www.nationalreia.com.

ALABAMA: AIA Associated Investors of Alabama   205-823-9008   www.AIAclub.com

ALASKA: AK-REIA   907-248-7088   www.ak-REIA.com

ARIZONA: Phoenix RE Club   602-944-2906   www.phoenixrealestateclub.com

Arizona REIA   480-990-7092   www.azreia.org

AZ REIA-Prescott   928-830-2599   www.azreia.org

CALIFORNIA: Autumn Leaf REI Club   www.alreic.com

Desert REI Club   760-415-2250   www.desertreic.com

OCRE Forum   562-431-6828   www.ocreforum.com

Palm Springs REIA   602-301-6335   www.goldphoenixllc.com

Santa Barbara REIA   866-853-0803   www.santabarbareia.com

SJREI Assoc.   408-264-3198   www.sjrei.net

California & Nevada REI Club   925-846-2582   www.nreiclub.com

No. California Diamond Group   925-625-4151   www.simplesimmonsays.com

San Diego Creative Investors Assoc.   www.sdcia.com

COLORADO: Colorado Assoc. of RE investors   303-398-7035   www.carei.com

Colorado Springs RE Club   800-665-7051   www.csrec.com

Southern CA 6 Star REO   949-361-5550   www.6starreo.com

Boulder County REI   720-318-5445   www.BCREI.com

Investors of Northern Colorado   800-767-5085   www.theinclink.com

CONNECTICUT: BCA Women   203-948-3488   www.bcainvest.com

Connecticut REIA   860-561-8821   www.ctreia.com

Northeast REIA   888-637-3421   www.northeasteia.com

DELAWARE: Marshall Williams Group   610-368-6966

BiState Creative Investors   302-992-9056

Real Estate Investment Networking Group   610-804-1493   www.ringonli

FLORIDA: Broward REIA   954-318-6042   www.breia.net

Central FL Realty Investors   407-328-7773   www.cfri.net

DADE REIA   305-948-3378   www.DREIA.org

Future Wealth Club   239-248-2182   www.futurewealthclub.com

Investors Resource Center   407-831-2498   www.IRCFlorida.com

Real Estate Navigators-Emerald Coast   850-585-1257

SWFL REIA   239-247-5061   www.swflreia.com

Tampa Bay REIA   727-452-9648   www.tbreia.com

Real Estate Investors Network of NE FL   904-384-6400   www.rein-jax.co

Treasure Coast REIA   772-343-7338   www.tcreia.com

Urban REIA   305-479-2403   www.michaelchatman.com

Marion County REIA   352-307-4366

Panhandle Investors   850-215-0926   www.panhandleinvestors.com

Wealth Builders REEA   800-335-0256   www.reea.com

Sarasota REIA   941-726-4162   www.sarasotareia.com

Suncoast REIA   813-882-3170   www.sreia.com

GEORGIA: North Georgia REIA   770-877-9111   www.reioutpost.com

HAWAII: Maui REI Club   808-573-2219

Hawaii REIA   808-368-6548   www.hirei.org

IDAHO: Boise REIA   208-866-4041   www.soldteamboise.com

ILLINOIS: Chicago Creative Investors Assoc.   630-858-4663   www.ccia-info.com

Hampton Marshall REIA   773-298-0707   www.hamptonma

Metro East Landlord Assoc.618-877-6352   www.melia-il.com

Northern Il REA   815-363-0233   www.NorthernIlREA.com

RPOA Alton   618-462-6654   www.rpoa-riverbend.com

Chicago area REIA   708-301-5123

INDIANA: REIA of No. Central Indiana   574-235-3634   www.mipoa.net

Central Indiana REIA   317-670-8491   www.cireia.org

IOWA: Two Rivers REIA of Central Iowa   515-633-3347   www.TwoRiversREIA.org

Greater Midwest REIA   712-389-5816   www.gmwreia.com

KANSAS: Kansas City Investment Group   816-292-2822   www.kcig.org

Bridge Real Estate   913-766-9999

KENTUCKY: REIA of Greater Cincinnati   859-292-7342   www.CincinnatiREIA.com

Kentuckiana REIA   www.kreia.com

Bluegrass REIA   859-278-0388   www.bluegrassreia.com

LOUISIANA: Baton Rouge REIA   225-329-8138   www.brreia.com

New Orleans REIA   504-364-5813   www.neworleansreia.com

MAINE: Southern Maine REIA 207-651-5536 www.mainereia.com

MARYLAND: Baltimore REIA 410-569-0345 www.baltimorereia.com

Maryland Real Estate Exchange 410-426-6000 www.mdrealestateclub.com

Mid-Atlantic Real Estate Investors Assoc. 410-738-3600 www.mareia.com

DC/Central Maryland REIA 301-218-4333 www.dcreia.com

Washington REIA Network 301-231-5437 www.washingtonreianetwork.com

MASSACHUSETTS: Investor's Real Estate Resource 508-371-4377

Mass REIA 781-405-1845 www.massrealestate.net

Boston Area REIA 866-378-3037 www.bostonareia.com

Mass REI & Apartment Owners Assoc. 508-987-8806 www.massreia.com

MICHIGAN: Michigan REIA 248-487-0123

National Real Estate Network 248-762-0800 www.megaeveningevent.com

REIA of Oakland County 800-747-6742 www.reiaofoakland.com

Rental Property Owners Assoc. 616-454-3385 www.rpoaonline.org

REIA of Detroit 313-486-0340 www.reiaofdetroit.com

Investors Education Network 269-685-5921

www.InvestorsEducationNetwork.org

REIA of Macomb 586-435-7113 www.REIAofMacomb.com

MINNESOTA: Minnesota Real Estate Investors Assoc 651-779-6446 www.mnreia.com

MISSOURI: Mid-America Assoc. of REI 816-523-4400 www.MAREInet.com

MONTANA: Montana REIA 406-546-6219

NEBRASKA: Omaha REI 402-680-1125

NEVADA: Prosper-Las Vegas 866-702-5188 www.prosper-REIA.com

NEW HAMPSHIRE: New Hampshire REIA 888-922-4500

REINGUSA 603-494-4294

New England REIA 603-887-5677 www.nereia.org

NEW JERSEY: South Jersey Investors 856-663-1133 www.sjclub.com

Garden State REIA 973-275-1442 www.gsreia.com

Metropolitan RE & Investors Assoc. 201-343-8629 www.mreia.com

NEW MEXICO: Capitol Investment Group Of New Mexico 505-998-9390

NEW YORK: New York City REIA 718-654-2694 www.nycreia.com

New York REIA 518-786-8896 www.nyreia.org

Mid-Hudson Valley REIA 877-571-0918 www.mhv-reia.com

Real Estate Investment Education Club 516-298-4135 www.reiec.com

N. CAROLINA: Carolina's REIA 828-255-2727 www.creianc.org

Charlotte REIA 704-777-7342 www.charlottereia.com

Eastern No. Carolina REIA 2520756-6068

LeCroix Investment Group   704-882-2780

Tidewater-Hampton Roads REIA 252-599-0459   www.visionmtgroup

Triangle REIA 919-719-7250   www.treia.com

Metrolina REIA 704-523-1570 www.metrolinareia.org

Coastal Carolina REIA   910-431-6497 www.coastalreia.org

OHIO: Mahoning Valley REIA 330-788-4450 www.mahoningvalleyreia.com

Newton Falls REIA 330-872-7046 www.newtonfalls-reia.com

REIA of Cleveland 440-808-9717 www.reiaofcleveland.com

Greater Dayton REIA 937-586-3726 www.gdreia.com

Tuscarawas REIA 330-339-3227 www.tuscreia.com

Sandusky County Area REIA 419-334-4477

Tiffin Area REIA 419-447-0487

Shelby REIA 937-968-5600 www.shelbyreia.com

Akron/Canton REIA 330-283-5771 www.acreia.org

OKLAHOMA: Millionaire Possibilities 405-286-2000 www.millionairepossibilities.com

Tulsa REIA 888-799-5550 www.tulsareia.com

OREGON: Oregon REIA 541-915-8977   www.oreig.com

PENNSYLVANIA: Delco Property Investors 610-490-1934 www.delcopropertyinvestors.com

Capitol Area RPOA 717-608-8363

Diversified Investment Group 215-712-2525 www.digonline.org

ACRE of Pittsburgh 888-422-7340 www.acrepgh.org

Monroe County REIA 570-504-9722

RHODE ISLAND: Northeast REIA 888-637-3421   www.northeastreia.com

S. CAROLINA: Carolina Coast REIA 843-424-3940 www.carolinacoastalreia.com

Coastal Investment Network 843-368-2935

Main Street REIA 803-417-5467

PD-REIA 843-206-9353 www.pd-reia.com

Grand Strand REIA 800-758-0845 www.gsreia.com

Upstate CREIA 864-787-6400 www.upstatecreia.com

Capital City REIA 803-948-8033 www.screi.com

TENNESSEE: Memphis Investors Group 901-414-2729 www.memphisinvestorsgroup.com

Armed Forces REIA 931-378-0875 www.afreia.com

RE investors of Nashville 615-353-7056 www.reintn.net

Mid-South REIA 901-454-4987   www.midsouthreia.org

TEXAS: Women Investing in RE 214-793-4831   www.womeninvestingre.com

Texas REIA 972-671-7346

The RE Investment Club of Houston 713-947-7424 www.richclub.org

DFW REIN 972-671-7346   www.DFWREIN.com

San Antonio REIA   210-662-0297   www.sareia.com

UTAH: Salt Lake REIA   801-830-4830   www.slreia.com

Utah Creative REIA   801-913-6195

Southern Utah REIA   435-632-9358   www.sureia.com

Northern Utah REI Club   801-430-1576

Utah Valley REI Club   801-342-9260

VIRGINIA: REIA of Dulles   703-798-8155

Virginia REIA   757-875-9251   www.virginiareia.com

DC/VA REIA   800-383-3138   www.dcvareig.com

Richmond REIA   804-314-4575   www.reia.org

WASHINGTON: Bellingham RE Investor Network 360-220-2529   www.breinonline.org

Northwest REI   503-730-8495   www.northwestrei.org

RE Assoc. of Puget Sound   425-458-4797   www.reapsweb.com

WEST VIRGINIA: W. Virginia REIA   304-412-6000

WISCONSIN: Milwaukee RING   414-762-6849   www.milwaukeering.com

INDEX

www.ingramcontent.com/pod-product-compliance
Lightning Source LLC
Chambersburg PA
CBHW051210200326

41519CB00025B/7064